A Narrative Commentary on Matthew 5–7

The Way of Restoration

Following Jesus in the Sermon on the Mount

RACHEL STARR THOMSON

The Way of Restoration: Following Jesus in the Sermon on the Mount

Published by 1:11 Publishing
An imprint of Little Dozen Press
Welland, ON, Canada
littledozen.com

Copyright © 2021 by Rachel Starr Thomson
Visit the author at rachelstarrthomson.com.

Unless otherwise noted, all Scripture quotations are taken from the Holman Christian Standard Bible®, Copyright © 1999, 2000, 2002, 2003, 2009 by Holman Bible Publishers. Used by permission. Holman Christian Standard Bible®, Holman CSB®, and HCSB® are federally registered trademarks of Holman Bible Publishers.

Scriptures marked AMP are taken from the AMPLIFIED BIBLE (AMP): Scripture taken from the AMPLIFIED® BIBLE, Copyright © 1954, 1958, 1962, 1964, 1965, 1987 by the Lockman Foundation Used by Permission. (www.Lockman.org)

Scripture quotations marked "NIV" are taken from the Holy Bible, New International Version®, NIV®. Copyright © 1973, 1978, 1984, 2011 by Biblica, Inc.™ Used by permission of Zondervan. All rights reserved worldwide. www.zondervan.com The "NIV" and "New International Version" are trademarks registered in the United States Patent and Trademark Office by Biblica, Inc.™

Scriptures marked "NASB" taken from the New American Standard Bible® (NASB), Copyright © 1960, 1962, 1963, 1968, 1971, 1972, 1973, 1975, 1977, 1995 by The Lockman Foundation. Used by permission. www.Lockman.org

Scriptures marked "ESV" are taken from The ESV® Bible (The Holy Bible, English Standard Version®). ESV® Text Edition: 2016. Copyright © 2001 by Crossway, a publishing ministry of Good News Publishers. The ESV® text has been reproduced in cooperation with and by permission of Good News Publishers. Unauthorized reproduction of this publication is prohibited. All rights reserved.

Scriptures marked NLT are taken from the HOLY BIBLE, NEW LIVING TRANSLATION (NLT): Scriptures taken from the HOLY BIBLE, NEW LIVING TRANSLATION, Copyright © 1996, 2004, 2007 by Tyndale House Foundation. Used by permission of Tyndale House Publishers, Inc., Carol Stream, Illinois 60188. All rights reserved. Used by permission.

Scriptures marked NKJV are taken from the NEW KING JAMES VERSION (NKJV): Scripture taken from the NEW KING JAMES VERSION®. Copyright© 1982 by Thomas Nelson, Inc. Used by permission. All rights reserved.

Scriptures marked "KJV" are taken from the Holy Bible, King James Version. Public domain.

All Rights Reserved. This book, or any portion thereof, may not be reproduced or transmitted in any form or by any means, electronic or mechanical, including photocopying, recording, or by an information storage and retrieval system (except by a reviewer, who may quote brief passages in a review or other endorsement, or in a recommendation to be printed in a magazine, newspaper, or on the Internet) without written permission from the publisher.

ISBN: 978-1-927658-64-2

Volume 2 of this series contains material adapted from my blog, where I have been writing verse by verse through the gospel of Matthew since the fall of 2015. It covers Matthew 5–7. All the original posts (going far before and beyond this book) can be viewed at: rachelstarrthomson.com/category/gospel-of-matthew.

Contents

INTRODUCTION
Jesus Is Not "Just a Teacher."
But We Should Listen to Him. 13

PART 1: THE THINGS WE RECEIVE: A STUDY IN THE BEATITUDES

1 The Shadow Life of Moses and
How We Know We Can Trust the Storyteller 25

2 Beatitudes: Blessing and Resurrection
and Why Jesus Is Better Than the Law 33

3 Blessed Are the Spiritually Impoverished,
for the Kingdom of Heaven Is Theirs 41

4 Happy Are the Wrecked,
for God Will Draw Near to Them 47

5 Blessed Are the Patiently Battered,
for They Will Inherit the Earth 55

6 Blessed Are the Starving
for Things to Be Made Right 63

7 The Hidden Gospel in
the Heart of the Beatitudes 71

8 Blessed Are the Merciful,
for They Will Obtain Mercy 79

9 "They Shall See God":
Purity of Heart and
the Greatest Blessing of All 85

10 Blessed Are the Makers of Reconciliation:
Peacemaking and the Heart of God 93

11 Blessed Are the Persecuted Prophets,
Part 1: This Means You 99

12 The God Who Respects Our No 107

13 The Gospel According to Jesus 115

PART 2: THE LAW OF LOVE: JESUS ON MORALITY, RIGHTEOUSNESS, AND BECOMING LIKE GOD

14 Why You Are Here 123

15 You Weren't Saved Just for
Your Own Sake 131

16 Not to Destroy But to Fulfill:
How Jesus Gets the Job Done 139

17 Super-Righteousness
and the Law of God 145

18 Good-bye, Frustration:
How the Law of the Spirit Sets Us Free 161

19 Higher Vision:
Why Jesus's Morality
Is Better Than Ours 167

20 What's So Bad About Anger
and How Jesus Calls Us to Freedom 175

21 Why Sin Is Serious
and How Your Personal Salvation
Can Change the World 185

22 Raca, Respect, and the Agape Love of God,
Part 1 193

23 Raca, Respect, and the Agape Love of God,
Part 2 201

24 Raca, Respect, and the Agape Love of God,
Part 3 209

25 The Way of Reconciliation:
How Mercy Triumphs Over Judgment 219

26 Talking Slant:
Jesus on Lust, Love, and Fidelity 227

27 Recalibrating Our Religion:
Jesus on Divorce 241

28 Everything Sacred:
Jesus on Telling the Truth 249

29 Righteousness Redux:
What Is the Point? 257

30 Justice According to Jesus,
Part 1 263

31 Justice According to Jesus,
Part 2 271

32 How to Be Perfect:
Loving Our Enemies and Becoming Like God 277

PART 3: TRUST AT THE CORE:
JESUS ON SPIRITUAL DISCIPLINES

33 Keeping Secrets and Finding Right Rewards:
Jesus on Spiritual Disciplines 289

34 The Spiritual Discipline
of Giving to the Poor 299

35 "Your Father Knows":
Why It Matters
Who You Pray To 311

36 "Pray Like This":
How to Pray the Pattern
in the Lord's Prayer 319

37 How to Find Yourself in the Words
"Our Father" 329

38 Honoring the Other:
What Holiness Means 337

39 Kingdom Come, Part 1:
A Brief History of the Kingdom of God 345

40 Kingdom Come, Part 2:
Why Do We Pray "Your Kingdom Come"? 355

41 The Will of God and the War for Life:
Why Praying "Your Will Be Done"
Is an Act of Warfare 363

42 The Power of Embracing Our Need:
Meeting God in the Prayer
of Daily Dependence 371

43 The Centerpiece Prayer:
Why "Forgive Us Our Debts"
Is the Central Step in the Lord's Prayer 377

44 "Lead Us Not Into Temptation":
The Prayer You Didn't Know
God Wanted You to Pray 385

45 "Deliver Us from the Evil One":
What the Devil Has to Do With It 393

46 Praising the King of Heaven:
The Controversial Doxology 401

47 Secret Sorrow and Private Fasting:
How Jesus Meets Us
in Our Brokenness 409

48 Free and Full of Light:
What Jesus Taught about Scarcity,
Generosity, and Abundance 417

49 Free and Full of Light:
What Jesus Taught about Scarcity,
Generosity, and Abundance 425

50 Money Can Be a Good Thing—
But It's Always a Terrible Master 433

51 Right Places, Right Times:
What Looking at the Birds
Teaches Us about Provision 441

52 Provision, Responsibility,
and The Waste of Worry 447

53 "Won't God Do More for You?"
How Jesus Confronts Our Low
Expectations of God 453

PART 4: SEEKING THE KINGDOM: A SPIRITUALITY FOR THE HUMBLE AND HUNGRY

54 Trust at the Core:
Why Jesus Lived in a Different World
than We Do 458

Jesus was going all over Galilee, teaching in their synagogues, preaching the good news of the kingdom, and healing every disease and sickness among the people.

Then the news about Him spread throughout Syria. So they brought to Him all those who were afflicted, those suffering from various diseases and intense pains, the demon-possessed, the epileptics, and the paralytics. And He healed them.

(Matthew 4:23–24)

Introduction

Jesus Is Not "Just a Teacher." But We Should Listen to Him.

The pages you are about to read are a personal, in-depth exploration of the Sermon on the Mount—which means they're an in-depth exploration of Jesus's teachings. These teachings mostly revolve around things we should do and things we should not do, attitudes we should cultivate and attitudes we should abandon. They give us spiritual disciplines we should take up and specific words we should pray. Jesus taught us about morality and love and human behavior. The Sermon is a kind of *torah*, a law given by Jesus for his disciples to follow.

The perspectives you'll find here are, thankfully, not the last word on anything. They've grown directly out of my personal study and my feeble attempts to do what Jesus said. Without any doubt, there is far more wisdom in his teachings than I've managed to glean, and my approach is probably skewed and lacking in various ways. Even so, the insights I attempt to share here have been deeply impactful in my own life, and I hope they can be a gift to you on your own journey.

Before we can even get there, though, I think we need to address the context of our present day, in which it may come as a surprise to many that Jesus taught us *anything* about behavior, and in which you may find yourself uncomfortable with the very suggestion that he gave us a law.

Yet this is the reality. Jesus was a teacher and a moral genius,[1] and every bit as much as he gave us something (Someone) to believe in, he also gave us things to do.

In Matthew 4:23–24, which opened this introduction, we see the shape of Jesus's early ministry. Jesus taught, preached, and healed, and these three things flowed into and out of one another and all together offered people the kingdom of God. Jesus's teaching was an integral part of this, and from the Sermon on the Mount, we know he didn't just teach ancient prophecies or a set of truths about himself. He taught people how to live.

In *all* that he did and said, Jesus led his followers in the way of restoration. He restored bodies, souls, and relationships on his way to kingdom come, to the full realization of God's rule and reign among us. And he called us to live in a way commensurate with this ultimate goal—to actively partner with God in recreating the world. In a very true sense, his law is life.

---

[1] H/t to Dallas Willard for this phrase.

Today I think we are more comfortable with Jesus the preacher and Jesus the healer than we are with Jesus the teacher and lawgiver. That's ironic on several levels: while the world wants to dismiss Jesus as just another teacher, the church doesn't like him to be a teacher at all. As a teacher he blurs the lines between "faith" and "works" to an uncomfortable degree; he makes demands on our lives; he insists we see and do things differently. If we listen to him too closely, we may find our very definition of salvation shifting and changing—that we can't be satisfied with any definition that falls short of the entire transformation of our lives.

Connecting with the Seekers of God

Thankfully, total transformation is exactly what Jesus offers us. There is a strong participatory element to this transformation, and it's laid out in his teachings, especially in the Sermon. Yet many Christians today grow nervous as soon as we begin to echo Jesus's moral teachings, or claim that *there is a way God wants us to live*. Even using words like "morality" or "righteousness" leaves us open to the charge that we are Pharisees: preaching a works-based religion and laying heavy burdens on the backs of our hearers, which we won't lift a finger to help carry.

In a related phenomenon, there's a myth abroad that Jesus had no use for "religious people"; that if he were here today, he probably wouldn't darken the door of a church. Actually, the "local churches" of the day were the synagogues, and that's where Jesus launched his ministry. He went to people who were already trying to live in a better way, a way that was faithful to God. Why not, after all? If you were in a synagogue, to some degree you identified yourself as a seeker of God, as someone desirous of connection with God. Jesus went straight to those people to establish the connection they wanted. So did Paul, if you look. Paul went first to the Jewish synagogues and then to already God-fearing Gentiles. But I digress.

Jesus came to people who were seeking God and taught them "with authority." He spoke from his own experience, he spoke with deep understanding, he spoke with power. His teaching was life-changing.

The entire Bible presents God—Father, Son, and Holy Spirit—as one who is eager to teach. He is eager and even longing to share the wonders of the universe and of his own heart with the people he created.

Paul expressed his desire for the churches in Laodicea: "I want their hearts to be encouraged and joined together in love, so that they may have all the riches of assured understanding and have the knowledge of God's mystery—Christ. All the treasures of wisdom and knowledge are hidden in Him" (Colossians 2:2–3).

Everything about relationship with God is an invitation into knowledge: into the secrets of creation and into the kind of personal, intimate knowledge of God that, lived out, constitutes righteousness.

Righteousness is more than a moral code: it is right-relatedness to God and to everything he has made.

The Heart of Righteousness

So where do all the objections come from? Why do we shy away from Jesus the teacher, and why are we so quick to cast suspicion on anyone who wants to talk about righteous living?

Well, some probably do it because, like the apostle John so scathingly said, "they loved darkness rather than light, because their deeds were evil" (see John 3:19). But that's not all of us. Some of us really do want to run to the light, and to walk with Jesus, yet we're still suspicious of anything that sounds like moral teaching in the church. Why? Well, in our defense, there *is* a thing people call "righteousness" that is rigid and legalistic, and if you've been around at all, you know it brings oppression, heaviness, and hardship. It doesn't do nuance or compassion. Rather than setting people free, it breaks up families, causes unnecessary hurt and offense, shuts down personality, and traps people in unhealthy cycles and habits. It lacks wisdom and is therefore not really righteousness at all: it's a sham, a satanic substitute. It's not the way of restoration, and it's not the way of Jesus.

But just because poison exists does not mean that food does not.

Jesus is the one who is wiser than Solomon, and Solomon's heart for people, expressed in the opening chapters of Proverbs, lies behind Jesus's teaching as well:

> My son, don't forget my teaching,
> but let your heart keep my commands;
> for they will bring you many days, a full life,
> and well-being ...
> Happy is a man who finds wisdom
> and who acquires understanding,
> for she is more profitable than silver,
> and her revenue is better than gold ...
> Long life is in her right hand;
> in her left, riches and honor.
> Her ways are pleasant,
> and all her paths, peaceful.
> She is a tree of life to those who embrace her,
> and those who hold on to her are happy ...

> Maintain your competence and discretion.
> My son, don't lose sight of them.
> They will be life for you
> and adornment for your neck.
> Then you will go safely on your way;
> your foot will not stumble.
> When you lie down, you will not be afraid;
> you will lie down, and your sleep will be pleasant.
> (Proverbs 3:1–2, 13–14, 16–18, 21–24)

If we want to really know Jesus, and if we want to really live in the reality of the kingdom of God which he ushered in, we have to take him seriously as a teacher. We have to become seekers, learners, disciples. We need to hunger and thirst for righteousness and be consumed with the desire to know and to live out the truth. We have to lose our fear of God's law and learn to love his morality, which flows directly out of his nature. We need to discover the things God has given us to *do*.

The wisdom of God, given to us in Jesus's teachings and the ongoing ministry of the Holy Spirit, is one of his greatest gifts to us.

Learning How to Live

In his marvelous book *The Divine Conspiracy*, Dallas Willard wrote, "It is the failure to understand Jesus and his words as reality and vital information about life that explains why, today, we do not routinely teach those who profess allegiance to him how to do what he said was best. We lead them to profess allegiance to him, or we expect them to, and leave them there."[2]

Indeed, Jesus's teaching is *truth*—and as he himself said, "If you continue in My word ... you will know the truth, and the truth will set you free" (John 8:31a, 32). To the extent that we don't practically engage with truth and "continue in it," we miss out on the freedom and power it can bring. When we see the gospel as primarily a message of believing the right thing so we can have a happy afterlife, we may miss the reality of the kingdom now. Access to Jesus's teaching is one of the central benefits of the kingdom come: we can learn how to live, how to think, and how to relate to reality from the Son of God himself.

When Jesus's teachings are lived out—with wisdom and not just a rigid legalism that is far from the way he modeled his own teachings—they impact the world in astounding ways because they impact *us* in astounding ways.

The Sermon on the Mount is widely considered the greatest and most influential moral teaching ever delivered. In it I hear the echoes of Solomon as

---

[2] Dallas Willard, The Divine Conspiracy (New York: HarperOne, 1997), xiv

Jesus calls us to listen:

> My child, don't forget my teaching,
> but let your heart keep my commands;
> for they will bring you many days, a full life,
> and well-being.
> (Proverbs 3:1–2)

"Your righteousness," Jesus told the crowds early in the sermon, "must surpass that of the scribes and Pharisees. If it doesn't, you will never enter the kingdom of heaven" (paraphrased—see Matthew 5:20).

Jesus calls his followers to a higher righteousness, a higher way of relating, a way that lines up with the invisible kingdom and the rule of God. Rather than bringing judgment and death, this kind of righteousness brings freedom and life. It is the way of restoration—surpassing indeed.

Today, fellow children of God, let's believe Jesus when he says his ways lead to life. Let's listen to him, not just as a Savior but as our Teacher—the one who can actually help us figure this thing out. He knows what he is talking about. We just need to open our ears and listen.

PART 1:

The Things We Receive: A Study in the Beatitudes

When He saw the crowds, He went up on the mountain, and after He sat down, His disciples came to Him. Then He began to teach them, saying …

(Matthew 5:1–2)

1

The Shadow Life of Moses and How We Know We Can Trust the Storyteller

When Moses declared some fourteen hundred years before Jesus walked the earth that God would "raise up a prophet like unto me,"[1] it's doubtful anyone thought he was talking about a specific person to come. Moses, the deliverer of Israel and the one through whom God gave the Sinai Covenant and its law, was contrasting the way the nations sought their gods to the way God would speak to his people. Rather than practicing divination and sorcery, the children of Israel would have prophets, like Moses, through whom God chose to speak.

This promise was partially fulfilled throughout Israel's history, through all of the prophets whose words are recorded in the Scriptures and many others whose messages have not lived on. But at the same time, there never was a prophet quite like

---

[1] Deuteronomy 18:15

Moses—one who saw God face-to-face and heard him speak directly.

Never, that is, until Jesus.

So the book of Acts clearly proclaims that Moses's words were about Jesus (Acts 3:19–23). The early church, ethnically Jewish and steeped in Jewish history, understood from Moses's life and prophecy who Jesus truly was.

At the same time, Jesus pushed Moses's prophecy to a whole new level. It wasn't just that this prophet-to-come would hear directly from God. This prophet—Jesus—would also be a deliverer. He would also instate a covenant. And like Moses, he would reveal God to the people in a whole new measure.

It wasn't just Moses's *words* that pointed to Jesus. It was his entire *life*.

Shadows of Messiah

Matthew seems acutely aware of the Moses-Jesus parallels, and he more than any other gospel writer draws them out. Because of course, when an omnipotent, storytelling God is directing events, they will be fraught with significance.

Jesus's life as laid out in Matthew mirrors the life of Moses in a way that's almost eerie considering that no human being was consciously trying to create the parallel:

- Jesus leaves the "king's palace" of heaven to identity with God's oppressed people on earth.
- He is born in a time of oppression.
- He narrowly escapes genocide by a pagan king.
- He flees to Egypt.
- In his baptism, he is drawn up out of the water into a new life of favor.
- He is driven from that favor into the wilderness for forty days.

After encountering God and accepting his mission, Moses led the people of Israel to a mountain, Sinai, where he delivered ten commandments. Jesus gathered disciples and then went up on a mountain in Galilee, where he delivered eight blessings—the Beatitudes.

Throughout his account, Matthew is consciously paralleling Jesus with Moses: showing him as the fulfillment not only of Moses's law and Moses's prophecy but of Moses's whole life, which was a type and shadow of the Messiah to come.

A Life of Seconds

I think Moses lived his whole life knowing that

he wasn't God's final prophet, and by extension, that the law he delivered wasn't God's final word and plan for his people. That is foreshadowed over and over again. Moses's life was a life of "seconds," where the second always has some kind of superiority to the first. For Moses, this often meant a kind of demotion. Maybe this is partly why God honored Moses's humility so deeply. He lived out a picture that always pointed to someone else.

So Moses is called as God's prophet, but it's Aaron who speaks. Moses establishes the priesthood, but Aaron serves as high priest. Moses is given the law, but the first tablets are broken when the people apostatize and have to be replaced by a second set. Moses spends forty years in the wilderness as a refugee and a shepherd of sheep and then a second forty years in the wilderness as a deliverer, prophet, and shepherd of God's people. Moses is called to lead the people into the land, but it's Joshua (whose name is the Hebrew form of "Jesus") who actually does so.

Living Out the Story

In a very real sense, Moses was a Messiah—an anointed one. He was called and anointed by God to deliver his people. But he wasn't *the* Messiah, and all his life, he looked ahead—ahead to the end of the law, ahead to the faithfulness of God that would reach further than the people's failures to believe, ahead to the second Messiah, the real Messiah, the one Moses's entire life was a picture of.

Types fascinate me, because these are not just literary conventions being added to a story by a human author. The Old Testament is full of types of Jesus, but these were *real* people—human beings living out real lives that seemed to them to be just as random and prone to the vagaries of time and chance as any other life. Everything mattered, though they couldn't have known it then. Even the "wrong turns" of Moses's life came together to foreshadow the coming of Jesus.

According to Paul, we're no longer living in the law's types and shadows but in the reality to which they pointed. Speaking of the law's rituals and sacrifices, he wrote, "These are a shadow of the things that were to come; the reality, however, is found in Christ" (Colossians 2:17, NIV).

At the same time, we are still living in something of a shadowland:

> Now our knowledge is partial and incomplete, and even the gift of prophecy reveals only part of the whole picture! But when the time of perfection comes, these partial things will become useless ... When I was a child, I spoke and thought and reasoned as a child. But when I grew up, I put away childish things. Now we see things imper-

> fectly, like puzzling reflections in a mirror, but then we will see everything with perfect clarity. All that I know now is partial and incomplete, but then I will know everything completely, just as God now knows me completely. (1 Corinthians 13:9–12, NLT)

We are still living out a story we don't fully understand. We have one foot in the glorious reality of the kingdom of heaven and one foot in the murk of the world. Yet, if the Bible demonstrates anything, I think it demonstrates this: everything matters. God may not directly cause everything that happens in our lives, but there are no accidents.

Life is a story, a story with layers and themes, a story with a plot and characters, a story with a predetermined ending. And we are living it, not because we just happen to be here, but because our lives are an integral part of the whole. We mean something. It *all* means something.

Trusting the Storyteller

Like Moses, we can be aware that our lives are fraught with significance and still not see it. We can be convinced that even our wrong turns mean something, yet never really come to understand what they mean.

For Moses, that awareness created humility and

a deep trust in God, rather than arrogance or resentment. May our response be the same!

What we have now is partial and incomplete, yet it's enough to tell us that what is still to come is truly wonderful. When we "know everything completely," when we know God as fully as he knows us, the shadows will take form and the puzzling reflections will make sense.

Perhaps some future chronicler will remember our lives the way Matthew remembered Moses: as contours and parallels of a reality so incredible it could hardly be conceived until it happened.

We can't know what every twist of the plot means as we're living it. All we can do is trust the Storyteller, who knows where all this is going and has proven that he knows how to direct the story well.

When He saw the crowds, He went up on the mountain, and after He sat down, His disciples came to Him. Then He began to teach them, saying:

"The poor in spirit are blessed,
for the kingdom of heaven is theirs.
Those who mourn are blessed,
for they will be comforted.
The gentle are blessed,
for they will inherit the earth.
Those who hunger and thirst for righteousness are blessed,
for they will be filled.
The merciful are blessed,
for they will be shown mercy.
The pure in heart are blessed,
for they will see God.
The peacemakers are blessed,
for they will be called sons of God.
Those who are persecuted for righteousness are blessed,
for the kingdom of heaven is theirs.

"You are blessed when they insult and persecute you and falsely say every kind of evil against you because of Me. Be glad and rejoice, because your reward is great in heaven. For that is how they persecuted the prophets who were before you.
(Matthew 5:1–12)

2

Beatitudes: Blessing and Resurrection and Why Jesus Is Better Than the Law

When Moses went up into a mountain, he delivered the law, summed up in the Ten Commandments.

In biblical symbolism, ten is a number of completion: it presents a finished form—in the case of the law, a rounded righteousness.

Jesus also climbed a mountain and delivered a *torah*—a "teaching" or "law"—but he began his differently. He began with *eight blessings*.

Those blessings are known as the Beatitudes (from the Latin meaning "supreme blessedness") and we're going to examine them in detail. But before we do, I want us to step back and see them with a wide lens.

The Beatitudes are as significant to Jesus's teaching on the kingdom as the Ten Commandments were to Moses's teaching of the Sinai law.

But their form immediately shows us that what Jesus is bringing surpasses what Moses brought.

The end of the law, as Paul tells us, was a curse and death. Jesus, from the outset, brought life.

THE MEANING OF BLESSING

I wrote about blessing (Hebrew *barak*) in the prequel to this book, *When God Walked in Galilee*. There, we looked at Jesus as the fulfillment of the promise to Abraham to bless the nations:

> A study through the Bible passages that use the word "barak" shows it to be the source of life, righteousness, prosperity, and salvation. Fundamentally, to bless is to fill with the capacity and potential for life. To curse is the opposite—it is to wither, dry up, make barren. Blessing is a kind of empowerment given through the spoken word of God. It is as significant to human origins as creation itself: immediately after creating mankind, God *blessed* them.
>
> For this reason, we are empowered to be more in the world than animals or plants; for good or for ill, we create, we rule, we influence through our wills and actions. We are creatures of real significance because we are blessed ...
>
> Through Jesus, the blessing of Abraham—life,

salvation, prosperity, healing, creative power, influence, righteousness—comes on all the children of faith.[1]

That Jesus opens his sermon by giving not commandments but *blessings* marks a fundamental difference between the Sinai Covenant and the covenant Jesus brought: where one depended on human ability for a positive outcome, the other begins with the direct empowerment of the Word and Spirit of God.

And while blessing in the Sinai Covenant had to be earned through obedience (see Deuteronomy 28–30),[2] blessing in Jesus is given at the outset, as a gift.

Obedience is still the goal, of course (why would you *not* live in a relationship of hearing-and-doing with a Lord, Savior, and Teacher whose will is perfect goodness and whose teachings are the deepest possible wisdom?), but we arrive there from a new direction.

Blessing, empowerment, being filled with the capacity for life—that's where it *starts*.

---

[1] Rachel Starr Thomson, When God Walked in Galilee (Little Dozen Press, 2019), 32–33.

[2] This is not to suggest that there was no prior, unearned blessing in the case of the children of Israel: the law was given in the context of the Abrahamic blessing. Nevertheless, Paul tells us that the law was weak through the flesh: it could not bring righteousness because human beings could not carry it out. Thus, what was intended to bless brought a curse. But even here God had a bigger plan: deliverance from the curse by the Son, who comes with blessing that is not attached to human ability but to his own accomplishment.

The Power of Eight

The number of Beatitudes is significant too. Bible numbers are often symbolic, with some more familiar than others: one and three for God, seven for divine perfection, forty for testing/purification, etc. Eight is the number of resurrection, new life, and eternity. It indicates a new creation after the finish of the old one. Eight is both an end and a beginning: it comes after seven, the last day of the week, but since the week starts over, the eight is also a one—a new start.

The Ten Commandments presented a finished law: a completed, closed system. Jesus acknowledges this when he says that everything written in the law must "be accomplished": the law is finite and can be finished.

The Eight Blessings of Jesus's teaching, on the other hand, give life without end. They are blessings of resurrection that continue into eternal life.

Not a To-Do List

The Beatitudes don't get talked about enough, in my opinion—but even when we do talk about them, we sometimes miss what these blessings *are*. They are not tasks, nor do they declare that certain states (like poverty and mourning) are somehow more godly by nature than others. Instead, they bless *peo-*

ple in the midst of those states, and the blessings themselves impart life and strength to those who receive them.

That's why the Beatitudes begin with "Blessed are the poor in spirit"—not because being spiritually impoverished is a virtue, exactly, but because God's gift has come on those with absolutely nothing to offer. A state that is ordinarily barren and even cursed becomes blessed because the Lord enters into it.

That's our starting point: We have nothing. Our hands are empty. Our souls are a graveyard of dreams.

To us, Jesus says, "The kingdom of heaven is yours."

We Are Blessed

John the Baptist could announce the kingdom of God by preaching "Repent, you brood of vipers"[3] because when you are at open enmity with an existing monarch, the arrival of that monarch on your home turf is very bad news.

But for everyone willing to receive it with open hands and open heart, the coming of this kingdom is the best possible news—truly a gospel ("good news") of the highest order. This king has ascended his mountain to give a law, and he opens his mouth with blessing.

---

3 Matthew 3:7

The Greek word *makarios*, blessing, denotes us as happy, blessed, to be envied. Jesus comes preaching "Happy are you"—or at least, "Happy you can be, if you will receive." Our gospel is a gospel of happiness, the charter of a happy people who are to be envied, for their king has come, their king brings life, and their king loves them.

The only thing we need to qualify is empty hands.

The poor in spirit are blessed,
for the kingdom of heaven is theirs.
(Matthew 5:3)

3

Blessed Are the Spiritually Impoverished, for the Kingdom of Heaven Is Theirs

The first blessing Jesus gives in the Beatitudes makes no sense at all.

Poverty is not a naturally "happy" state (*makarios*, the Greek word for "blessed," is also translated "happy"). To be poor is a devastating condition, not a blessed one. It is not ordinarily a virtue to be poor in spirit. To be poor in spirit means we have no inner resources, no inner life, absolutely nothing to give. To be poor in spirit is to be depressed and oppressed; to be so inwardly destitute we can hardly get ourselves out of bed in the morning. The addict, dependent on outside substances to feel any glimmer of well-being, is spiritually poor. The suicidal is spiritually poor. The debilitatingly depressed is spiritually poor.

What Jesus says is nonsense … until we realize

what he is really saying. This is not so much a blessing on one's current state as an offer to transform it.

If you are spiritually impoverished, inwardly devastated, a graveyard of dreams—

To you Jesus speaks blessing.

To you, he speaks life.

In fact, to you he gives a gift:

A kingdom.

His kingdom.

Blessed are the poor in spirit, for the kingdom of heaven is theirs.

All We Need Is Nothing

Jesus's words are so radical, so outlandishly (outworldishly?) generous that we can't wrap our minds around them. What does it mean to be *given* a kingdom, after all? We know what that means; we've all read stories of people given kingdoms. David was given a kingdom. Arthur was given a kingdom. Aragorn was given a kingdom. To be given a kingdom is to be given position, authority, power, privilege, wealth, honor, responsibility.

You have been given a kingdom (or, more accurately, a place in God's kingdom), provided you meet one qualification:

Nothing.

All you need in order to receive from God is nothing.

All you need in order to qualify for greater riches than you can imagine is deep personal poverty.

Thankfully, we all qualify.

The Graveyard of Dreams

Years ago during a time of immense personal struggle, I found myself coming to a point where I recognized how deeply impoverished I really was. I'd been through a spiritual battle, and inwardly, it had left destruction and devastation in its wake. As someone who always wants to have something to offer, it was hard for me to realize just how poor I had become. I did not have anything to give God, or others, or even myself.

But God met me there. Sitting in the wreckage of my soul I became aware of his presence and his acceptance. I wrote a poem about the experience that included the lines, "So we join hands and dance / In the graveyard of dreams."

The truth is that all of humanity is a graveyard of dreams. Created for glory, we lost that glory through sin. We "fell short," as Paul so perfectly puts it (Romans 3:23). Some of us, in some seasons, are acutely aware of this. Others are not. To those who feel the depth of their own depravity and need, and to those who don't feel it but are willing to acknowledge it regardless, Jesus offers to give our glory back. He offers to seat us on high with himself. He offers to anoint us as kings and priests.

Hannah sang:

> He raiseth up the poor out of the dust
> And lifteth up the beggar from the dunghill,
> To set them among princes,
> And to make them inherit the throne of glory.
> (1 Samuel 2:8, KJV)

When Mary rejoiced over the child in her womb, she sang an echo of Hannah's prayer: "He has toppled the mighty from their thrones and exalted the lowly; He has satisfied the hungry with good things and sent the rich away empty" (Luke 1:52–53). In a strange twist of history, the most blessed are the most helpless. In a real sense, even the state of spiritual poverty *becomes* blessed, because it is a place of encounter and transformation. This is good news for all of us because, as it turns out, we're all poorer than we think. When we embrace this truth as a friend, our poverty can open us up to the presence and work of God.

A Spiritual Kingdom

When Jesus offers the kingdom as the answer to spiritual poverty, he points to the nature of this kingdom: it, too, is spiritual. That doesn't mean it has no effect or manifestation in the material world—all material begins in and is upheld by the realm of spirit. But the wealth and power of the kingdom answer directly to our spiritual poverty and weakness, going straight to our deepest need and offering to meet it.

The destitute will be rich. The blind will see. The mostly dead and entirely hopeless will find a well of life spring up within them, leading to eternal life.

And since this is a kingdom given as a gift to those who have absolutely no way to earn or pay for it, all we need to do is acknowledge our need and humbly, gratefully receive it.

Those who mourn are blessed,
for they will be comforted.
(Matthew 5:4)

4

Happy Are the Wrecked, for God Will Draw Near to Them

Like the first blessing in the Beatitudes, the second appears at first to be nonsense. "Happy are those who mourn" is a contradiction in terms. Jesus, I'm convinced, did this on purpose: he chose terms that were meant to shock and bewilder before giving way, upon closer inspection, to hope.

Like poverty of spirit, mourning is not a virtue in and of itself. Sorrow is a negative. To weep, to wail, to be wracked and wrecked by grief, undoes and devastates us.

I don't mean to suggest that mourning is a vice. In the world as it is, it's necessary and important to grieve. Jesus did so on multiple occasions. Sadness is a response to the curse of death and the hardships of corruption: an appropriate response, but not in itself a good thing.

The first four Beatitudes are what I think of as the "negative" Beatitudes: all four bless an inherently negative state (poverty, grief, meekness—which is submissive endurance in a state of affliction—and hunger). In every case, the blessing is the promise of a particular divine response of goodness poured into the low place. To borrow a phrase from another preacher, the negative Beatitudes are very like saying, "Blessed are they who have cancer, for they shall be cured."

This is very like the God we see all through the Scriptures—the God who cleanses lepers, fills empty wombs, and gives kingdoms to shepherd boys and refugees. Rather than disqualifying us or causing God to view us as less-than, our weakness, need, and trouble attracts his grace and compassion. His strength, after all, is made perfect in our weakness.[1]

It is not the state Jesus blesses but the person suffering in that state, and his blessing promises a way forward. Even more, it promises a transformation of the negative state itself: our places of greatest suffering can become our places of greatest encounter. We will look back on our graveyards and call them blessed.

Blessed Are Those Who Hurt

After blessing the spiritually impoverished with the

---

[1] 2 Corinthians 12:9

promise of all the wealth and power of a kingdom, Jesus blesses those who mourn.

There is here no hint of rebuke—"Why don't you just pull yourself together?"—or of spiritual pragmatism ("God is probably using this to teach you something").

In fact Jesus's response to those who mourn—and he doesn't say *why* they mourn, indicating that there isn't some hierarchy in which we are allowed to feel sad about some things but not about others—to those who hurt, who cry, who are sad, who grieve—is to bless them.

And the blessing is to me one of the most beautiful promises in all of Scripture: "For they will be comforted."

Even in English this is beautiful. The world these days is not really okay with sadness. *We* are not really okay with sadness. We are allowed a little time to grieve (if, say, someone dies), but then we're expected to get over it, grow up, move on, be happy.

Some things we are not allowed to mourn at all. The end of a marriage, we're told, should be celebrated as a new birth. A move or career change is a positive, even if it entails loss. We are not to see our losses as losses but as gains.

I am all for positive thinking, but we become emotionally disconnected and unhealthy when we cannot accept sorrow as a legitimate part of ourselves and of our lives in this world. The implication in our culture is that sadness is something we should be ashamed of, something we need to get over as quickly as possible.

If you have ever been truly, deeply sad, you know how much more wounding comes with that kind of shame. The story of Job's friends resonates for a reason. It's not just our culture—to some degree it's human nature. We aren't equipped to deal with our own grief, let alone others'. Better that we all just get over it.

But Jesus doesn't say any of that. He doesn't say "Blessed are those who mourn, for they shall move past it." Nor "Blessed are those who mourn, for they shall grow up." Nor "Blessed are those who mourn, for their gains are greater than their losses."

Rather, he says "Blessed are those who mourn, for they shall be comforted."

No shame. No rebuke. No "hurry up and get past it." Jesus validates our deep hunger to be comforted. To just be held and loved on. To be recognized as people who have truly lost something and truly suffer from it.

The Isolation of Grief

Because sorrow is so deep and so particular to every one of us, when we grieve we grieve alone. Even those with the unusual blessing of a strong and loving community will always encounter aloneness in the center of mourning. Personal grief isolates and alienates.

Even in English "they shall be comforted" is a beautiful promise, but in Greek it becomes even more wonderful. Because the literal meaning of the Greek word we translate "comfort" is "to come alongside."

Literally, the blessing of Jesus is that those who mourn will find God drawing alongside them. That in the center of their greatest alienation and suffering, they will find the Lord God who loves them to be very, very near. And he comes not as a Job's friend with a lesson to teach. He comes just to sit with us and let us cry.

In this is deep healing. Perhaps deeper than we know.

The One Who Is Near

Jesus's words echo some of the most beautiful of the Old Testament promises about the Messiah:

> The Spirit of the Lord GOD is on Me,
> because the LORD has anointed Me
> to bring good news to the poor.
> He has sent Me *to heal [lit. to "bind up"—to*

> *bandage, to tend the wounds of]*
> *the brokenhearted ...*
> to proclaim the year of the LORD's favor,
> and the day of our God's vengeance;
> *to comfort all who mourn,*
> to provide for those who mourn in Zion;
> to give them a crown of beauty
> instead of ashes,
> festive oil instead of mourning,
> and splendid clothes
> instead of despair.
>
> (Isaiah 61:1–3, emphasis mine)

Heaven Now

In proclaiming "Blessed are those who mourn, for they shall be comforted" as one of the eight kingdom blessings, Jesus proclaims himself to be the Messiah—the king who comes to fulfill Isaiah 61. The year of the Lord's favor has come, and with it the One who comes to comfort those who mourn.

These are promises that are true on a deeply personal level—the promise is to the individual who mourns. They are also true on a cosmic level. Jesus has come into a world reeling with loss, drawn alongside it, and offered comfort and companionship.

The healing of the world is in his name "Emmanuel": God with us.

Mindful of the Scripture's ultimate promises that in the new heaven and new earth every tear will be wiped away[2] and "sorrow and sighing shall flee away,"[3] we have a tendency to put the Beatitudes off till the afterlife: "Blessed are those who mourn," we say, "for when they die and go to heaven they will be comforted."

But that misses the whole context of Jesus's blessings. He is announcing the kingdom of heaven. He announced it *two thousand years ago,* and he ascended to the throne just forty days after his resurrection. The kingdom of heaven is *now,* and the kingdom blessings are for us now, not at some future date.

If you mourn, then, blessed are you, for the King of Kings sees, knows, and has promised to come alongside you—quietly at first, simply to comfort, but with healing and gladness in his wings.

---

[2] Revelation 21:4
[3] Isaiah 51:11, ESV

> THE GENTLE ARE BLESSED,
> FOR THEY WILL INHERIT THE EARTH. (HCSB)
>
> BLESSED ARE THE MEEK,
> FOR THEY SHALL INHERIT THE EARTH. (KJV)
> (Matthew 5:5)

5

Blessed Are the Patiently Battered, for They Will Inherit the Earth

The runner and missionary Eric Liddell, whose life inspired the movie *Chariots of Fire*, wrote a small booklet on the Sermon on the Mount in which he said, "Meek is kind and gentle and fearless. Meek is love in the presence of wrong."[1] Adopting this same idea, many Christians define meekness as "power under control."[2] We take pains to point out that being meek is not the same thing as being a doormat. But the fact is there's a reason people in the world tend to equate meekness with weakness and doormatliness: it often looks like it.

The British folk song "The Ballad of Accounting," written by Ewan MacColl in 1964 and sung with

---

[1] Eric Liddell, "The Sermon on the Mount for Sunday School Teachers." As quoted in Sally Magnusson, The Flying Scotsman (New York: Quartet Books, 1981), 165.

[2] A Google search will turn this definition up everywhere, though I haven't been able to find its original source. Despite claims to the contrary, it's not an exact definition of the Greek praeis.

the appropriate tone of bitterness, sums up how a posture of meekness often comes off to those who share in the affliction but don't share the posture: "Did you learn to keep your mouth shut, were you seen but never heard?" it mockingly asks; "Did you learn to be obedient and jump to at a word?" To many, an attitude of meekness deserves nothing but scorn. Jesus couldn't differ more strongly.

Unlike poverty and mourning, meekness is not in itself a negative—but it does imply a negative state. Rightly understood, meekness is an attitude of submission in the midst of affliction.

What Meekness Really Is

The biblical concept of meekness encompasses three basic ideas, always within a context of affliction or hardship—a state where evil seems to be winning. The three ideas are:

1. Humility and trust toward God, expressed in waiting on him.
2. Gentleness toward people.
3. Patience/endurance in a difficult circumstance.

As a response to suffering, meekness—especially its "gentleness" aspect—makes no sense unless there is a reason to trust that a Higher Power is in control and that a greater purpose is being worked through the current state of suffering. But because those two things are true, the results of meekness can be incredibly powerful.

In their efforts to create widespread social reform, Gandhi knew the secret of meekness. So did Martin Luther King, Jr., who was inspired by Gandhi. Both men patterned their strategies of non-violent response after the example and teachings of Jesus, whose third kingdom blessing essentially assures us that the reasons for meekness are true: there *is* a Higher Power, and a great purpose *is* being worked out through our suffering.

In fact, if you will endure affliction, oppression, and injustice with an attitude of submission to God and gentleness toward your fellow men, the end of your endurance will be inheritance. You will make it through to the other side.

Those who cannot respond in meekness cannot endure. They flare up, flame out, and burn themselves out in their zeal.

So meekness is not, as the "Ballad of Accounting" would suggest, simply a matter of licking a conqueror's boots. The submission of the meek is not actually to the conqueror at all, but to God. The gentleness shown toward people flows out of that response to God. Because we're not at war with God in our suffering, we needn't be at war with our brothers and sisters either.

The Old Testament Promise of Inheritance

Jesus's promise that the meek will inherit the earth was not actually new to the Jewish people—though to a generation struggling under Roman oppression, it was certainly salient. In Jesus's day, the people of Israel were *in* the land, but Rome controlled it and them. Various factions, including the militant Zealots and the religious Pharisees, eschewed the idea that meekness in the face of occupation would accomplish anything good. For many, the way of violence, hatred, and taking-matters-into-their-own-hands seemed the more truly blessed.

Jesus's blessing reassured his Jewish listeners that yes, an attitude of submission to God and gentleness toward men *would* result in inheritance—again, not a new idea. In fact, the promise is a direct quote from Psalm 37. Reading that entire psalm—with its series of parallel promises as to who will "inherit the earth" (or the land)—sheds a lot of light on Jesus's meaning here in Matthew 5.

The psalm begins by acknowledging the apparent triumph of evildoers, but urges God's people to keep their trust firmly in him:

> Do not be agitated by evildoers;
> do not envy those who do wrong.
> For they wither quickly like grass

and wilt like tender green plants.
Trust in the LORD and do what is good;
dwell in the land and live securely.
Take delight in the LORD,
and He will give you your heart's desires ...
Be silent before the LORD and wait
expectantly for Him;
do not be agitated by one who prospers
in his way,
by the man who carries out evil plans.
Refrain from anger and give up your rage;
do not be agitated—it can only bring harm.
For evildoers will be destroyed,
but those who put their hope
in the LORD will inherit the earth.[3]

(Psalm 37:1–4, 7–9)

MEEKNESS AND ACTION

Although meekness can look like weakness, it does not necessarily imply inaction. Jesus was not inactive when he healed his attacker's ear or called out for the forgiveness of his executioners. Moses, called the meekest man on earth in the Old Testament,[4] was not inactive when he confronted Pharaoh, led the people out of slavery in Egypt, and

---

3 The HCSB actually renders this word "land," as do many other translations. Either word is accurate, but I've used "earth" here to show the tie-in to Matthew more clearly.
4 Numbers 12:3

governed the recalcitrant children of Israel for forty years in the wilderness.

But for both these men, their response to evil was not anger, bitterness, violence, or strife. They did what David urges in Psalm 37:

They trusted in the Lord.

They did what was good.

They refused to be agitated and distressed by the apparent triumph of evil, remembering that goodness is always stronger and longer lasting.

They delighted in God.

They deliberately refrained from anger and gave up rage.

They put their hope, actively and constantly, in God.

And the result was inheritance. Their attitude of meekness in affliction enabled them to endure—and therefore to reach the finish line triumphant.

Running with Meekness

The power of this blessing can't really be overstated. I think of a time in my own life when it seemed to me that the enemy was winning. I was suffering personal blows that were manifestly unfair. Not only was the pain overwhelming, but the injustice of it all would rise in my throat and nearly physically choke me.

The temptation was very strong to become angry. To become bitter. To doubt God and blame others. To lash out against life, against the Lord, against those around me who were causing hurt.

And at times I gave in—of course I did. But this kingdom blessing offered a different path and a promise: that if I would walk in meekness, in the end, I would inherit the earth. I would be given the desires of my heart. I would last when the works of the enemy burned up like grass. Embracing humility, trust, and gentleness in the middle of intense trial allowed my heart to endure.

The race of life is at times incredibly hard. The temptation to burn ourselves out in anger and bitterness can be huge.

Jesus, like David, doesn't pretend everything is easy and fine. But he calls us to a hard way that turns out to be the only way that will allow us to thrive in times of hardship: a way of love and humility that will cause the fire to refine us instead of destroying us.

And he gives us a promise.

If you endure, you will inherit.

If you don't quit, you'll win.[5]

If you wait on the Lord, your trust will never prove to be empty.

He will give you the desires of your heart.

---

5 Thanks to Misty Edwards for this line.

Those who hunger and thirst
for righteousness are blessed,
for they will be filled.

(Matthew 5:6)

6

Blessed Are the Starving for Things to Be Made Right

This last of the "negative Beatitudes" once more blesses those who are in a naturally unblessed state. Hunger and thirst are not, in and of themselves, good.

I like to read this verse as, "Blessed are those who are starving, who are famished for things to be made right." We are hungry and thirsty for righteousness because we are not righteous. We desperately need righteousness within ourselves and in the world around us. It's a yearning we all feel, some of us more strongly than others—something much deeper than desire. We don't just want things to be okay in the world; we *need* them to be okay.

And they aren't. Those are the facts on the ground.

But Jesus's fourth kingdom blessing assures us that our hunger and thirst for righteousness will be filled.

Ancient Promises

Like everything else in Matthew, this promise is drenched in Old Testament context. Righteousness is the right ordering of everything in creation, especially within relationships—it is right-relatedness, between ourselves and everything else. It encompasses the ideas of justice and peace. Our desperate need for righteousness-within and righteousness-without goes all the way back to Eden and the brokenness introduced to the world there. And throughout the law and the prophets, God promised to answer this need.

In fact, the ultimate return of righteousness to the earth would be in the person of the Messiah, the Davidic king:

> Then a shoot will grow from the stump of Jesse,
> and a branch from his roots will bear fruit.
> The Spirit of the LORD will rest on Him—
> a Spirit of wisdom and understanding,
> a Spirit of counsel and strength,
> a Spirit of knowledge and of the fear of the LORD.
> His delight will be in the fear of the LORD.
> He will not judge
> by what He sees with His eyes,
> He will not execute justice
> by what He hears with His ears,
> but He will judge the poor righteously,

and execute justice for the oppressed of the land ...
Righteousness will be a belt around His loins;
faithfulness will be a belt around His waist.
The wolf will live with the lamb,
and the leopard will lie down with the goat.
The calf, the young lion, and the fatling will be together,
and a child will lead them.
The cow and the bear will graze,
their young ones will lie down together,
and the lion will eat straw like the ox.
An infant will play beside the cobra's pit,
and a toddler will put his hand into a snake's den.
None will harm or destroy another
on My entire holy mountain,
for the [earth] will be as full
of the knowledge of the LORD
as the sea is filled with water.
On that day the root of Jesse
will stand as a banner for the peoples.
The nations will seek Him,
and His resting place will be glorious.
(Isaiah 11:1–10)

The Beatitudes, as the inaugural blessings of the kingdom, proclaim Jesus as the Messiah: because he has come, those who hunger and thirst for righteousness will be filled.

To Lead a Hungry Life

The negative Beatitudes are ultimately blessings because they offer help for each negative state. But paradoxically, *because they accord with reality,* the negative states in themselves become blessed as well. If you are poor, better to accept it and go through life open-handed, rather than pridefully refuse help. If you are grieving, better to cry than to cut off your emotions and become hard. If you are going through affliction, the attitude of meekness will turn hardship into a refiner's fire instead of a ravager's flame. And if you are hungry and thirsty, it's better to know it than to grow so desensitized to your need for food and water that you starve to death.

Just as pain alerts us to danger so that we are able to avoid damage or seek healing, spiritual poverty, mourning, meekness, and hunger and thirst bring us face-to-face with the true state of things in our world and in our hearts.

The truth isn't pretty or easy. It's not what we'd like it to be. None of us wants to lead a hungry life.

But unless and until we embrace the truth of our need, we are not in a position for that need to be met. And the Meeter of Needs has in fact come. That is the whole point of the Beatitudes. Jesus identifies each of our deepest, most desperate needs and blesses them, because at long last, the answer to those needs has come.

Open your empty hands and let them be filled.

Open your grieving heart and let it be comforted.

Open your hungry soul wide and let the Lord of Creation feed you.

Repent, for the kingdom of heaven is here.

The Beginning of Righteousness

Everything about the kingdom of God in its present form has a now-but-not-yet aspect. Peter reminds us of this when, years after the ascension of Jesus, he writes,

> But based on His promise, we wait for the new heavens and a new earth, where righteousness will dwell. (2 Peter 3:13)

The kingdom of God came to earth with Jesus and was fully established when he sat down at the right hand of the Father in heaven. But the nature of the kingdom currently is that it's hidden inside of us—planted like a seed in our hearts.

The righteousness wrought within us will spill over into our world. The earth will be filled with the knowledge of God as the waters cover the sea—but first *we* will be filled with the knowledge of him, the experiential knowledge born of love, of fellowship, and of oneness of Spirit.

Perhaps the greatest miracle of the kingdom is that we don't have to wait for the new heavens and the new earth before righteousness will dwell in *us*—before we will be renewed and transformed into the image of Jesus from glory to glory.

The Ultimate Gift

To those who hunger and thirst for righteousness, Jesus offers not ultimately a change of circumstances or even a change of heart, but the gift of himself.

> I am the bread of life … No one who comes to Me will ever be hungry, and no one who believes in Me will ever be thirsty again. (John 6:35)

> Whoever drinks from the water that I will give him will never get thirsty again—ever! In fact, the water I will give him will become a well of water springing up within him for eternal life. (John 4:14)

We are truly blessed when we are hungry and thirsty for righteousness, for not only has Jesus promised to meet our need himself, but our fullness will overflow to fill the world. That too accords with reality, though it seems too good and too big and too abundant to be true. With the Lord as our shepherd, we shall not want for anything anymore.

The poor in spirit are blessed,
for the kingdom of heaven is theirs.
Those who mourn are blessed,
for they will be comforted.
The gentle are blessed,
for they will inherit the earth.
Those who hunger and thirst for
righteousness are blessed,
for they will be filled.
The merciful are blessed,
for they will be shown mercy.
The pure in heart are blessed,
for they will see God.
The peacemakers are blessed,
for they will be called sons of God.
Those who are persecuted for
righteousness are blessed,
for the kingdom of heaven is theirs.

(Matthew 5:3–10)

7

The Hidden Gospel in the Heart of the Beatitudes

Several years ago I was supposed to speak at a women's conference in Ontario on the Beatitudes and the kingdom of God. The theme was "seeing yourself through a kingdom lens." I'd suggested that topic in part because it was specific but still broad enough for me to develop my talk over time, as I prayed and thought about it. There was one problem: I prayed, I thought about it, I spent time with my Bible, and the evening before the conference arrived and I still had nothing to say.

I messaged a more experienced speaker friend in a mild panic. She laughed and said, "You'll be fine. Just say what the Spirit gives you to say."

Another friend reminded me that it wasn't like I didn't "know my stuff." I have studied and prayed through the Bible dozens of times over a lot of years, and all of that has laid a pretty solid foundation when I speak.

But even so. Going to speak in front of a hundred or so women with no talk outline was intimidating, and I felt irresponsible.

So that night, I lay down on my air mattress on the floor and continued to think about it. I realized part of the issue: While I found the Beatitudes enormously meaningful, I also found them scattered. The first half felt disconnected from the second half. I just didn't know how to teach them in a way that would be cohesive.

I knew there had to be a unifying principle in the Beatitudes somewhere. I just couldn't see it.

So I lay there staring up into the dark and asked God about it. What was I missing?

My roommates can attest to what happened next: in the dark at about one in the morning, I suddenly blurted out, "It's a chiasm!"

I flipped on my lamp and flipped through the pages of my Bible (apologies, roommates) with my heart racing. Was it true? Had I seen something that was really there, or was I making this up?

But as I read the lines of the Beatitudes again, armed with a bit of Greek knowledge, I saw it. Indeed the Beatitudes *are* a chiasm, and right at the heart of them lies their unifying principle: the gospel itself.

Chiastic Structure and the Heart of the Matter

The next morning I enthusiastically got up in front of that women's conference and proclaimed the chiastic structure of the Beatitudes to ... well, a lot of blank faces. Which wasn't unexpected, so I hastened to explain. In Greek literature, a chiasm is a particular structure in which points parallel one another at the top and bottom, and so on up and down the piece.

The structure gets its name from the Greek letter *chi,* which looks like an X. The main point—the "thesis statement," to use the lingo of contemporary essay writing—is right in the middle. This is very different from the structure we tend to use in our culture, where an argument builds to its high point at the end.

Chiasms are common in the New Testament, and understanding where the crux—the central point, the thesis statement—lies can help us get at the real force of a teaching. The parallels are illuminating as well, giving, as they often do, two different sides of a particular coin.

So far in this book, I've spoken of the first four blessings in Matthew 5 as "the negative Beatitudes." They all bless a particular state of lack. The last four are very different: each one blesses a virtue. This was why I found the Beatitudes so disjointed: how did the negatives and the positives relate? What was the central point of it all?

The answer is found in the heart of the chiasm, at the very center of the Beatitudes, where two parallel lines meet—and in their meeting, they transform. They transform not only the blessings of the kingdom, but our very lives.

Righteousness and Peace Have Kissed Each Other

Long before Jesus came, a psalmist prophesied, "Mercy and truth are met together; righteousness and peace have kissed each other" (Psalm 85:10, KJV). The fourth Beatitude is a double-edged sword. We are promised that those who hunger and thirst for righteousness will be filled. And we do need righteousness. We are famished for it, within ourselves and within the world. But anyone who hungers and calls out for righteousness to be established in the world has to come face-to-face with the necessity of judgment and the realization that our desire for things to be put right demands that we too come into the light—because we are part of the problem.

In another place, David—who was given to crying out for justice and righteousness—wrote,

> Do not bring Your servant into judgment,
> for no one alive is righteous in Your sight.
> (Psalm 143:2)

Paul sums the problem up neatly:

> Therefore, any one of you who judges is without excuse. For when you judge another, you condemn yourself, since you, the judge, do the same things. (Romans 2:1)

This isn't complicated theology: it's common human experience. Just as one example, you know the saying "hurt people hurt people"? You get hurt and are justifiably angry at the one who hurt you, but in your bitterness and anger you carry out the same actions toward someone else.

Or take prejudice. Few things upset me more than prejudice, especially racial prejudice. But can I honestly claim that I have no prejudice—no "pre-judgment"—of my own? That I don't even harbor prejudice against prejudiced people?

We human beings can get very black and white in our judgment of each other and our assessment of what would solve the problems around us. We know what "righteousness" would mean in our situation—what it would take to bring things into right order, to see justice come about and peace restored.

It's the kind of righteousness we see in every action movie where the hero seeks revenge. He scratched my car? Make him pay. She lied about me? Make sure everyone finds out the truth about her. They bombed us? Wipe them out. They hurt us? Damn them.

But then there's Paul, and Jesus too, with their warnings about judgment. When you judge another, you condemn yourself. "With the measure you use, it will be measured to you," Jesus says in Matthew 7:2. You can't have selective justice. We hunger and thirst for righteousness—but maybe all we'll get is a belly full of fire.

Into this dilemma the psalmist's words speak with haunting beauty. Is it really possible for righteousness and peace to embrace? Can mercy and truth sit down together as friends?

Indeed it is. They can. They do, here in the heart of the Beatitudes—in the middle of a chiasm, where two lines cross. And in the middle of *the* cross, where righteousness and mercy embrace in the person of Jesus Christ and flow out to the whole world.

Because of course, the very next blessing Jesus gives—the parallel tightly bound together with "Blessed are those who hunger and thirst for righteousness"—is "Blessed are the merciful, for they will obtain mercy."

Gospel Transformation

In the heart of the Beatitudes, righteousness and mercy meet. In the cross of Jesus, justice is done and mercy is offered. Sin is destroyed and life is bestowed. Righteousness is restored not through punishment but through forgiveness. It's a startling, breathtaking, indescribably counterintuitive way. It's Jesus's way. It's the way of restoration.

And it transforms. Reading the Beatitudes from top to bottom, a transformation occurs: four states of lack pass through mercy and are transformed. Suddenly the poor in spirit is one who possesses the kingdom. The one who mourns has become one who brings peace and comfort to others. The afflicted has become the pure in heart, who shall not only inherit the earth but actually see God. And the one who hungers and thirsts for righteousness has found everything put right at last—but in the obtaining and the giving of mercy, not in the strong hand of judgment.

The inaugural blessings of the kingdom promise new life to the people of this planet as we acknowledge our rightful king. He brings us hope, life, a better way.

He brings us the gospel—the good news—of the kingdom. With every layer we peel back, the better this news proves to be.

The merciful are blessed,
for they will be shown mercy.
(Matthew 5:7)

8

Blessed Are the Merciful, for They Will Obtain Mercy

I will never forget the awful, sick feeling that came over me the day I watched someone I knew get what he deserved.

He was a bitter, judgmental, hypercritical person. He'd brought negativity and pain into many lives. He never really had time or grace for others. That day, it came back to bite him.

He deserved it.

It was horrible.

I realized that day that I have often wanted people to get what they deserve. At least, that's what I thought I wanted. I'd probably wanted that for this particular person. But now that it was actually happening, all I could see was the truly heartbreaking consequences of sin. I couldn't rejoice in it at all. It broke my heart. Honestly, in that moment it didn't matter that he'd sown what he was reaping. It didn't matter that he deserved it. All I wanted was for people to forgive. To embrace the joy of grace freely given and transform his harvest into something he *didn't* deserve.

I'd never realized until that day how precious and beautiful mercy truly is.

Father, Forgive Them

The fifth blessing of the kingdom, tightly bound with righteousness in the very heart of the Beatitudes, is "Blessed are the merciful, for they will obtain mercy."

Few things reveal the character of God like mercy does.

Mercy, in both Greek and Hebrew, is more than just a judicial "letting someone off the hook." For some reason, when I view it that way, I always see it being offered with an air of indifference or even condescension. But the Greek word for mercy, *eleos*, is emotional. It's empathetic. The idea *is* that of a judge letting someone off, but doing so because he sees the misery that justice would bring. He sees the wretchedness of the accused and feels for him. In Hebrew, a similar word translated "mercy" is even stronger. It actually comes from a root word for "womb." The word is *racham*, and it indicates a deep, gut-level empathy and identification with the one suffering.

On some level, this is why Jesus came. Because

he saw what we had coming to us and couldn't stomach it. Because he looked at people who deserved to reap misery and desperately wanted to change their harvest. He came to let adulteresses off the hook and tell them to go and sin no more. He came to kick the demons out of people who'd been reduced to living among tombs in self-harm and self-hatred. He came to look sinful people square in the face and call them children of God.

When he was beaten, bloodied, mocked, betrayed, and about to die, Jesus looked at his executioners—people absolutely dripping with guilt—and prayed, "Father, forgive them, for they know not what they do."[1]

The High Cost of Mercy

Mercy does not come without a cost. Injustice is real, sin is real, and people really do get hurt. Sometimes it seems like our whole being screams out for retribution. If mercy is going to be shown to perpetrators, it's going to cost us. We will have to let go of our need to be satisfied.

This is why the blessing Jesus gives is conditional: he doesn't say "blessed are the whole human race, for they will all obtain mercy." Rather, he requires that we show mercy if we want to obtain it. We need God's compassion and empathy for us. We

---

[1] Luke 23:34

need his forgiveness desperately. But we also need to be willing to create a new cycle, to let go of our own demands for retributive justice.

Forgiveness is offered to us freely, but we have to empty our hands if we want to receive it. We can accept the gospel, but we also have to be the gospel. If you want mercy, live mercy. We must become mercy to others, to learn to share Jesus's heart of compassion. Otherwise we block our own blessing by insisting that we want to stay in the cycle of sowing and reaping sin and its consequence, death.

A New Cycle

As we've seen, our desire for justice is a catch-22 because we are not, ourselves, innocent. No one is. The more we insist that others should get what's coming to them, the more we agree that we too must get what's coming to us. We can't have it both ways: either we live in the cycle of sin and death or we don't.

Mercy offers us a way out. It acknowledges the wrongdoing for what it is—wrong, and deserving of punishment. But it chooses to bestow grace instead. It chooses to forgive. It hates the thought of anyone suffering through the consequences of their own actions because it realizes just how truly awful those consequences actually are.

Not everyone will obtain mercy. The Bible is clear about that. Jesus offers us a new cycle: "The law of the Spirit of life in Christ Jesus has set us free from the law of sin and death" (Romans 8:2). But it's up to each one of us individually to enter that new life or not, and that's between us and God. He offers mercy to all, but not everyone will receive it. Not everyone will be willing to pay the price: to receive forgiveness for ourselves means offering it to those who have hurt us too.

The Freedom of Forgiveness

Ultimately, the crux of the Beatitudes—the twin blessings of righteousness and mercy—underscore the incredible promise of the gospel: everything *will* be made right, creation *will* be reconciled, peace *will* reign, and life *will* triumph, but they'll do it through the back door—not by coming and slaying God's enemies in a flood or a fire, but by redeeming and transforming them through mercy. It's cosmically counterintuitive, and it's beautiful. It's hope, and it's freedom.

Mercy and forgiveness do cost us. But everyone who has embraced them will attest to the freedom they bring. Rather than binding us, letting go of our need for retribution sets us free from the whole cycle of judgment. It releases us, and the whole creation around us, into the possibility of newness: of a future loosed from the chains of the past.

Mercy is our only hope. Give it, receive it. If you do, you are truly blessed.

THE PURE IN HEART ARE BLESSED,
FOR THEY WILL SEE GOD.

(Matthew 5:8)

9

"They Shall See God": Purity of Heart and the Greatest Blessing of All

From the beginning, the Beatitudes have been full of outsized blessings.

You have nothing? I'll give you a kingdom.

Alone in your grief? God himself will come alongside you.

Struggling against oppression and injustice? Take heart; you will inherit the earth.

But perhaps none is so outsized, so outlandish as this: "Blessed are the pure in heart, for they shall see God."

"No One Can See Me and Live"

Moses, the greatest of God's prophets, once refused to take another step unless he could see God. He had led the people out of Egypt, witnessed God's unspeakable power and supreme authority over all creation, received the marvelous and mysterious law. But none of that was enough for him. He needed more. He needed to see not just God's outstretched hand but his *face*.

Isn't that the way of love, after all? Who among us would be satisfied, having fallen in love, with just receiving letters from our beloved, or with benefiting from something he had done—if we never actually got to *see* him, to be with him?

And besides that, Moses knew the task in front of him was too big for him. The people too difficult, too stiff-necked. The journey too long and too thirsty.

So he said, "Please, let me see your glory."

> [The LORD] said, "I will cause all My goodness to pass in front of you, and I will proclaim the name Yahweh before you ... but ... You cannot see My face, for no one can see Me and live." The LORD said, "Here is a place near Me. You are to stand on the rock, and when My glory passes by, I will put you in the crevice of the rock and cover you with My hand until I have passed by. Then I will take My hand away, and you will see My back, but My face will not be seen." (Exodus 33:18–23)

So Moses.

But here is Jesus, sitting on a hill overlooking a vast crowd of ordinaries, of you-and-mes. A crowd of people who are poor in spirit, who have nothing to offer; who are curious and impoverished and ignorant. And he promises them, almost casually:

You will see God.

Yes, you.

Whosoever will.

A Two-Sided Promise

Of course, there is a condition: only the pure in heart will see God.

Here we come face-to-face with the changed nature of the Beatitudes: *they are no longer negative.* We have passed through the middle, through the gospel in the heart of the chiasm, and now the conditions are positive. These promises belong to the merciful, to the pure, to the peacemakers, to the prophets.

But who is pure in heart?

The prophets are unanimous on this:

No one.

Moses wasn't. Isaiah wasn't. David wasn't.

Since the fall in the garden, no one has ever been pure enough to see God and live. That is the conundrum of his holiness: we need to see his glory, we need to see his face, but if we do, it will kill us.

But then there's Jesus.

The only one who *is* pure enough, in his own right, to see the face of his Father. The only one who has not lost the pure vision of his Creator. The only one without a log in his eye or a sin in his heart.

Here he is, offering his vision. To us.

The Transformation

The chiastic structure of the Beatitudes means the lines parallel one another as they ascend and descend. The gospel lies right at the heart: mercy and righteousness have met together. The fulfillment of our longings is coupled with the forgiveness of our sins.

Passing through that heart means something dramatic happens—in this case, the transformation of the afflicted.

The parallel line to "Blessed are the pure in heart" is "Blessed are the meek, for they shall inherit the earth." Earlier I talked about the nature of meekness, that it's a particular response to affliction. The whole Bible promises that God's people will not be destroyed by affliction, as long as they embrace trust in God in the midst of it. Romans 8:28 promises that God will work all things together for good to those who love him.

And here is the greatest good:

That the fire of affliction, rather than destroying us, will purify.

Passed through the gospel, the meek will become the pure in heart.

And the pure in heart will see God.

The Nature of Sanctification

In Christian parlance, we call this transforming work of God "sanctification." It's easy to think sanctification is our responsibility, that the work of being sanctified is all on our shoulders. But if you read Paul, especially in Romans 6, you get the sense that sanctification is just as much a miracle as justification is. God hasn't pulled a switch: we're not given the gift of mercy and righteousness only to find ourselves kicked out of the kingdom until such time as hardship makes us worthy to get back in.

That's not it at all. Rather, Jesus, who can see God, has invited us into himself. He joins us with his body and blood and spirit. He places us in the rock that is himself, covers us with his hand, and says, "Look—see the face of the Father."

The heart of God has always been to bless us. The same people of Israel who could not see the face of God were given the Aaronic blessing:

> May Yahweh bless you and protect you;
> may Yahweh make His face shine on you
> and be gracious to you;
> may Yahweh look with favor on you
> and give you peace.
> (Numbers 6:24–26)

The face of God is shining on us. The hand of Jesus is covering us. The fire is necessary to remove the blinders that prevent us from seeing the grace in Yahweh's gaze.

This is the truth about sanctification: it's all a gift. It all starts with the Father's shining face—his smile. His desire. His wish to be known, stronger than our desire to know.

Far from being a matter of us flagellating ourselves into the kingdom, it is all a gift of grace.

We do not know what it will take to get us there—to bring us from our current partial blindness to a full view of God. But he does. And he has committed himself to taking us there.

Gift Upon Gift

From here on out, the Beatitudes are double blessings. The gifts that lead us into the heart of the gospel—the kingdom, the nearness of God, the inheritance of reward through affliction, the quenching of our thirst—now transform us.

We are not pure in heart. But we will be.

We cannot see God. But indeed, we will.

And miracle of miracles, when we do, we will not be destroyed. Instead, we will bask in the light of his face. And we will be transformed.

Of every promise in the Bible, this one fills me most with fearful wonder: *Beloved, we are God's children now, and what we will be has not yet been revealed. We know that when He appears, we will be like Him because we will see Him as He is.*[1]

---

[1] 1 John 3:2, HCSB and ESV

> THE PEACEMAKERS ARE BLESSED,
> FOR THEY WILL BE CALLED SONS OF GOD.
>
> (Matthew 5:9)

10

Blessed Are the Makers of Reconciliation: Peacemaking and the Heart of God

Discovering the gospel in the heart of the Beatitudes made me read the whole list very differently. Rather than a disjointed list of random blessings, the Beatitudes are a journey.

They take us from our starting point (impoverished, broken, grieving, afflicted), gift us outrageously, and pass us through the gospel of mercy and truth to what we become: pure, peacemakers, prophets.

Where the first four Beatitudes pull us out of our brokenness, the last four set forth our victory: This is what we are saved for. This is what we become.

Blessed Are the Peacemakers

In the chiasm of the Beatitudes, "Blessed are the peacemakers, for they shall be called the children of God" parallels "Blessed are those who mourn, for they shall be comforted." As we saw, in the Greek, this latter blessing is literally that God will come alongside the grief-stricken. He will personally draw near to them.

When we have experienced that—when we have come through the gospel and known God as our Comforter—we find ourselves with a mission. As God has drawn near to us, so we are to draw near to others. As God has come alongside us, so we are to come alongside others.

And even more, it is our mission—our beautiful work—to make the comfort given to us available to others. Paul says it best:

> Therefore, we are ambassadors for Christ, certain that God is appealing through us. We plead on Christ's behalf, "Be reconciled to God." (2 Corinthians 5:20)

To be a peacemaker means far more than calming a situation down or negotiating between people. "Peace" in biblical language is a much more far-reaching idea than that. Peace is reconciliation. It is wholeness. It is healing and prosperity and blessedness.

It is shalom.

CHILDREN OF GOD

Jesus declares that the peacemakers will be called children of God. In Greek, the word translated "children" doesn't just identify paternity; it emphasizes resemblance. When our primary mission is to come alongside those who suffer, to identify with them and to bring them near to God, the world will look at us and see him. We will resemble our Father.

Our mission here is to do as God has done and to bring his presence near to others:

To see the hurting for who they truly are.

To come near them.

To sit with them, to mourn with them, to encourage and strengthen them.

And to offer them the most beautiful thing of all:

Peace.

To offer them healing and wholeness in the midst of their brokenness.

Not through our own power or our own ability,

But through the availability of an incredible blessing:

Blessed are those who mourn, for they shall be comforted.

On Christ's behalf we plead, "Be reconciled to God."

Blessed Are the Reconciliation Makers

It can be easy to get militant about our faith in a way that isn't helpful. There is a way to be militant that is good; Paul used military language for a reason. But we can't forget that the New Testament never identifies other people as the enemy. Our enemy is spiritual, and the weapons of our warfare are not carnal.[1]

It's my opinion that many of us need to re-vision our identity through the lens of the Beatitudes.

We need to understand ourselves as something other than condemnation bringers.

We are not right opinion expressers.

We are not (primarily) sin identifiers.

We are not (primarily) apologists.

Certainly not argument winners.

We are reconciliation makers.

Wholeness makers.

Healers.

We are children of God.

Comfort and the Heart of God

We have been comforted. In Jesus, God came to us when we least deserved it. The Creator of the universe has drawn close to us, not with condemnation or shame, but with love, encouragement, tenderness, and an offer of new life.

That comfort is given to us, Paul says, to pass along. We aren't just saved to be saved. We're saved to catch a vision. We're saved to become like God.

---

[1] 2 Corinthians 10:4

We're saved to learn to care.

> If we are afflicted, it is for your comfort and salvation. If we are comforted, it is for your comfort, which is experienced in your endurance of the same sufferings that we suffer. (2 Corinthians 1:6)

In this blessing, the seventh Beatitude—interestingly the number of divine perfection—we see the heart of God. We see what he wants us to become and what he wants us to offer. We see what he wants to give the world.

I know it sounds flaky. I know it sounds all flower-power and too warm and fuzzy and good to be true. And yes, there is a lot of fire and suffering and purity that comes into the picture. But in the end, it's true:

What God wants to give the world is himself.

He wants to draw near.

He wants to comfort us.

He wants to give the whole world a hug.

To say "I understand."

And to say "Come home to me."

"We can be reconciled. You can be whole again. I know you're hurting. I know. I care."

We plead, on Christ's behalf: "Be reconciled to God."

Those who are persecuted
for righteousness are blessed,
for the kingdom of heaven is theirs.

You are blessed when they insult and
persecute you and falsely say every kind
of evil against you because of Me. Be glad
and rejoice, because your reward is great
in heaven. For that is how they persecuted
the prophets who were before you.

(Matthew 5:10–12)

11

Blessed Are the Persecuted Prophets, Part 1: This Means You

The last of the Beatitude blessings is the longest and in some ways the most perplexing. To quote it again in the beautiful King James:

> Blessed are they which are persecuted for righteousness' sake: for theirs is the kingdom of heaven. Blessed are ye, when men shall revile you, and persecute you, and shall say all manner of evil against you falsely, for my sake. Rejoice, and be exceeding glad: for great is your reward in heaven: for so persecuted they the prophets which were before you.

In the middle of this final blessing, Jesus looks his disciples in the eye, and rather than repeating "blessed are they," he says "blessed are you."

In other words: *This means you.*

Who Wants to Be Persecuted?

This blessing always strikes me as a double-edged sword: the promise of persecution is frightening, yet the rewards promised are apparently staggering. "Rejoice and be exceeding glad" is *strong* wording. Luke says it, "Rejoice ye in that day, *and leap for joy: for, behold, your reward is great in heaven.*"[1]

In our North American context, where few of us ever experience actual persecution (we live in a society that has been profoundly shaped by the gospel, whether we realize it or not, and that kind of society tends to weigh against persecution in general), this blessing can cause some consternation. We read it as "real Christians get persecuted," and I think that sometimes has us manufacturing persecution so we can feel like real Christians.

But ultimately this blessing is not so much about circumstances as it is about a change in identity, and "persecuted" is not the identity word here. "Prophet" is.

Who Wants to Be a Prophet?

In Numbers 11 we read about a day during the Israelites' wilderness wanderings when Moses was instructed to call seventy elders together and impart the Spirit to them. When this happened, they began to prophesy; and Joshua, Moses's personal atten-

---

[1] Luke 6:23, KJV, my emphasis.

dant, friend, and eventual successor, was concerned. He went to Moses and urged him to stop them.

Here Moses reveals the heart of God for his people:

> Are you jealous on my account? If only all the LORD's people were prophets and the LORD would place his Spirit on them! (Numbers 11:29)

That desire was largely thwarted in the Old Covenant era due to hardness of heart. But it was always God's heartbeat: *If only all the LORD's people were prophets. If only all the LORD's people were full of the Holy Spirit.*

What would it mean to this world if all the Lord's people heard from him? If all were capable of speaking his heart and mind into specific situations? If all had the power to release the Word of the Lord into culture, into circumstances, into lives?

During the age of the prophets, this desire took the crystalized form of a promise: a new covenant would come in which, indeed, all the Lord's people *would* be prophets.

> "Look, the days are coming"— this is the LORD's declaration—"when I will make a new covenant with the house of Israel and with the house of Judah ... I will put My teaching within them and write it on their

hearts. I will be their God, and they will be My people. No longer will one teach his neighbor or his brother, saying, 'Know the LORD,' for they will all know Me, from the least to the greatest of them." (Jeremiah 31:31, 33–34)

I will give you a new heart and put a new spirit within you; I will remove your heart of stone and give you a heart of flesh. I will place My Spirit within you ... you will be My people, and I will be your God. (Ezekiel 36:26–28)

After this I will pour out My Spirit on all humanity; then your sons and your daughters will prophesy, your old men will have dreams, and your young men will see visions. I will even pour out My Spirit on the male and female slaves in those days. (Joel 2:28–29)

You Are Greater than John the Baptist

The Beatitudes have enacted a transformation: through the gospel, the blessing of Jesus turns people who were poor in spirit—having nothing, entirely without spiritual resources, bereft and poverty-stricken—into prophets.

Jesus once declared that among all the prophets known to history, none was greater than John the

Baptist. John was greater than Elijah, greater than Elisha, greater even than Moses or Abraham. And then he said, "But the least in the kingdom of heaven is greater than he" (Matthew 11:11).

This means you.

Prophets of a New Era

John's greatness wasn't so much about his personal qualities as it was about his position in history. Other prophets had spoken for God, but no other prophet directly heralded his coming.

John, in the womb, was the first to recognize the incarnate Creator in the earth. As a prophet, he literally prepared the way for God. He baptized him. John was the prophet who finally, after thousands of years, declared "The kingdom of heaven is at hand."

So what makes *you* greater than John the Baptist?

John lived in the era of the kingdom near. You live in the era of the kingdom come. And if you have received the blessings of Jesus, you have been given the kingdom. If you have received the Holy Spirit, you have become united to God in a way no one before John ever experienced.

Welcome to the *real* "New Age"—the age of the kingdom of God.

In the chiasm of the Beatitudes, this is where we see the transformation most starkly. Those who were spiritually poverty-stricken have become prophets of God.

How? Simply by receiving the kingdom of God in the person of Jesus Christ—and this is entirely a gift of grace.

The paupers become kings. The dumb sing the songs of God. The world is turned upside down.

As Mary sang, "He has toppled the mighty from their thrones, and exalted the lowly. He has satisfied the hungry with good things and sent the rich away empty."[2]

Jesus is almost casual about it: "Rejoice and be glad when this happens to you, for the world treated the other prophets the same way."

Not every believer will receive the charismatic gift of prophecy described in 1 Corinthians, and of those who do, not everyone will exercise it in equal measure. Certainly, the twelve apostles—the original "you" addressed by Jesus in this passage—had a prophetic role different from mine or yours. And yet, every believer with a Bible possesses a prophetic word for the world. Every Christian who can hear the Shepherd's voice call his or her name has a gift to give through that same voice. Each and every one who lives in the kingdom of God has a crucial role

---

[2] Luke 1:52–53

to play in that kingdom, and our roles in a fallen world are intrinsically prophetic.

This means you. Your identity has changed. You are no longer a pauper, but one who lives on this earth in fellowship with God, able to speak to, with, and sometimes for God. You who were nothing but dust now hear the secrets of eternity whispered in your ear. You who were a mud hut have become a temple.

If, of course, you have received the kingdom—a gift only given by Jesus.

Elect Yourself

The Beatitudes are blessings, and the thing about blessings—gifts as they are—is that you have to receive them. When Jesus looked at his disciples and the crowd all around them and said "Blessed are *you*," he knew not everyone would accept the blessing. Some would turn their backs; some would even end up opposing him. But others would step up, hold out their empty hands, and say "Yes, please."

Do you want to be transformed?

Do you want to go from poor to prophet?

Do you want to live in fellowship and communication with the very Creator of the universe?

Then elect yourself.

Step up to the altar and say, "I do."

12

The God Who Respects Our No

The gospel is a comedy in the Shakespearean sense: it ends with a wedding and turns expectations on their heads along the way.

It's often said that the people of Jesus's time expected the Messiah to come in military power, overthrow Rome, and rule Israel from a literal throne in Jerusalem. That is surely the truth—even though the Old Testament gave hints, all along, that that wasn't exactly how it would be. God's plan was more subversive, more transformational than that.

And so when Jesus calls us his prophets at the end of the Beatitudes, he also promises persecution. He's actually quite specific: you will be *persecuted, insulted,* and *slandered* for the sake of righteousness and because of Jesus.

But when that happens, he lets us know, we ought to rejoice and be exceedingly glad, because our reward is great in heaven.

Why Persecution Comes

In a sense, it seems backward that persecution should be allowed to come against the people of God. If God is sovereign (which he is), if Jesus is triumphant (which he is), and if the kingdom of God has come (which it has), why isn't persecution a thing of the past? Why aren't the righteous immediately vindicated, and the wicked—here defined as those who reject the gift that would transform and save them—just forced into compliance?

The answer lies in God's respect and love for all people, and in the subversive nature of his plan. He did not come to destroy the people in whom the kingdom of darkness reigns, but to transport them out of it into the kingdom of light.

Forces of Heaven

At Jesus's trial, Pilate asked him whether he was the King of the Jews. Jesus answered:

> My kingdom is not of this world. If My kingdom were of this world, My servants would fight, so that I wouldn't be handed over to the Jews. As it is, My kingdom does not have its origin here. (John 18:36)

Only hours earlier, the disciples had experienced

what this meant in a visceral way. When soldiers and a mob showed up to arrest Jesus, Peter leapt forward with great courage and drew his sword to defend his friend and rabbi, as he had sworn to do. He struck the servant of the high priest and cut off his ear. It was a classic showdown: good versus evil, the children of light springing to the defense of the innocent.

Except that Jesus held out his hand to stop Peter. He knelt down and replaced the servant's ear. And he said:

> Put your sword back in its place because all who take up a sword will perish by the sword. Or do you think that I cannot call on My Father, and He will provide Me at once with more than 12 legions of angels? How, then, would the Scriptures be fulfilled that say it must happen this way? (Matthew 26:52–54)

A Roman legion could include six thousand soldiers, so Jesus revealed here that he could immediately call more than seventy thousand angelic soldiers into action.

But he didn't. He respected his enemies and left them alive so that he could secure the means of their salvation and forgiveness only a little way down the road.

The Seed Kingdom

The kingdom of heaven does not work the way the kingdoms of the world do. Historically, the kingdoms of the world advance through conquest and force. By contrast, Jesus came and planted his kingdom as an invisible force in the lives of his people. He chose empty people and made them prophets, able to give voice to the heart of God in the world. Our lives are seeds. The kingdom does not come from outside and force its way in; it comes from inside, germinates in secret, and grows.

Until it changes the world.

For that process to work, the kingdom cannot rely on violence. Every time Christians have tried to advance the kingdom through violent means, it has backfired. We have driven people away from God, not drawn them to him. God's desire isn't to cut off the enemies' ears; it's to heal them.

How else can they hear the Word that would save them?

Violent Realities

The kingdom has come as a seed and a message. It will literally transform lives, and it will bring the rule of God into every place where it's invited. It does so in a way that is not violent ... on an earthly level. On a spiritual level, this is violence indeed.

The gates of hell will not prevail against the church, Jesus declared. The kingdom of light invades, raids, and guts the kingdom of darkness.

So the kingdom of darkness fights back.

It's interesting that out of the three types of persecution Jesus promises here, two are spoken: insults and slander (lies). The kingdom of God advances primarily through word; the kingdom of darkness fights back the same way. Truth is powerful; so are lies.

But since truth is *more* powerful, and since it brings with it freedom and transformation, the kingdom of darkness is not above good old-fashioned physical violence either. Persecution happens, especially when the gospel first advances in a region. So many Christians died in the Roman Empire during the early Christian era that the second-century apologist Tertullian wrote, "The blood of the martyrs is the seed of the church."[1]

The God Who Died for Us

God is on a rescue mission. The goal is not to destroy the world, as happened with Noah's flood, but to save it. A violent world fights back. God is constantly rejected. Those who speak for God shouldn't expect that they won't be affected by this.

---

[1] A loose translation from Tertullian's Apologeticus, AD 197.

So God tells us to turn the other cheek, love our enemies, bless those who curse us. The kingdom of light will win in this way.

We shouldn't think this means God delights in our suffering. He wept over his own in Gethsemane. But we live in a violent reality, and God invites us to join him in loving his enemies, in pursuing those who reject him, in blessing those who curse, in replacing the ears of those who come to cut off our message.

God respects the "no" of those who reject him every day. His plan is long-term and transformational. He is giving a full harvest time to grow. More seeds drop all the time. Some are germinating deep in the earth. Others are already changing the landscape. Some fields are new; some have been bearing fruit for hundreds of years. The fight is a riot of weeds in the midst of the wheat—but the wheat is there.

The Great Invitation

So we are invited into God's mission. We are invited into his patience. We are promised persecution in the process—that just as he met with opposition, slander, and trouble, so will we.

We don't have to manufacture our own persecution complexes in order to feel genuinely Christian. We can thank God for times and places of peace even as we keep up the work of sowing, watering, growing, and transforming in whatever ways present themselves.

But where we do encounter trouble, we're also promised reward. Reward so great that we should, as Luke says, "Leap for joy." There is trouble on earth, where so much of this-worldly reality is still violent. But in heaven—the parallel reality, the invisible world in which we already live through the Spirit—there is unspeakable reward.

13

The Gospel According to Jesus

The Beatitudes, so familiar and easy to gloss over, are breathtaking when we see them clearly. Far from just a disjointed list of niceties, these kingdom blessings encompass the gospel according to Jesus. The kingdom of God is here, and so we are transformed by the grace of God—and the whole world with us.

Can there be a clearer picture of God's transforming goodness?

In the Beatitudes we come empty, mourning, afflicted, and hungry. We leave merciful, pure, peacemaking, and prophetic.

You Are the Gospel

The gospel is not just "you are a sinner, so you must repent and be forgiven so you can go to heaven when you die." It is so much more than that. The gift of God is eternal life that begins now, a heaven that comes to earth, grace that not only amazes but overwhelms and transforms.

Lord, forgive us for making it so small!

The gospel of the kingdom is a huge story, one that began long before us and is much, much bigger than our personal needs and concerns. Yet it's so intensely personal that it can be summed up in the eight blessings of Jesus to individuals who are hungry and thirsty and spiritually impoverished, in the gifts God promises to give to all who come to him.

The gospel of the kingdom is more than "asking Jesus into our hearts." And yet the gospel is incarnate in us when we receive the goodness and grace of God. We are the flesh and bones of the good news. We are clay jars housing the Holy Spirit. We are the Beatitudes lived out—as individuals, and still more perfectly, as the community of God knit to one another in love.

The gospel isn't magic. For many people, the journey of transformation begins with "praying a prayer," but praying a prayer in itself doesn't work the change God promises in our lives. The gospel is a matter of receiving the blessings of God and living out their results.

It's important to remember that the blessings aren't given as a result of our efforts or our suitability for the job. To receive them, we just need open hands.

Remember, the first half of the Beatitudes—what you might call the requirements for receiving the kingdom—are all negatives. You just have to be poor. Sad. In trouble. Hungry. Go to God with that kind of resume, and you are going to get hired. His blessings are intended to turn your poverty into untold spiritual riches.

Relational Transformation

The gospel of the kingdom isn't magic, because transformation doesn't just happen through a prayer or a set of rules or rituals. Every transformation in the Beatitudes is relational, and the blessings work relationally.

Look at them again:

> Blessed are the poor in spirit: for theirs is the kingdom of heaven.
>
> Blessed are they that mourn: for they shall be comforted.
>
> Blessed are the meek: for they shall inherit the earth.
>
> Blessed are they which do hunger and thirst after righteousness: for they shall be filled.
>
> Blessed are the merciful: for they shall obtain mercy.
>
> Blessed are the pure in heart: for they shall see God.

> Blessed are the peacemakers: for they shall be called the children of God.
>
> Blessed are they which are persecuted for righteousness' sake: for theirs is the kingdom of heaven.
>
> Blessed are ye, when men shall revile you, and persecute you, and shall say all manner of evil against you falsely, for my sake. Rejoice, and be exceeding glad: for great is your reward in heaven: for so persecuted they the prophets which were before you. (Matthew 5:3–12, KJV)

We receive a kingdom ruled by a king, and that King chooses to speak to us and through us as his prophetic people.

In our mourning, God himself promises to draw near to us and comfort us, making us agents of reconciliation in the process.

In our affliction, God promises to work through our trials for our good, to purify our hearts, and to fulfill all his promises to us.

Jesus feeds our hunger and thirst with himself and pours his undeserved mercy and compassion on us.

The gospel of the kingdom is the good news of God highly, deeply, personally engaged with us, effecting transformation in our lives, working his purposes through our pains and hopes and relationships. The gospel Jesus actually preached is not a system for getting to heaven or a set of teachings to embrace, but a promise that God himself will walk with us in the nitty-gritty of our lives and do something eternal and heavenly through our tiny earthly selves.

Do You Actually Want To Be Changed?

The last Beatitude includes the paradoxical exhortation to rejoice and be wildly happy when we are persecuted for the sake of Jesus and the gospel. What God promises to do in us is incredible, but it will come with trouble in this world. That's just the nature of things when you're at the center of a battle to save the universe. But it has the effect of testing our allegiance too.

Do we want to be changed?

Do we want to be healed?

Do we want to become agents of reconciliation and carriers of the Spirit?

The gospel Jesus preached isn't the kind of message that just allows us to go on living the status quo. It requires a total shift in our priorities, our perspective, and our purpose.

Are you in?

PART 2:

The Law of Love: Jesus on Morality, Righteousness, and Becoming Like God

You are the salt of the earth.
But if the salt should lose its taste,
how can it be made salty? It's no longer
good for anything but to be thrown
out and trampled on by men.

(Matthew 5:13)

14

Why You Are Here

It's one of my pet peeves, and I hear Christians say it all the time, usually with an air of superiority: *"We shouldn't be surprised things are getting so bad. The only thing that's going to fix it is Jesus coming back."*

We say it about politics. About cultural trends. About R-rated movies. About the irresponsible kid next door.

Jesus said something different. He said:

> You are the salt of the earth. But if the salt should lose its taste, how can it be made salty? It's no longer good for anything but to be thrown out and trampled on by men. (Matthew 5:13)

The people of God are the salt of the earth. Which should change the conversation.

Jesus coming back isn't "the only thing that's going to fix it."

Your presence is.

WHAT'S THE DEAL WITH SALT?

Salt has two properties that I believe are key to understanding this verse:

> 1. It makes us thirsty, and conversely, enables us to become hydrated by actually holding on to water. Without proper salt in our diet, water just runs through us.
>
> 2. It guards against rot. Even today, salt is used as a preservative. In the ancient world, it was *the* preservative.

What does it mean that you are the salt of the earth?

It means that *you*—by your presence, by your lifestyle, by your faithfulness to God—act as a preservative in our culture. You keep it from going completely rotten and corrupt.

Not only that, but you have the potential to make people thirsty for God and enable them to retain the grace he gives them.

SALT IN SODOM AND GOMORRAH

In Genesis 18, Abraham sparred with God about the destruction of the twin cities Sodom and Gomorrah. God said the cities had become so wicked that he was going to destroy them, but Abraham pleaded with God to spare Sodom and Gomorrah if even fifty righteous people remained in them. God agreed. Abraham, realizing that fifty righteous people in these cities was too tall an order, lowered the limit to forty-five. Then forty. Then thirty. Then twenty. Then ten.

God agreed on every count. But there weren't ten righteous people in the cities.

God sent two angels into Sodom and Gomorrah to bring out the four people who did qualify as righteous, and after they were gone, he rained fire and brimstone from heaven and destroyed the cities.

Here's the key: As long as a certain number of righteous people remained, the cities could not be destroyed. Their presence there acted as a preservative, preventing judgment from coming.

Had there been more righteous individuals in Sodom and Gomorrah to begin with, the cities might never have needed to be destroyed. Their wickedness might actually have been beaten back by the presence of light.

Remember Lot's wife? She failed to act as salt in Sodom and Gomorrah, instead succumbing to the force of the wicked culture around her. When she looked back, she was turned into a pillar of salt.

That's called irony.

Noah's Flood and the Family of Israel

Genesis tells us that in the beginning, evil and violence spread very quickly through the earth. The descendants of Adam and Eve plunged into rampant wickedness so thoroughly that by the time of Noah, he was considered the only righteous man alive. Of everyone else, God said that every thought of their hearts was only evil all the time.[1]

Think about that. *Only evil all the time.* What kind of world would that be to live in?

But God promised that after Noah, he would never again destroy the world with a flood, which meant he needed a plan to keep things from getting that bad again. He had one: a family.

Early in the history of the reconstituted, post-flood world, God called a man named Abraham and promised to bless the world through him and his descendants.[2] Abraham's chosen line became the nation of Israel, and in Exodus 20, God did something unprecedented: he gave this family a law. He opened up the vaults of heaven and gave them teachings, principles, and strictures that would keep them from succumbing to the rot of wickedness.

Why?

Ultimately, to provide a family for the coming Messiah, whose presence would save the whole world.

---

1 Genesis 6:5
2 Genesis 22:15–18

And in the meantime, to salt the earth.

One small nation, historically persecuted and in biblical times rarely actually faithful to their own call, nevertheless acted as a preserving agent in the earth and stopped the pre-flood world from ever becoming a reality again. They created a thirst for God and allowed God's grace and blessings to linger here.

It was to a crowd of people from this nation that Jesus first said, "You are the salt of the earth."

Stand Up and Salt Something

Today, disciples of Jesus have the same call. We are not just supposed to sit back and shake our heads at how bad things are. We are to understand ourselves as agents of hydration and preservation.

We are here in our country, our culture, our time for a reason—and the reason isn't shaking our heads at other people.

We're here to intercede for them. We're here to bring godly perspectives into play, to bring them up in conversation, in business, in ministry. We're here to bring other people into the kingdom. We're here to conduct our own lives in a way that counteracts the corruption around us.

Jesus warned his hearers that salt can lose its saltiness, and if it does, it's no longer any good as a preservative. It won't work. Corruption will win, and the salt will be thrown out and trampled on.

Today, don't lose your saltiness. This is so much bigger than you. Most of us grieve where our world is going these days, but what are we doing to stand in the gap?

Jesus will come back and fix things. But in the meantime, he's already provided an answer to the rot.

The answer is you.

You are the light of the world.
A city situated on a hill cannot be hidden.
No one lights a lamp and puts it under a
basket, but rather on a lampstand, and it
gives light to all who are in the house.
In the same way, let your light shine before
men, so that they may see your good works
and give glory to your Father in heaven.

(Matthew 5:14–16)

15

You Weren't Saved Just for Your Own Sake

In the progression of the Sermon on the Mount, Jesus began with the offer of the kingdom. The kingdom is a gift of grace, given to the empty-handed, the poor in spirit. It is a blessing, a gift empowered with the quality of fruitfulness and the capacity to bring forth life.

This gift is transformational, bringing our lives into alignment with the heart and character of God.

But blessing is never given just for its own sake. The nature of blessing is to grow, to empower, to give life and bring forth more life. So a blessing always comes with a commission. Remember the first commission to mankind: be fruitful and multiply.[1] Our commission as Christians is not so different.

In Matthew 5:13–14, Jesus reminds the crowd of their commission. This was not a foreign or new

---

[1] Genesis 1:28

calling to them, particularly. It was as old as the blessing of Abraham, the law of Moses, and the calling of the Jewish people to be holy. But as Jesus warned, it had often been neglected and even lost.

At times in history, the cause of neglect was apostasy. In Jesus's time it was an inward focus so strong that religious leaders had forgotten that Israel was not called for its own sake but to impact the world. The blessing of Abraham was to bless the nations.

Our calling is much the same.

The City on a Hill

After salt, Jesus used the metaphor of light to remind his Jewish listeners of their purpose as God's chosen people.

As Christians, this is also our purpose.

We were not called, saved, and filled with the Holy Spirit in order to escape this world and go to heaven. We were empowered with a blessing in order to bless.

> You are the light of the world. A city situated on a hill cannot be hidden. No one lights a lamp and puts it under a basket, but rather on a lampstand, and it gives light to all who are in the house. In the same way, let your

light shine before men, so that they may see your good works and give glory to your Father in heaven. (Matthew 5:14–16)

The "city on a hill" was easily pictured by Jesus's hearers. In some sense at least, he was referring to the city of Jerusalem, which is literally situated on "a hill"—actually on a plateau, twenty-five hundred feet above sea level, and on four other hills including Mount Zion. This is why the psalms speak of "ascending" or "going up" to the house of the Lord.[2]

Jerusalem was a literal city on a hill. As such it was both highly visible and pretty much impregnable: armies can't sneak up on a hilltop, and the enemy is always at a disadvantage when he has to come from below! The city on the hill has the high ground. By its very nature it's a refuge, an inspiration, and a watchtower.

Lighting the Way

Jesus changes the metaphor a verse later by stating that no one lights a lamp and sticks it under a basket. If you turn a light on, it's because you want *light,* not because you want to hide the light. To get the best effect, you put the light on a stand so it will spread its rays as far as possible and do the most good in the house.

---

[2] Psalm 24:3, for example, or all of the Psalms of Ascent—Psalms 120–134.

Here's the point:

You weren't saved just for your own sake.

God didn't fill you with the Holy Spirit so he could hide the Spirit in you.

God didn't give you a kingdom so you could keep it under wraps.

The Sermon on the Mount lays out a powerful vision of righteousness and relationship with God through the gift of the kingdom. Again, this is a *gift*. We need to learn to use it, of course; but at base it's a gift of grace. This is clear from the Beatitudes. The gospel of the kingdom is intensely personal. It's life-changing. But it's also epic and grand. It's world-changing, because your changed life is meant to light the world.

The Christian Call to Leadership

Whether we like it or not, a call to follow Christ is a call to become a leader. God doesn't light lamps in order to hide them, but in order to lift them up and use them to give light to everyone else.

We have to speak up.

We have to act.

We have to have the courage to lead and not just follow.

Look around you.

People are stumbling around in deep darkness.

People are becoming deeply wounded because they cannot see, and what they do see they don't understand.

Sin and Satan are wrecking lives.

There's a simple solution to ending the damage of darkness.

Turn on a light.

You are the light God has turned on.

I don't know exactly what your individual "good work" entails. I don't know how God intends to use you, in what circles, or in what capacity.

But I do know that you are blessed to be a blessing. I know that you are a light God has lit, and his goal is *not* to hide you. God is not ashamed of you. He has a purpose for your presence on this earth.

You are a citizen in the city on a hill, offering light, refuge, and high ground. You are a fire meant to dissolve the darkness.

Wherever and whoever you are, if you are a child of God, he has lit a fire in you and placed you on a lampstand.

There will always be people who hate the light and avoid it. Jesus said they do this because their deeds are evil. But there will always be others who come to it—who run with relief and gratitude to the light that can save their souls.

The light that is in you. The light that *is* you.

The Father's Face

The ancient Aaronic blessing speaks into the lives of people who look into the face of God and see his light:

> May Yahweh bless you and protect you;
> may Yahweh make His face shine on you and
> be gracious to you;
> may Yahweh look with favor on you and give
> you peace.
> (Numbers 6:24–26)

Through our lives, the world around us may find the shining face of our Father, be blessed and protected, and find peace.

Jesus said the goal of your light was that people should "glorify your Father in heaven."

Through our light, people will see God and respond to him. This is our purpose here.

Don't assume that I came to destroy the Law or the Prophets. I did not come to destroy but to fulfill. For I assure you: Until heaven and earth pass away, not the smallest letter or one stroke of a letter will pass from the law until all things are accomplished.

(Matthew 5:17–18)

16

Not to Destroy But to Fulfill: How Jesus Gets the Job Done

The Sermon on the Mount begins with a charter: the eight blessings of the kingdom. That's followed by a purpose statement: that we might be salt and light. Next comes Jesus's discourse on the law. He says:

> Don't assume that I came to destroy the law or the Prophets. I did not come to destroy but to fulfill. (Matthew 5:17)

Entire theological paradigms are built around that statement, and I'm not going to go deep on them here. But I want to draw out the central point: whatever the law and the Prophets were given to accomplish, it is Jesus who will get the job done.

JESUS FULFILLS THE LAW AND THE PROPHETS

Some take this verse to mean that Jesus kept the

law perfectly, but while that's true, I think it misses the point. "Fulfill" is a prophecy word and a purpose word, not an obedience word. When I drive 100 kilometres an hour in a 100 km zone, I don't say I "fulfilled" the speed limit. Jesus didn't just keep or obey the law and the prophets; he fulfilled them.

Paul later makes it clear that the law of Moses would have accomplished certain things if it had been able to do so, but it wasn't able because of our weakness. In other words, the problem wasn't the law; the problem was our inability to keep it. On a highway, a law that says you may not drive under 60 miles an hour is a good law that will accomplish a smooth traffic flow if you can keep it. If you're driving a car, you're all set. But if all you've got is a bicycle, you've got a problem.

Our frail, sinful human lives are a bicycle on a highway. So in the final analysis, the law was inadequate to accomplish what it set out to accomplish.

But Jesus is not inadequate. Everything the law and the prophets set out to do, he can do and *did* do. He picked up where they faltered and finished the job.

The Checklist of Jesus's Life

The list of things the law and the prophets were meant to do is long. In a way you could say it was the checklist of Jesus's life.

Through its sacrificial rituals, the law was meant to redeem and atone for human souls.

It was meant to set apart a holy people for God.

It was meant to restore relationship with God.

It was meant to create a prophetic people whose lives brought blessing to the world.

It was meant to make people righteous in their actions, words, and even thoughts.

It was meant to bring the rule of heaven (i.e. the kingdom of God) to earth.

It was meant to be a channel of blessing and life.

It was meant to be a light to the nations.

("I have set before you life and death, blessing and curse. Choose life so that you and your descendants may live, love the LORD your God, obey Him, and remain faithful to Him. For He is your life …" Deuteronomy 30:19–20)

The law ultimately failed to do all these things. Some of its goals were partially met, but the ultimate vision remained unfulfilled. The law was broken and forsaken, and so it brought a curse. But it had another function: that of a schoolmaster, a temporary tutor to lead and protect the children of God until the fulness of sonship arrived (Galatians 4:1–7).

At that point our allegiance transfers to Jesus, and we swap our bicycle for a Mercedes-Benz.

Look to Jesus

Jesus fulfilled the law and the prophets. He accomplished everything the law and the prophets pointed to, taught us about, and attempted to get us to.

Through his sacrifice, he redeemed and atoned for our souls.

He set apart a holy people for God.

He restored our relationship with God.

He created us as a prophetic people whose lives bring blessing to the world.

He makes us righteous in our actions, words, and even thoughts.

He brings the rule of heaven to earth (i.e., he inaugurates the kingdom of God).

He is a channel of blessing and life.

He is a light to the nations, inviting all to come up the mountain of God and take their place in the city on a hill.

This is tremendously practical and tremendously wonderful. It means we cannot and do not have to try to save ourselves, make ourselves righteous, earn holiness, or become channels of blessing by obeying a set of rules and rituals. If a *person* has fulfilled the law and accomplished its mission, then our role in the divine story becomes incredibly relational.

If I am not looking to a system but to an individual to redeem me, atone for me, teach me, shape me, and pour life into and through me, then my life is no longer a burden or a struggle to live up to obligations but is instead the greatest relational adventure ever offered.

The law is good, but the law does not know me. The law is good, but the law cannot shape itself to my needs, my heart, and my hurts. The law is good, but the law cannot offer a comforting shoulder to cry on, a deep conversation, or an understanding gaze.

Look to Jesus. Whatever you think a system or law might be able to accomplish in your life, Jesus actually *can* accomplish it.

As he hung on the cross, Jesus cried out "It is finished!" He had accomplished the greatest mission any human being ever set out to fulfill. He did not do this by destroying or abolishing the law, but by finishing it—by fulfilling and accomplishing what it set out to do.

Therefore, whoever breaks one of the least of these commands and teaches people to do so will be called least in the kingdom of heaven. But whoever practices and teaches these commands will be called great in the kingdom of heaven. For I tell you, unless your righteousness surpasses that of the scribes and Pharisees, you will never enter the kingdom of heaven.

(Matthew 5:19–20)

17

Super-Righteousness and the Law of God

What does the law of God have to do with being a Christian?

This might be one of the biggest points of confusion facing many Christians today. Since we are saved by grace—do we need rules? If not, why did Jesus give us rules? Was it just to teach us that we can't keep rules? Are Christians free from all law, or are we still under a law of some kind? And if we are—will that law free us? Judge us? Crush us? Kill us? Or empower us to live a good life?

Jesus spends a lot of the Sermon on the Mount talking about law, and he starts by saying that he did not come to destroy the law and the prophets (i.e. the law of Moses). Rather, as we saw, everything the Old Testament law and prophets set out to do would be accomplished in him. And yes—this does mean that large swaths of the Mosaic law are no longer applicable to Christians. We don't offer animal sacrifices, for example, because Jesus has offered himself on our behalf, once and for all. We don't keep the dietary and other cleanness laws, because Jesus has atoned for us—he has made us clean. And so on.

But he *doesn't* just say, "So you can forget about any kind of law now." Nowhere does the Bible even hint that lawlessness is a goal we should strive for. In fact, one of the Bible's strongest words for sin, *iniquity*, literally means "lawless" or "without law." From a biblical perspective, being without law is never a good thing. To be lawless is to be disordered and chaotic, ruled by our own passions and lorded over by idols that are far below our dignity. To be lawless is to be a slave of entropy, slipping into corruption and the grave.

Not only that, but after he said that he would personally fulfill the law and the prophets—rendering some aspects of the Mosaic law obsolete—Jesus highlighted the need to go on doing and teaching God's commands. And he wasn't alone in this. The rest of the New Testament stresses that we as Christians are very much under God's law—the law of Christ:

> To those who are without that law, [I am] like one without the law—not being without God's law but within Christ's law. (1 Corinthians 9:21a)

> Carry one another's burdens; in this way you will fulfill the law of Christ. (Galatians 6:2)

> But the one who looks intently into the perfect law of freedom and perseveres in it, and is not a forgetful hearer but one who does good works—this person will be blessed in what he does. (James 1:25)

Rather than claiming that we should now feel free to cast off all the restraints of law, Jesus said that those who practice and teach the commands of God will be called great in the kingdom, while those who break and teach others to break them will be called least. And then he went on to give commands and call us to a high standard of living. A *very* high standard of living—one that takes us all the way to the perfection of our Father in heaven.

Super-Righteousness and the Kingdom of God

We don't say it, but many of us understand the moral teachings of the Sermon on the Mount as one giant losing proposition. We cannot possibly be as righteous as it calls us to be. It's the law squared and compounded.

And honestly, Jesus's original hearers may have felt the same way. After all, once he had affirmed the importance of God's commands, Jesus went on to tell them that their righteousness would need to *surpass that of the scribes and Pharisees* if they were even going to enter the kingdom of God, much less live a long and productive life within it. This word "surpasses" could be more literally translated "abounds above." It means something overflowing, excessive, exceeding the ordinary or necessary—*more*, in both quality and quantity. The Pharisees practiced righteousness. Jesus called his followers to super-righteousness instead.

To really understand how this impacted Jesus's hearers, forget what you think you know about the Pharisees for a moment. We have them so typecast as villains that we've lost our ability to really hear this. For the average God-fearing Jew seeking to live a more godly life in the first century AD, the scribes and Pharisees were the people you went to if you wanted to know what righteousness *was*. They taught the Bible and called people to faithfulness through precise, careful keeping of the Mosaic law. They hoped that their righteous actions would usher in the age of the Messiah. And here Jesus was saying that not only wouldn't their kind of righteousness make you great in the kingdom, *it couldn't even get you in*.

The Pharisees were trying hard. At first glance, Jesus seems to be saying that we'll need to try even harder.

If the thought of this makes you feel impossibly burdened and oppressed by the weight of God's demands, there's a good chance you're reading the Sermon with the eyes of a Pharisee. The Pharisees came from a starting place that basically assumed God was offended with Israel and distant from them. Because of their sins, he had given them into the hands of their enemies. Their answer to this was to dial down on the law and its holiness codes, amplifying even the most minute commandments and applying the strictest standards to themselves, even outside of what was normal for God-fearing Israelites. When they made themselves holy enough, the hope was that God would see their good works, accept them, and draw near to Israel again—specifically in the person of the Messiah, the long-awaited deliverer from Rome. In an attempt to recover right standing with God, they took God's law and made it harder, stricter, and more exacting. (And if it made you look better than your neighbor, you got bonus points.)

Being spiritual Pharisees ourselves, we might be inclined to think that Jesus did the same thing in the Sermon on the Mount. But he didn't. Jesus didn't give a harder, stricter, deeper law which we must now try and fail at so we can rescued by the gospel. Instead, in this passage he points us to a kind of righteousness that is of a completely different order.

Some years later, lamenting over the unwillingness of many of his fellow Israelites to trust in Christ, Paul lamented:

> Brothers, my heart's desire and prayer to God concerning them is for their salvation! I can testify about them that they have zeal for God, but not according to knowledge. Because they disregarded the righteousness from God and attempted to establish their own righteousness, they have not submitted themselves to God's righteousness. (Romans 10:1–3)

Saving righteousness, he goes on to say, is "the righteousness that comes from faith" (Romans 10:6). This is the same super-righteousness of which Jesus spoke. It's a righteousness that comes from God, and which we receive through faith, which works through love.[1]

Righteousness by Relationship

The Hebrew concept of "righteousness" isn't easy to translate. It is closely linked to the ideas of justice, judgment, mercy, faithfulness, and peace. Fundamentally, to be righteous is to be *rightly ordered or rightly related*—that is, to be in right relationship to God and to everyone around you, from your fel-

---
1 Galatians 5:6

low humans to the earth itself. To be righteous is to be in right relationship, and this is first of all a gift, one we receive from our Father in heaven only by faith—in other words by believing, trusting in, and committing ourselves to him. So in a very real sense, *righteousness that comes by faith is righteousness that comes by relationship.*

The real key to Jesus's words in this passage is that the Pharisee kind of righteousness was not really right-ordered at all. It didn't come out of relationship. It didn't place them in a right relationship with their neighbors, or with God, or even with themselves. It didn't come out love, nor did it lead to love. It was scrupulous and exacting, but it was also very self-focused, judgmental, and proud.

Kingdom-of-heaven righteousness is superior because it is first of all based in relationship with God, which is given to us as a gift; and because every aspect of it comes from and leads to love. This is why Jesus said that we can't enter the kingdom unless our righteousness exceeds that of the Pharisees, *and* that we can't enter the kingdom unless we are born again.[2] Both depend on God. Both depend on our being made new and sovereignly placed into a new relationship with God, by grace. The new birth and the surpassing righteousness of the kingdom are closely linked.

---

2 John 3:3, 5

Remember, Jesus didn't make this statement about righteousness and the kingdom in a vacuum. The Beatitudes ground everything in the Sermon in the Mount. And in the Beatitudes, both righteousness and the kingdom of heaven are gifts given to those who qualify by virtue of empty hands, hungry hearts, and the faith and humility to receive.

Unlike us, God isn't a legalist. He doesn't judge people as righteous or unrighteous based on how well we keep rules, *even his rules*. He knows we are weak and frail, and he extends grace to us. That's why in the kingdom of heaven, *saint* and *sinner* describe the same people. Every saint is a sinner saved by grace. Even in the Old Testament, righteousness was not a function of sinless behavior. Abraham, David, Moses, and many others—sinners all—were made righteous by their faith, not their perfect works. To quote Paul again, they were "justified by faith."[3] And from the very start, faith was only effective because it responded to God's grace—his *a priori* love for us, and the gifts he chooses to extend to us.

The reason our righteousness as kingdom citizens can so vastly surpass that of the Pharisees is that through Jesus, God invites us into a vastly superior relationship with him. It's the difference between relating to God as a servant and relating to

---

[3] Romans 3:28. In the New Testament, "righteousness" and "justification" are two ways of translating the same Greek word.

him as his child. This changes us not only positionally—we are children of God, and made righteous through the blood of Jesus—but also practically, in measure as we live in accordance with this new relationship. I am like my parents in many ways, not because when I was born I was given a bullet-point list of actions I should adopt in order to be like them, but because they raised me, because I have their DNA, because we have been through countless situations together in which I watched them respond and learned how to go and do likewise. Not only that, but even today, I have their presence and support when I need it. God offers us the same kind of righteousness. We are right-ordered and right-related because we are first of all related to him, as children to their Father.

It's Paul who frames this change of relationship most clearly:

> When the time came to completion, God sent His Son, born of a woman, born under the law, to redeem those under the law, so that we might receive adoption as sons. And because you are sons, God has sent the Spirit of His Son into our hearts, crying, "Abba, Father!" So you are no longer a slave but a son, and if a son, then an heir through God. (Galatians 4:4–7)

In the kingdom, we are never expected to go it alone. The surpassing righteousness Jesus taught is a righteousness that begins and ends in the words "our Father."

Therefore, Live Rightly

If surpassing righteousness is a gift from God, and is characterized by our being in right relationship with him through *his* initiative, does that mean righteousness doesn't have a practical, this-world application anymore? Does it mean that Christian lives shouldn't really be expected to look different from the world's?

("God forbid," I can hear Paul saying.)

It does not. The Sermon on the Mount, and actually the entire Bible, makes it crystal-clear that with all the gifts we have been given, Christians should absolutely live righteous lives, both inwardly and outwardly. The gifts of God empower us to walk by the law of God—not the Mosaic law, which was temporary, but the for-all-time, rooted-in-God's-nature moral law, which is explored by Jesus in the Sermon on the Mount.

The law of God is not a set of arbitrary rules. It is a description of how *God* is—of his nature and the way he designed the universe to interact with his nature. We are given the opportunity to be governed by the same law. As Christians, we can enter into and be governed by "the law of the Spirit of life in Christ Jesus" (Romans 8:2, NKJV). Our lives can function according to the same laws that describe the life of God. In other words, we can learn to live like God does.

Those who want to say Christians are without law, and that we really shouldn't talk about "rules" in the church, need to explain why the Bible is full of commands if they have nothing to do with us. Not just the Old Testament—the New Testament too. Unless we're unwilling to teach Paul, and Peter, and John, and James, and most of the Sermon on the Mount, we *have* to teach commands. In fact, Jesus told us to do exactly that: "Go, therefore, and make disciples of all nations ... teaching them to observe everything I have commanded you" (Matthew 28:19–20).

According to the New Testament, Christians constitute a distinct people group in the earth—a "holy nation" (1 Peter 2:9). When a law is given to a nation, it constitutes that nation, or gives it a distinct form. (That's why the foundation document of the United States is called the "Constitution.") A nation's character will be good or bad depending on the nature of its laws. Good laws empower the righteous, protect the weak and the poor, and disempower evil.

The law of Moses, given to ancient Israel, was a gift that constituted a righteous nation. And now, Jesus has come with a new law, as the prophets promised—but this is a law of the Spirit, written on the heart. Reforming us from the inside, it constitutes our hearts and then transforms the world around us through the salt and light of our influence. "I will put My teaching within them and write it on their hearts," God promised in Jeremiah 31:33, speaking of the New Covenant. "I will be their God, and they will be My people."

In the New Covenant, we are governed by the life of God within us, and his law inside of us changes who we are.

The People God Wants

When we live by the law of the Spirit of life in Christ Jesus, we live out of God's life.

So we are not just people who don't murder; we are people who don't hate, who don't dismiss, disrespect, and look down on one another.

We are not just people who don't commit adultery; we are people who don't lust, who don't objectify one another, and who are not controlled by our sexual urges.

We are not just people who don't divorce without good cause; we are people who are deeply faithful to one another in the marriage bond.

We are not just people who don't lie and intentionally manipulate and mislead one another; we are people who understand words as sacred and powerful and who honor that power and holiness in all that we say.

And we are not just people who carry out religious duties: we are people who have a real and personal relationship with God in the secret place of our inner lives, and who live that relationship out in public.

The Science of Righteousness

As we continue through the Sermon on the Mount, we'll encounter many specific commands—the law of Christ, clearly spelled out for us. You might wonder why, if God is writing his law in our hearts, we also need it written down on paper. I would say it's because God is very generous with his gifts! He is clear throughout the Scriptures that he wants us to pursue wisdom and understanding. He wants us to seek him. He wants us to be intentional in pursuing righteousness, learning to live as a child of God, and loving and worshiping our Father. He does not want us to be ignorant or stuck or lazy. So he shares with us secrets of the universe: truths about ourselves and the way the world works that empower our true identities, disempower evil, and protect the poor and weak.

I like to think about the teachings of Jesus in

terms of science. Why do we study science, if the laws of physics and biology and cosmology are all going to work without us anyway? Because the more we understand about science, the freer and more powerful we become. We are able to access realities that have always been there, but which could never help us before we understood them—before we could harness electricity, for example; or generate energy; or send communication through cables and wires and radio waves. The laws of nature benefit us as we understand them.

The laws of righteousness are the same way. That's why God writes them down. He's giving us a massive head start on the kind of life available to us—not by our making ourselves into proud, scrupulous Pharisees, but by the Spirit of God working in us and our own humble willingness to believe, receive, and obey.

Our righteousness can be universes beyond that of the Pharisees because it's not about perfecting ourselves by keeping rules. It's about being made perfect by love. It's about becoming God's children and learning, through a committed relationship of faith, to live like he does.

After all, faith is deeply relational. Faith listens to God. It believes him. It trusts him. It goes to him. It chooses to walk with him. It prays to him. It commits to him.

Every New Testament command is an open door, an invitation to a new kind of life. This life will make us fully human and empower us to live a life of grace and goodness. It will rightly order us and rightly relate us to everything and everyone around us. It is a life of peace, mercy, justice, love, and stability. When it comes right down to it—it is the life we all truly want.

Psalm 119, the longest chapter in the Bible, is a song of yearning for righteousness. David, its author, sang, "Oh, how I love thy law!"

David loved the law of God and understood that it represented his greatest freedom, his greatest joy, his most exquisitely realized humanity.

We have an even greater law than David did, both written on our hearts and revealed to our minds through the Scriptures. Having received new life as God's children, let us pursue practical righteousness as ardently, as joyfully as David did—knowing that it is a gift to us, and that learning to live like our Father in heaven means bringing heaven to earth and transforming not only our own lives but also everything around us.

For I tell you, unless your righteousness surpasses that of the scribes and Pharisees, you will never enter the kingdom of heaven. You have heard that it was said to our ancestors ... But I tell you ...

(Matthew 5:20, 21a, 22a)

18

Good-bye, Frustration: How the Law of the Spirit Sets Us Free

Jesus came to change our lives in an actual, practical, daily sense. This doesn't happen without our participation. But it doesn't happen by our own power, either.

The story so far is this: Jesus came to give us a kingdom. He didn't come to destroy the law of Moses, but to accomplish what it couldn't. He requires—and gives us—a righteousness that far surpasses that of the best legalist. He reconstitutes our hearts so that we function according to the laws of God on the inside.

So does this affect how we live our lives?

Of course it does. That we even *ask* this question is proof of how lost in the trees we can tend to get, when a forest is staring us in the face.

Yes, there is such a thing as "the Christian life,"

and yes, we can and should live it, and no, believing that does not constitute legalism or dead works. In a very real sense, it's the whole point.

Jesus didn't come to give us some fuzzy ideas and make us feel better about ourselves. He actually came to change our lives.

And our world, when it comes to that.

Welcoming the Rule of God

From the very beginning, I've stressed that Jesus came to bring a kingdom. God's kingdom. The kingdom is a gift, and we can do exactly nothing to earn it, which is why Jesus said it was for the poor in spirit. The people who have nothing except empty hands: that's who is best positioned to receive. As we saw earlier, Jesus offers the poor in spirit position, authority, power, privilege, wealth, honor, and responsibility.

But to be given a kingdom is to be given something else as well: *When you receive a kingdom, you receive a government.*

You receive the rule of the King—in this case, God.

You agree to be governed by another.

The kingdom of God is a spiritual kingdom ("kingdom of heaven" = "kingdom of the spiritual realm"), so to receive the rule of God is to receive governance over your spirit. Your inner life comes into alignment with God's life. The law is no longer something external to you, something you comply with through outward observance only, but something internal to you, which you comply with through trust and surrender and obedience from the heart.

In fact, this is the essence of Christian spirituality: that we leave behind the lower law that has governed our lives since the garden of Eden and become governed by the higher law of the Spirit of God.

We trade the law of sin and death for the law of the Spirit of life in Christ Jesus.

Eden, Babel, and Why We Get So Frustrated

Humanity currently is living a life oriented around "the flesh"—the body and its needs. As such, we are anchored to decay and death and tuned in to externals, functioning according to what our five senses tell us. But we weren't supposed to be this way. We were created as spiritual beings, partaking of God's eternal life and tuned in to the higher laws of the spiritual realm.

When Adam and Eve fell, they fell from that spiritual existence to a fleshly existence. Don't get me wrong, they *had* flesh before they fell, and God said that it was good—but their orientation changed at the fall. The part of them that was meant to function as a servant became a master instead, and at the same time, humanity found itself trying to function in a state of severe lack. We were created to be in relationship with God. Separated from our Creator, we lack the resources needed to live as we were originally designed to do.

As a result, humanity ended up in a constant cycle of frustration, because, as Galatians 5:17 informs us:

> The flesh desires what is against the Spirit, and the Spirit desires what is against the flesh; these are opposed to each other, so that you don't do what you want.

To me, the tower of Babel is the best illustration of this. Mankind, ruled by their flesh—i.e. governed by the law of sin and death—wanted to build a tower to heaven. They would actually have been able to do this, whatever exactly it was, but the Spirit of God did not want them to do it, so he frustrated their plans by scrambling their ability to communicate with each other.

The flesh and Spirit are opposed to each other; you want to do what the flesh wants; hey presto, you cannot do what you want. The Spirit will frustrate you every time.

History is a long tableau of mankind's frustrated desires.

But then along comes the kingdom of God, and suddenly things change.

Because when we welcome the rule of God in our hearts, the law of the Spirit of life in Christ Jesus becomes the governing force in our lives. When we walk after the Spirit, we get out of the cycle of frustration and into the will of God ... which, as it happens, is the desire of the whole righteous universe. Good-bye frustration, hello freedom.

Getting with the Program

Jesus's kingdom mission was and is to bring the kingdom of heaven to earth—to see the will of God done on earth as it is in heaven. When we receive the kingdom, *this* is the program: we are being governed by a new law, reoriented from flesh to Spirit, pulled out of the cycle of frustration and placed in the glorious freedom of the children of God. What was lacking is restored in and through Jesus.

All of this is a gift.

It also requires our participation.

I can hand you a million dollars, but it won't do you much good if you don't use it.

The Scriptures tell us that we are new creatures in Christ, but we are still in bodies that are used to the old law and the old orientation. It takes time and active participation to learn to live by higher laws. That's why Jesus teaches us and gives us commands: they help us get our new lives off the ground. They show us how we will function best.

Discipleship, or the act of following and learning from Jesus, is an active lifestyle. It is entirely based on the gifts and empowerment of God, but it does require us to get up and walk.

Learning to follow Jesus is not a complicated process. It involves identifying and abandoning deception; accepting and receiving truth; changing our thought patterns and attitudes to line up with God's reality. It involves yielding to the Spirit, ceasing to fight, learning to rest, letting ourselves be loved. It means learning to walk out a new identity that, in the end, was always who we were meant to be—a people created in the image of God, walking with him in a trust relationship, and drawing our life from his.

When we accept the rule of God in our lives, we do not find ourselves bound and burdened. We find ourselves set free.

That's what it means to live a Christian life.

That's what it means to receive the kingdom of God.

19

Higher Vision: Why Jesus's Morality Is Better Than Ours

"Morality is the herd-instinct in the individual," Friedrich Nietzche wrote. Einstein said, "A man's ethical behaviour should be based effectually on sympathy, education, and social ties and needs." Human morality, in other words, is determined by our surroundings: by the needs, expectations, and ties of the people around us.

Morality Is:

Nietzche and Einstein got it right, partly. In English, the word *morality* derives from *mores,* "the customs, values, and behaviors" that govern a society, whether through law or simply through cultural pressure. Every society has cultural mores by which we judge behavior, set expectations, and separate those who are acceptable from those who are not.

That's why nonconformity is so often treated as a crime against society and why shame is such a significant part of traditional morality: shame is what happens when our behavior doesn't conform to social expectations and we are, in a sense, put out of the tribe. In our society as in every other, shame is one of the primary ways we keep one another in line.

In our age of moral relativism and the belief that the individual is supreme, however, many voices cry out that traditional morals are just a cover for control, for manipulation, for the shameless shaming of one another. Traditional morals are there to force us to conform, and so they are bad.

But the Bible offers a different kind of morality—a standard for behavior that isn't based primarily in society's needs and expectations but in the character of a transcendent God. That's why Judeo-Christian thought has always insisted that morality is absolute, not relative.

Freedom from Shame

At this point in Matthew 5, we've reached the beginning of Jesus's moral discourse: a set of five teachings that begin with the morality of the Mosaic Covenant but then go on to transcend it. Jesus, like Moses, relates a vision of morality that goes deeper and higher than the mores of society, and when it is taken to heart, shame is no longer central to controlling behavior.

Because here's the thing: a lot of human morality—traditional, postmodern, and every other kind—is about control, manipulation, and shame.

We do reward conformity and punish nonconformity. That's how the human race survives with sin in the camp. We control and shame people so they don't become murderers, so they don't act out every twisted fantasy they have, so there are social consequences to keep us all cowed. Yes, sometimes it backfires on us and the "misfits" go on a killing spree, but for the most part it works. In fact, the fear of shame probably averts a lot more evil than strength of conscience does. That may be why certain sins become rampant as soon as the media, the government, and the entertainment industry approve of them. They're no longer shamed, so a lot more people suddenly feel free to carry them out. It's not that people are worse than they used to be; "young people" haven't come loose from their moorings in any fundamental way. We've just changed the moorings as a society.

So yes, people who feel that morality is all about control are feeling something true, to an extent. And it's not all bad—there are times when shame is good, when it humbles us in a healthy way and leads us to do what is right. But I *am* saying that human morality, based on "sympathy, education, and social ties and needs," is a poor substitute for the real thing—for morality that is not only based in the character of God but sourced in our hearts.

Jesus's Morality Is Better Than Ours

Jesus's vision is not about conforming to social norms. It has nothing to do with living up to societal expectations or even creating new expectations, as many social reformers have tried to do. The William Wilberforces of history go after laws and culture, creating new norms which people must heed if they wish to be seen as decent and respectable. This can be a very good thing, but Jesus didn't do it. He didn't bother with externals at all. Instead he went straight for the heart.

We've already dealt with this at length: the righteousness Jesus taught was a righteousness that comes from being rightly related to God, that flows out of a heart reconstituted after the good law of God. It is, in a sense, more stringent than any external law can be: it doesn't just modify our behavior but transforms our inner selves.

And at the same time, and for the same reason, it is exponentially more freeing.

When our hearts get reconstituted after the law of God, when we actually change on the inside and become like the one who is Goodness and who is Love, we don't need society to control us. We don't act righteously in order to conform but in order to be true to our deepest nature, to the deepest wellsprings of our heart. We don't have to be manipulated or controlled. We're free to be free and to express everything that we truly are, because everything that we truly are is of God.

The first principle of Jesus's kind of morality is that it's absolute because it's transcendent: it's based in the unchanging nature of God, not in the culture around it.

The second principle is that it's internal. It's not about our surroundings. It's about our source.

The Third Principle: It's Your Fault

The third principle of Jesus's kind of morality is that it's individual.

Let me rephrase that: *Jesus's kind of morality requires us to take total responsibility for ourselves.* We cannot blame our behavior on anyone or anything else. In order to live from our source and walk out the righteousness of God, we have to give up blaming and take complete responsibility for our own words, thoughts, and actions.

That's the foundation of repentance, after all. We can't repent and move forward in a new direction as long as we are pointing fingers and crying victim.

In our culture today, we seem to be pursuing a doubly destructive path: We cast some people as eternal victims, depriving them of the ability to take responsibility for themselves, while we cast others as eternal villains, worthy of nothing but blame and undeserving of forgiveness. Yet we're rarely quick to accept blame ourselves, and we excuse the wrong actions of the victims as someone else's fault. Maybe this is because we realize that if we hold other people responsible for their sins, we also have to hold ourselves responsible for ours. *Mea culpa*, as the liturgical confession goes. *Through my fault.*

This principle is on full display when Jesus begins his moral teachings, because he doesn't begin by addressing stealing, or vandalism, or swearing, or failing to recycle. He begins by addressing anger and lust: probably the two sins we are most prone to blaming on the other person.

With his words "You have heard that it was said to the ancients—but I say to you," Jesus calls us out of the realm of social responsibility and hits us with personal responsibility before the God who knows our hearts, minds, and motivations.

Jesus's teaching on morality is relatively simple—on the surface. But its principles of transcendence (and therefore absoluteness), internality, and individualism make it deeply profound and practically life-changing.

You have heard that it was said to our ancestors, Do not murder, and whoever murders will be subject to judgment. But I tell you, everyone who is angry with his brother will be subject to judgment. And whoever says to his brother, "Fool!" will be subject to the Sanhedrin. But whoever says, "You moron!" will be subject to hellfire. So if you are offering your gift on the altar, and there you remember that your brother has something against you, leave your gift there in front of the altar. First go and be reconciled with your brother, and then come and offer your gift. Reach a settlement quickly with your adversary while you're on the way with him, or your adversary will hand you over to the judge, the judge to the officer, and you will be thrown into prison. I assure you: You will never get out of there until you have paid the last penny!

(Matthew 5:21–26)

20

What's So Bad About Anger and How Jesus Calls Us to Freedom

According to Jesus, people don't make you angry. You do. And if you want to be free, you have to take responsibility for it.

Remember, morality as Jesus teaches it follows these principles: it's transcendent and therefore absolute; it's internal; and it's individual. As such, it's demanding.

Jesus doesn't pull his punches. He goes straight for a very painful, very personal sin: anger. And where we universally want to blame our anger on others, Jesus puts the responsibility for it—and the impetus to change—squarely on us.

Who Made You Angry?

Nowhere is the principle of individual responsibility more obvious than in the first two moral issues Jesus addresses: anger and lust. Maybe more than any other sin, we automatically blame these on the other person.

You can hear it in the language we use. We rarely say "I got angry." We say "He made me angry" or "That made me really mad." Our language makes it clear where we stand: It's not our fault. Someone else did it to us. We couldn't help it. We are the victim here.

> You have heard that it was said to our ancestors, Do not murder, and whoever murders will be subject to judgment. But I tell you, everyone who is angry with his brother will be subject to judgment. (Matthew 5:21–22)

Anger, Jesus says, is not okay; and furthermore, you are responsible for it. Not the other person, not the circumstance. You. You are so responsible, in fact, that by kingdom rules you can be hauled into court for it.

Here we see one of the major differences between the law of God and the laws of men: men can only judge us, or haul us into court, for externals. They can only judge what we *do*. The law of God is in our hearts and deals with our hearts, and because of that, it can call us to judgment over things we feel, things we think, and things we say in the heat of the moment.

The law of God is strict. Not graceless or soul-crushing, but strict. This kind of righteousness runs deep, much deeper than that of the scribes and Pharisees.

It requires us to own up to a whole lot more.

Is Anger Sin?

Is anger, in and of itself, sin? This passage would seem to say so.

But the issue isn't totally black and white. Some New Testament manuscripts add the phrase "without cause" here in Matthew 5, so that the passage reads, "everyone who is angry with his brother *without cause* will be subject to judgment."

It's also clear that God gets angry—sometimes really angry—and never sins. Paul elsewhere instructs us to "be angry and do not sin" (Ephesians 4:26).

There is an anger that isn't sin. We call it "righteous anger" because it's justified.

There is also a kind of anger that is a simple, unchosen emotional response. It is, perhaps, stretching to call this sin—but the moment we choose it, the moment we entertain and invite it in, at that moment we are not walking righteously.

(I'm sure we can all think of a list of real justifications off the top of our heads. Mind you, that doesn't make anger an optimal response. Unlike

God, we don't handle anger well. When we can say with God that we are "compassionate and gracious, slow to anger and rich in faithful love and truth," [Exodus 34:6], then maybe we'll handle anger okay. In the meantime, what if we chose another route? What would happen to the world if those who are radicalized by real oppression and real injustice instead took the route of social reformers who have taken Jesus's words seriously? "Forgiveness is nothing less than how we bring peace to ourselves and our world," wrote Archbishop Desmond Tutu in *The Book of Forgiving*. "In South Africa, we chose to seek forgiveness rather than revenge. That choice averted a bloodbath. For every injustice, there is a choice … you can choose forgiveness or revenge, but revenge is always costly. Choosing forgiveness rather than retaliation ultimately serves to make you a stronger and freer person.")

And again, I'm also not sure we can say that any instinctive emotion is sin in and of itself. Anger certainly has an emotional component, and at the point where that is *all anger is*—not an action, not a thought that is kept and sustained, not an ongoing attitude—I'm not sure Jesus would call it sin.

When we are "subject to judgment" because of it, we might get off without a guilty sentence.

But here's what I've noticed. We are very quick to bring up the subject of righteous anger when

Matthew 5 is quoted, as if the possibility of righteous anger means our anger is probably fine. But 99 percent of the time, our anger isn't righteous. It is not rightly ordered; it is not rightly related. It's just anger. And when it flares up in us, offering us a choice of response, many of us *do* choose it.

When Jesus says, "everyone who is angry with his brother will be subject to judgment," his use of the word brother suggests he's talking about the kind of anger we turn on people close to us. We're having a rough time, so we make our loved ones suffer.

Most of the time, our anger isn't really even about the other person. It's the result of some undealt-with issues in our lives, and the pressure of those issues explodes at somebody else.

I'm hormonal, so I bite your head off when you track mud on the floor after I cleaned it.

I'm late for dinner, and my relationship with my spouse is already on the rocks because of a fight we had last night, so I curse at the guy who cuts me off in traffic.

I feel hurt, unloved, and rejected because of deep wounds in my past that aren't healed, and I let the negative emotion of all that come out in my interactions with you over stupid things I wish I could just let go of—over the annoying way you eat your food, or how you're always late, or how you can't seem to get a grip on your finances, or how you forgot to pick up milk when I asked you three times today.

The anger is my problem, born out of other problems which are also mine. But if someone calls me on it, I'll say, "But she made me mad." "He made me angry."

It's not *my* fault.

What's So Bad About Anger

As Jesus goes on to teach about this, the crux of this particular subject becomes clear: *No matter what you may be feeling, it is not okay to demean another human being because of it.*

Angry people wound those around them deeply and constantly through their words, their tone, sometimes their actions. But if you call them on it, often they don't even seem to be thinking about the other person. "I'm just having a bad day. I needed to let off a little steam. I know I shouldn't have said it, but it felt good at the time."

That is the issue Jesus is pinpointing. He's pointing to our tendency to justify things that make us feel better even though they hurt other people and in the process reveal what we think of others when push comes to shove—that they really don't matter that much.

According to Jesus, anger and murder are equivalent. *This is why.* This thing inside of us that says our needs are more important than someone else's in the moment, that what we feel is more pressing than watching out for our impact on other people, that our need for release justifies hurting others—that other people are actually in some way less than ourselves—is the impulse behind murder.

Subject to Judgment

An externally based morality system can tell me, "If you blow up like that again, you will be fined. Do not raise your voice, or it's ten demerit points. Treat your colleagues with respect, or you will be dismissed." And of course—"You should be ashamed of yourself. Get a grip on your actions so you don't expose yourself to shame again."

An internally based morality system—the kind Jesus teaches—says, "Clean up your heart."

God knows and cares about our pain. He cares about the stuff that's going on in our lives, and he gives us his own Spirit to dwell within us and empower us to take a better road. But first we have to repent.

Take responsibility. Own up: it's not okay. It's not okay what I'm feeling. It's not okay what I'm expressing. It points to things being off in my heart. Anger is happening in me, and it points to something in me.

If you struggle with anger, if you find you are being "called to judgment" by the Spirit of God in this area, don't just try to modify your behavior. Recognize conviction as the call to freedom that it actually is.

Healing and change begin when we own up to our stuff and take responsibility for it.

We aren't asked to change on our own, without God's intimate, compassionate, gracious, faithful, and loving help. (And I should note—this can take very very practical shape, like going to see a therapist, or giving ourselves time to be still.)

But if we struggle with anger, if we demean and devalue others through our words and behaviors, *we* are asked to change.

That's central to Jesus's vision of morality.

You have heard that it was said to our ancestors, Do not murder, and whoever murders will be subject to judgment. But I tell you, everyone who is angry with his brother will be subject to judgment.

(Matthew 5:19–20)

21

Why Sin Is Serious and How Your Personal Salvation Can Change the World

Most of us can justify anger pretty easily. It's bad, but not that bad. Anger isn't murder.

Except that it is.

In Jesus's first moral teaching in the Sermon on the Mount, he makes the outrageous equivalence of anger with murder: "You have heard that it was said to our ancestors, Do not murder, and whoever murders will be subject to judgment. But I tell you, everyone who is angry with his brother will be subject to judgment" (Matthew 5:21–22).

Apologists and street preachers point to this verse all the time when trying to explain to people why sin is so bad. It's a helpful exercise, because even as Christians, we rarely see sin for what it is. Jesus pulls back the curtain and shows us the bad and the ugly.

In the process, he makes it clear just how incredibly good his salvation is.

The Seed Principle

In the kingdom of God, most things work on a seed principle. The Word of God is like seed. Our bodies are resurrection seeds. Our presence on earth—the kingdom itself—is seed.

Sin also works on a seed principle. At first glance, calling anger and murder the same looks a little extreme. But Jesus doesn't just see things in their current form; he sees them all the way through to their full potential—from the acorn to the full-grown tree bound up in its DNA.

That's why all sin is so serious. Many of us may wonder why something like "telling a white lie" is so bad. In a way, it isn't. But it's an early expression of something—a spirit of deceit—so awful it can destroy trust and ruin an entire world.

In fact, deceit is the seed that ruined ours.

It's not fun to think of the anger that wells up in us when we're stuck in traffic or confronted by an annoyance or faced by a particularly aggravating loved one as the seed of murder. We don't want to think that spirit could possibly have any place in us. I'm not so bad, we think, especially comparatively. Yes, I spout off sometimes, but I'm not a terrorist.

I'm no Hitler.

But what if Hitler just expressed a few things in full-grown splendor that are still mostly dormant in you and me as seeds?

Horrifying, that thought. If we took it seriously it would drive us to desperation for salvation. *For someone to save us.* For someone to root the sin-seeds out and give us new ones. For someone to save our lives while getting rid of any possibility that those things in us will ever grow. If I truly believed I was a ticking time bomb, I'd be desperate to find someone who could put out the fuse.

Of course, that's what Jesus does—saves us, purifies us, gets the bad seeds out and replaces them with new ones. God's solutions are always incredibly pertinent to our actual needs.

Suddenly being freed from sin sounds a lot more necessary. And a lot more amazing.

In Genesis 3 there's an intriguing passage where God expresses the result of mankind's fall into sin. After the fall, he takes away their immortality, saying that he can't let them eat from the tree of life "lest they should live forever—"[1]

The thought in Hebrew actually trails away. It's too horrific to be finished. What would mankind become, if death didn't halt the growth of the seeds inside us? If our lives weren't bounded by the need

---

1 Genesis 3:22

to survive and thus to cooperate with social mores, and instead we could just reach our full potential—in everything?

Here is the incredible truth of salvation:

Because Jesus has freed us from sin—its presence and power—we can live forever again. We *can* live a life that's not bounded by the need to survive. We don't have to play societal games; instead we're free to pursue God's vision for us. And we *can* reach our full potential, the full potential we were designed for when God knit us together in our mothers' wombs. We can reach our potential to love, to enjoy, to create, to fellowship, to be like God.

Romans 8 tells us that all creation groans and travails, waiting for the sons of God to be revealed. Waiting for us to become what we will be, because in Jesus that is no longer a nightmare but the saving of the world.

Meanwhile, on the Ground

Meanwhile, here we are. Sin, we're told, no longer has power over us. Which means it's time to stop living like it does. Which means it's time to learn how God thinks about morality and agree with it.

The Sermon on the Mount's moral teachings—which are simple, clear, and short—are all about this.

To sum them up, it's time to get real.

Jesus says we need to clean out our hearts. But he doesn't say that in a vacuum. He's already given us the kingdom, drawn near to us in our pain and sorrow, promised to shape us through our afflictions, shown us mercy, called us his children, met all our hunger and all our thirst.

We *can* get real about what we're dealing with, and we *can* deal with it, because we're not alone. He's given us everything we need to come out the other side whole and healed.

And then the whole impetus for unrighteous anger vanishes away.

Because it was never about the other person anyway.

The Kingdom of God and the Culture Around Us

I said earlier that Jesus wasn't a social reformer, but the kind of morality he taught has more power to transform a society than any external law, shaming code, or cultural expectation in the world.

If you live in the West (and a lot of other places now), you experience the benefits of exactly that transformation every single day. I don't have room to go into it here, but our culture with its general ideas of human rights, respect for others even when they are different from us, and protection of the weak did not happen by accident, and it's not historically normative.

External controls do help keep dangerous criminals off the streets and curb violent behaviors, but imagine a society full of people who:

1. Value other human beings

2. Take full responsibility for their responses to those human beings, and

3. Have cleared anger and all of its roots fully out of their hearts.

If that kind of morality reached critical mass, we wouldn't need half the laws we have. We would all be safe with each other. And we would all be free.

Jesus's kind of morality is higher and better than human moral relativism because it doesn't just help us get along with society, it empowers us to completely transform it.

That's what salvation is.

That's why we can change the world.

It starts with you and me.

But I tell you, everyone who is angry with his brother will be subject to judgment. And whoever says to his brother, "Fool!" will be subject to the Sanhedrin. But whoever says, "You moron!" will be subject to hellfire.

(Matthew 5:22)

22

Raca, Respect, and the Agape Love of God, Part 1

Anger is not a victimless crime. Anger is aggressive. To have someone's anger turned on you—especially when it's "without cause," not your fault or out of proportion to your fault—is emotionally and physically traumatizing.

At first glance, Jesus's moral teachings in Matthew 5 can look almost trite or arbitrary. Given a chance to address the greatest evils of his day, he starts with anger. But the more we look at it, the more serious anger is seen to be.

Watch a little child react when an adult in their space gets angry. Their reaction—the very evident fear, insecurity, confusion, and hurt, even if the anger is being aimed at someone else entirely—is how we all, deep down, react to anger.

Anger makes us instantly unsafe. It assaults our well-being and demeans our personhood.

Anger left unchecked, and directed as it so often is at those who don't deserve it, becomes sniper shootings and terrorists driving trucks into a crowd, firing at will. It becomes racial and xenophobic and without reason or empathy.

But is anger the real problem?

After all, sometimes anger is righteous. God is angry every day, and he should be. So it seems unlikely that anger itself is the root Jesus is after here.

Where does our problematic anger come from, anyway?

The Root of the Problem

Jesus begins by addressing anger—flying off the handle at "your brother," at someone close to you. But then he takes it farther.

The Amplified Bible breaks it down well:

> And whoever speaks [contemptuously and insultingly] to his brother, "Raca (You empty-headed idiot)!" shall be guilty before the supreme court (Sanhedrin); and whoever says, "You fool!" shall be in danger of the fiery hell. (Matthew 5:22b, AMP)

Raca is an Aramaic word, a serious insult. The Amplified's "fiery hell" is the Greek *Gehenna,* a name for the Valley of Hinnom just south of Jerusalem (more about this later).

It's this further development of anger that really makes the link between an angry response to another person and murder apparent. The problem isn't actually anger, the flare-up that comes against another. Murderers aren't always angry when they kill. The problem is something more, something deeper at the root of both.

The Destructive Power of Words

It's interesting that while anger in itself—apparently unexpressed—is enough to bring a person "into judgment," the spoken expression of anger brings things up to a more serious level—in Matthew 5:22, the judgement escalates along with the seriousness of the offense.

God does not take words lightly. We see this everywhere in Scripture: words are real things with a real impact.

Angry or demeaning words can be more damaging than any physical blow, with their ability to get into our minds and hearts and deconstruct us from the inside, for days and years and decades. Spoken words are in fact physical things: they create sound waves that physically impact the tympanic membrane inside our ears. They manifest the spirit of the one speaking, so that words spoken in anger or contempt affect us physically like blows and get into our own spirits like canker worms.

The specific words Jesus uses here are significant too. We mustn't get legalist about this: I have never in my life called anyone *raca*, and it's unlikely that I ever will; Aramaic insults aren't part of my daily vocabulary. But the spirit behind the word is familiar.

Vine's Expository Dictionary gives helpful insight:

> *Rhaka* is an Aramaic word akin to the Hebrew *req*, "empty" ... It was a word of utter contempt, signifying "empty," intellectually rather than morally, "empty-headed."

"Stupid," in other words, is what *raca* means; "dummy"; "retard." *What an idiot.*

Still, the *Vine's* entry assures us that the next word and attitude Jesus condemns is worse: "[Raca] does not indicate such a loss of self-control as the word rendered *'fool,'* a godless, moral reprobate." That word is *moros*, root of our "moron" though expressive of considerably more, and again *Vine's* is very helpful. Of Matthew 5:22 it says:

> Here the word means morally worthless, a scoundrel, a more serious reproach than "*Raca*"; the latter scorns a man's mind and calls him stupid; *moros* scorns his heart and

character; hence the Lord's more serious condemnation.

We have plenty of modern equivalents for *moros*. I've heard even Christians use them. Loser. Faggot. A-hole. Waste of space.

I shudder at the things we say about people of other religions, other political parties, people who struggle with certain temptations. People who are different than we are and therefore, we think, deserving of our scorn.

The Real Root of Murder

Jesus begins by addressing anger, but he goes deeper, to the real problem, the real issue at hand. Anger, it turns out, is just a front.

The real issue is contempt.

In 1992, Dr. John Gottman of the Gottman Institute conducted a much discussed study in which he watched the interactions of couples who were having marital troubles. In that study he was able to predict with a 94 percent success rate which couples would divorce and which would stay together. The number one cause of divorce? Contempt, of course.

The real reason for racism, for domestic violence, for injustice against the poor, for classism, for fraud, for religious persecution, for ethnic warfare, for our world of broken and battered relationships?

Contempt for others lies at the base of them all.

The Moral Genius of Jesus

Jesus, the absolute master of morality, is not just picking an arbitrary list of petty sins and smacking our hands for them. Nor is he leveling outlandish consequences on minor infractions of a list of rules.

Jesus is a moral genius, and in Matthew 5 he goes directly for the roots of our problems, individual and societal.

Contempt is the first one he identifies. But the antidote to it may surprise you—it lies in the little-understood agape love of God for all people.

But I tell you, everyone who is angry with his brother will be subject to judgment. And whoever says to his brother, "Fool!" will be subject to the Sanhedrin. But whoever says, "You moron!" will be subject to hellfire.

(Matthew 5:22)

23

Raca, Respect, and the Agape Love of God, Part 2

This should not be shocking to any Christian, but to me it was when I discovered it: God respects, values, and esteems people. *All* people, simply because they are human beings, created in his image and created with worth.

To this point, we've been exploring Jesus's moral teaching on anger, which he equates with murder. We've identified the root problem of anger as actually being contempt, an attitude that demeans and devalues other human beings.

The reason this is such a problem is that it's totally contrary to the Spirit of God. God, who made men and women in his image, doesn't just "love" people in some sentimental way, he respects them.

If you look up agape online or in a dictionary, you'll get a lot of definitions like the following:

> This is the Greek word for love at its ultimate. Agape love is not like a brotherly love or a love between a husband and a wife. It is the most self-sacrificing love that there is. This type of love is the love that God has for His own children. This type of love is what was displayed on the cross by Jesus Christ ... That is the type of love which is always the highest, most supreme love there is. It is a love where one is willing to die for another, even if that person is unworthy, sinful, undeserving and is an enemy of the one who died for them.[1]

Personally, I've always found this type of definition unhelpful. It's not that there isn't truth to it—of course there is, and *agape* is the most-used word for God's love in the New Testament. But it's lacking a fundamental definition, a definition I can really work with and put into action in my own life. To me this is like asking "What is a dog?" and being told "A dog is man's best friend! A dog is loyal to the end!" True, but I still don't know what a dog is, fundamentally—that it's a four-legged mammal, a canine, a pet.

So what is *agape*, anyway?

---

[1] Jack Wellman, "What Is Agape Love?", Patheos.com. http://www.patheos.com/blogs/christiancrier/2014/05/02/what-is-agape-love-a-bible-study/

The Truth about Agape Love

I tried for years to get hold of this slippery answer. Eventually I noticed that some Internet definitions hinted at the existence of a more fundamental definition for the word. "Outside of the New Testament, the word agape is used in a variety of contexts, but in the New Testament it takes on a distinct meaning," says an article at *Got Questions*.[2]

Finally I found it. Here it is in a scholarly work discussing 1 Peter 2:17:

> "Love the brotherhood": St. Peter says next: "Love the brotherhood." The agape he prescribes is not a higher quality than respect … it is simply a special, affectionate kind of respect reserved for brothers. *Agape* keeps the fundamental sense it has in classical usage and in the Septuagint: "to venerate, respect, show esteem for."[3]

Fundamentally, agape love is the love that respects.

Agape means to honor, respect, and esteem others.

Read 1 Corinthians 13, "the love chapter,"

---

2 http://www.gotquestions.org/agape-love.html
3 Ceslaus Spicq, O.P., Agape in the New Testament vol Two: Agape in the Epistles of St. Paul, the Acts of the Apostles and the Epistles of St. James, St. Peter, and St. Jude, trans. by Sister Marie Aquinas McNamara, O.P., and Sister Mary Honoria Richter, O.P. (Eugene, OR: Wipf & Stock Publishers, 2006)

through that grid. Read John 3:16 through it: "God so honored the world, so esteemed, so respected and valued all people, that he sent his only begotten Son."

In the New Testament *agape* takes on a special, technical nature as the word for love that specifically denotes the love of God, but in doing so, it doesn't depart from its original meeting. It underscores the incredible grace and love in God's heart that he sees past the rebellion, sin, and guilt of human beings to highly value and esteem them anyway.

Misrepresenting God?

I am afraid we Christians have been guilty of misrepresenting the heart of God. We have sometimes taught people that God views them as disgusting worms, worth saving out of some inexplicable, detached "agape" in his character that urges him to glorify himself, but not actually worth anything in themselves. We do not tell people, often—although I think on the whole we're getting better about this—that God honors and respects them.

That he values them.

Esteems them.

Please don't misunderstand me: human beings often are despicable.

We can be wretched.

And God must judge.

But even in his judgments, God is respectful. He respects our free will. He respects our personhood. He goes to every length to save us but gives us the right to choose.

Honored Sinners

I have mixed feelings about sin—the way we talk about it, I mean. On the one hand I think it gets too much attention, considering that Jesus has killed it off in our lives. On the other hand, I think we could stand to talk about it a lot more, or at least to understand it better.

It would be good, I think, if we understood better what sin is, and why it's so bad, and why it makes judgment so necessary and important.

Talking to a group of young teens about sin, I said, "You know, most of us are a little uncomfortable with the word 'sin,' and we don't really like to say we're sinners. But 'sin' is really not that complicated or strange a concept. It means to miss the mark. It means to be kind of messed up. You don't have to raise your hand, but who here is messed up?"

The teens laughed. They looked relieved.

And every single hand went up.

"Sin" is such a loaded word that we've become uncomfortable with it; we're not quite sure what we're *saying* when we say we're sinners, and we're not sure we want to lay claim to all it might mean. But ask us if we're messed up? Sure we are. Of course we are. We get that. We all miss the mark all the time.

And yet, the greatness of grace.

The majesty of God's love.

The depth of the *agape* in his nature.

Despite our sin, despite our constant mark-missing and our deep messed-upness, *he respects us*. He values us so highly that he launched a rescue mission at the cost of his own life, and he esteems us so greatly that he is devoted to ridding our lives of sin and bringing us back to our original, created image.

His image.

The Love We Show

As Christians, we have a clear mandate to love. The apostle John makes this undoubtable:

> Beloved, let us love one another, for love is of God; and everyone who loves is born of God and knows God. He who does not love does not know God, for God is love. (1 John 4:7–8, NKJV)

Love may take on many different expressions and forms. It may look like feeding the hungry. It may look like laying down our lives on the mission field, or for many, in contexts of persecution. It may look like giving counsel, being a good spouse or parent, being a good friend.

But fundamentally, first of all, it looks like respecting one another. If you cannot speak of a Democrat or a Republican with respect; if you cannot esteem the homeless person on the corner; if you can't speak of those who oppose your values in a way that values *them,* you don't really love.

When I realized that agape fundamentally meant respect, it made intuitive sense, and it immediately made the task of loving others seem both easier and harder. Easier to grasp, easier to define; harder to walk out.

But also, in the process of walking it out, transformative.

But I tell you, everyone who is angry with his brother will be subject to judgment. And whoever says to his brother, "Fool!" will be subject to the Sanhedrin. But whoever says, "You moron!" will be subject to hellfire.

(Matthew 5:22)

24

Raca, Respect, and the Agape Love of God, Part 3

In his discussion of anger and contempt, Jesus also spoke of levels of judgment—ending in his indictment of those who call their brother "fool" as subject to hellfire, or more literally, "the Gehenna of fire." It's easy to think we know exactly what that means, but we may miss a lot if we just skim over it—so let's take a closer look.

When Jesus talks about anger, he takes it in levels, and he gives levels of judgment that come with it.

He begins with the simple act of "being angry with your brother"—of flaring up, lashing out, taking your frustration out on someone else. For this he says we become "subject to judgment": the verdict is not certain and the judge isn't specified, but when we are angry, we subject ourselves to judgment.

The second level is that of calling one's brother "raca," empty or stupid, idiot or retard. Here we aren't just lashing out in a moment of anger; here we are making a value judgment of our own, counting another's mind as vapid and useless. This, Jesus says, subjects us "to the Sanhedrin," the Supreme Court of the day. Judges of our brothers, now we're judged by our brothers.

But it's the last, the word translated "fool"—moron or loser, essentially "waste of space"; our judgment of the actual value of another person's heart—that is most serious.

When we go this far, Jesus said, we are subject to fire.

Open Questions ...

In the last few chapters, I've talked about anger being a surface problem, something that comes up from the deeper root of contempt, which is the real issue Jesus is addressing.

I'm not sure that's always the direction, though. Maybe contempt, rather than necessarily lying at the root of anger, is the fruit of it. Maybe anger comes out of our sense of powerlessness, of frustration or angst about our own lives, and turned often and heavily enough upon others it becomes contempt for them. Perhaps anger and contempt move in one direction or the other, or perhaps they move in both. These are questions worth contemplating, because Jesus raised them, and because as we grow to know ourselves, so we are better able to grasp hold of grace.

Gehenna and the Judgment of Fire

Gehenna, which is variously translated "hellfire" or "hell," is Jesus's primary word for the place of judgment. It's actually the name of a real place: the Valley of Hinnom, located south of Jerusalem.

What exactly the word connotes in Jesus's teaching is a matter of debate.

The Valley of Hinnom, also called Topheth—literally "the fireplace"—was notorious in the Old Testament as the place of Israel's most appalling rebellion against God, a place where they sacrificed their own children in fire as offerings to pagan gods.

Because of this, God said, Hinnom would become a place of terrible judgment:

> "For the Judeans have done what is evil in my sight." This is the LORD's declaration. "They have set up their detestable things in the house that is called by My name and defiled it. They have built the high places of Topheth in the Valley of Hinnom in order to burn their sons and daughters in the fire, a thing I did not command; I never

entertained the thought. Therefore, take note! Days are coming"—the LORD's declaration—"when this place will no longer be called Topheth and the Valley of Hinnom, but the Valley of Slaughter." (Jeremiah 7:30–32)

In a related prophecy—one Jesus quotes elsewhere in connection with Gehenna—God's anger is pictured as fire: "The LORD will come with fire ... to execute His anger with fury and his rebuke with flames of fire" (Isaiah 66:15). After this, Isaiah said, the nations will come to worship God and will pass by the dead: "As they leave, they will see the dead bodies of the men who have rebelled against Me; for their worm will never die, their fire will never go out, and they will be a horror to all mankind" (Isaiah 66:24).

Gehenna, in other words, is a symbol for the burning, fiery, and angry presence of God as he goes to war against his enemies.

The Fire of Anger

We're all familiar with the terms "heaven" and "hell," so we quickly read a lot of theology into what Jesus says here. But I don't want us to miss some of the more subtle meaning in his choice of words.

With his three levels of judgment, Jesus said

something very clear and powerful about the kind of anger that is spoken, contemptuous, and pointed at others: *It burns.*

Throughout Scripture, God's anger and wrath are constantly described as a fire. His anger burns; his wrath is fiery and consumes his enemies. Gehenna is the ultimate expression of that.

People too, made in God's image, flush and grow hot when they are angry. We speak of an angry person as "hot-headed" and "hot tempered"; and we tiptoe around them lest they "explode" or "blow up."

Our anger burns, just like God's does.

The difference is that God's wrath is not arbitrary, is not misdirected, and is not quick to fire: his wrath takes hundreds and thousands of years to heat up.

Ours is often careless and quick.

The victims of human anger and contempt carry scars just as any burn victim does. Blasted by anger and contempt, we are shaped by it—disfigured and misdirected by words, spoken with power and aggression, that tore down our personhood and should never have been spoken.

Often, if we've been hurt by anger we become angry ourselves. We take the pain of our scars and turn it on others, "burning" one another in our anger, just as the people of Israel burned their children in the fire to Baal.

Jesus's warning in Matthew highlights the justice of God: we who have burned one another unjustly in our anger become subject to Gehenna, when God's just and righteous anger will spill over as fire.

The God Who Sees

In a story early in the Bible, God is given a name by a runaway slave who calls him "Thou God seest me"—or "the God who sees."[1]

Jesus's words in Matthew 5:21–23 are strong. He is not soft on anger.

But this tells us several things.

It tells us we are seen.

If we have been hurt by anger, if we have been scarred and torn apart by contempt, God sees.

He saw it happen, and he did not think it was okay.

He didn't think it was no big deal.

He didn't let the offender off the hook because they'd had a bad day.

He saw how deep and how real those burning words were to you, and he thought they were an atrocity.

---

1 Genesis 16:13, KJV

He's angry about it. Emotionally, truly angry.

I hope that in some way, that heals you. God isn't fine with what happened to you. He's angry *for* you.

He will heal you if you will allow it.

And if our hurts have turned into anger in our own lives, God sees the root of it. He knows how we got this way. He lays the blame where it belongs. He sees, and he cares, that we were damaged.

But God doesn't excuse us, either, when we choose to turn the weapons on others that were turned on us.

He can't. He's just. Will he blame you for things that aren't your fault? No. But some things are. To some degree, at some level, we make our own choices. Our responses, our retaliations, those are ours.

If we burn others with our tempers or with our contempt, God sees. He knows the damage it's doing to them. He loves us. He cares. But he won't excuse the damage we do to others no matter how much we want to justify ourselves.

This is the paradox of love and judgment. God loves us all, so deeply he gave his only begotten Son to die a brutal death for our sakes. His desire is to rescue, redeem, forgive, purify, clean up, cover, and transform every one of us.

So we don't burn others anymore.

So we don't come under the judgment of Hinnom.

So we can come to God to be healed ourselves, and so we can become conduits of healing to others—maybe even to those who bear scars we gave them.

But we have to let him. We have to surrender to love. If we choose to remain at enmity with God all our lives, Gehenna will find us on the wrong side of judgment.

The Hard Road of Healing

Jesus isn't easy on anger, because he doesn't think it's no big deal. But neither does he just dismiss the angry. On the contrary: he invites them.

Invites us.

All of Matthew 5 is an invitation. An invitation to trade our empty hands for the kingdom of God. An invitation to get real, to repent. To confess that our no-big-deal sins are a big deal after all, that God has a right to be angry and is the only one who can help us and heal us.

The Sermon on the Mount invites us to take the hard road to healing.

And every step of the way, the one preaching it—Jesus himself, Lord of heaven and earth—offers his friendship, his forgiveness, and his help.

It used to be a lot more common than it is now to hear the gospel presented in terms of sin and judgment and forgiveness: we've all sinned, judgment is coming, we need to repent and get right with God.

We don't hear it much anymore, but it's still true. That's the human predicament: we're damaged, and we damage others, and we need to be held accountable for it.

This is the offer of God: that though he sees the reality of our sins, he also sees the reality of our hurts; he will forgive the one and heal the other, transforming our lives if we will allow him to do so.

God looks at us and sees victims and perpetrators simultaneously, and his heart is big enough for us just the way we are.

But big enough, too, not to leave us this way.

So if you are offering your gift on the altar, and there you remember that your brother has something against you, leave your gift there in front of the altar. First go and be reconciled with your brother, and then come and offer your gift. Reach a settlement quickly with your adversary while you're on the way with him, or your adversary will hand you over to the judge, the judge to the officer, and you will be thrown into prison. I assure you: You will never get out of there until you have paid the last penny!

(Matthew 5:23–26)

25

The Way of Reconciliation: How Mercy Triumphs Over Judgment

Jesus is relentless in his examination of anger: its roots, its ugliness, the damage it does, and the guilt we incur because of it. Along the way he continually underlines the fact of judgment.

We might be tempted to see the judgment of God as something arbitrary or cruel, but the truth is that because morality flows from the nature of the Creator God, judgment is woven into the fabric of our existence. That which does not align with God's nature *will* come under judgment, not because God is petty, but because that is the way the universe operates. When we live in anger and contempt we will come under judgment within ourselves, among our peers, and finally before God himself.

Judgment is an end point, involving a whole process of accusation, exploration, and finally condemnation or acquittal. It brings consequences and labels one *guilty* or *innocent*.

Ultimately, judgment is good. Ask anyone in a country where justice is not practiced, and the poor (for example) cannot get redress for wrongs done against them. In fact, Scripture testifies that the whole world cries out for God to come and "judge the world with righteousness and the peoples with His faithfulness" (Psalm 96:13). If you have ever been in a situation where you needed justice to be done for you, you understand how deep a need this actually is.

And yet, Jesus teaches us, there's a better way. Judgment is good. But reconciliation is better.

The Way of Reconciliation

In Matthew 5:23–26, Jesus concludes his discussion of anger and judgment by urging us to get ourselves out of the judgment loop completely.

As much as we all desire judgment on our own behalf, we human beings live in a catch-22: we are sinners too, just like the person who has sinned against us, and so when we haul another into court we find ourselves facing charges also. Jesus recognizes this, but rather than urging us to pursue justice at all costs and take our own consequences bravely, he urges us to another course of action.

Reconcile.

First go and be reconciled, he says. Reach a settlement quickly with your adversary. Don't take it before a judge at all. Instead, recognize your wrongdoing and go to the one you've wronged. Apologize. Ask forgiveness. Humble yourself. Make things right where you can. Mend what's broken to the best of your ability.

Get out of the judgment loop long before you ever meet the Judge.

Be Reconciled to God

If we understand who Jesus, the God-man, truly is, we can see the startling truth of God's own course of action. God has a long list of grievances against mankind. Judgment Day will in fact come, when we all stand before the throne, and those who have never gotten out of the judgment loop will find they are hauled up on charges from which they cannot escape.

But before we ever reach that day, God comes to us in the person of Jesus and offers to reconcile.

This is all backwards, of course. It's supposed to be the wrongdoer who goes to the offended party in humility and apology, seeking to settle, not the other way around. But this is the grace of God: while we were yet sinners, he loved us—so much so that he urges us to step out of the catch-22, to seek forgiveness, to be washed clean, to be restored in a relationship of peace and favor with the One we have wronged.

Some years after Jesus's ministry, the apostle Paul wrote about his missionary work:

> Everything is from God, who reconciled us to Himself through Christ and gave us the ministry of reconciliation: That is, in Christ, God was reconciling the world to Himself, not counting their trespasses against them, and He has committed the ministry of reconciliation to us. Therefore, we are ambassadors for Christ, certain that God is appealing through us. We plead on Christ's behalf, "Be reconciled to God." (2 Corinthians 5:18–20)

God's love for us is so great that in the person of Jesus, he urges us to be reconciled with him now: to accept his forgiveness, be released from eternal consequences, be restored instead of put away.

And then he urges us to turn our eyes to one another and do the same: to share his heart for reconciliation, put aside our right to be vindicated and paid back, and embrace restoration with others instead.

The Cosmic Monkey Wrench

Satan, who is called "the accuser of the brethren"[1] and is said to accuse mankind like a court prosecutor day and night, thought he won when he intro-

---

[1] Revelation 12:10

duced sin into the world. He pitted God and humanity against one another, and since humanity will always be guilty, our ultimate fate could only ever be in a courtroom, hearing the gavel come down.

But Satan didn't reckon with the power of forgiveness and the whole new pathway it opens up.

Forgiveness and reconciliation are not quite the same thing. I can forgive another without ever being reconciled to them; reconciliation takes two people, and it will not always be realized. Jesus offers forgiveness to all, but many refuse to be reconciled to him.

Even so, forgiveness is a giant monkey wrench in Satan's careful machinations: it wrecks everything he has attempted to do. When we go one further and actually reconcile with one another, bringing peace and wholeness where brokenness and ruin existed before, the satanic plan is forever ruined. We have returned to the garden, with God and with one another, and we need no longer fear the courtroom.

The Heart that Hurries

We do not live in a perfect world, and I know from experience that reconciliation is not often simple. Sometimes our efforts to reconcile with others will be turned down or blocked from the outset. But Jesus's teaching in Matthew 5 reveals the Father's heart: if you find yourself in worship at the altar, offering your gift to God, and there remember that you have wronged someone and are not yet reconciled to them, leave the gift right there. *Hurry* and be reconciled. Close the gap as quickly as possible. Don't delay restoration any longer than you absolutely have to.

God will not be offended that you left him hanging. Rather, he'll smile on your heart, because it's his heart. Even as he sat on a hillside teaching the Sermon on the Mount, Jesus's life was an invitation to be reconciled. He left heaven in a hurry to be reconciled to us.

You have heard that it was said, Do not commit adultery. But I tell you, everyone who looks at a woman to lust for her has already committed adultery with her in his heart. If your right eye causes you to sin, gouge it out and throw it away. For it is better that you lose one of the parts of your body than for your whole body to be thrown into hell. And if your right hand causes you to sin, cut it off and throw it away. For it is better that you lose one of the parts of your body than for your whole body to go into hell!

(Matthew 5:27–30)

26

Talking Slant: Jesus on Lust, Love, and Fidelity

Jesus can be slippery, so that when his words seem most stark, most black-and-white, perhaps they are not stark but slant.[1] Stare at the black-and-white and it becomes something else, one of those 3-D images where you look at a pattern hard and long and suddenly see an unexpected picture.

Or maybe it is stark, and it is black-and-white, and yet it's also unexpected and layered.

Matthew 5:27–30 (and on into 31–32, because the discussion about divorce is all one piece with this passage even though many Bibles split them

---

[1] "Tell all the truth but tell it slant —" wrote Emily Dickinson:

Success in Circuit lies
Too bright for our infirm Delight
The Truth's superb surprise
As Lightning to the Children eased
With explanation kind
The Truth must dazzle gradually
Or every man be blind —

into separate topics) is one of these slippery passages for me.

"You have heard that it was said, Do not commit adultery." We have heard that, it's true. It's one of the best-known of the Ten Commandments, and even today most people would not argue with it. We like to support people's right to run around in theory, but no one ever told a wronged wife that her husband's adultery was no big deal. We tell her throw the bum out the door and good riddance.

"But," Jesus says, in one of his usual caveats where you wouldn't think there would be one—and his audience holds their breath.

Is he going to give them a loophole?

(They thought they had one in divorce; see verses 31–32.)

An instance in which adultery might be permissible?

No, he says, "But I tell you, everyone who looks at a woman to lust for her has already committed adultery with her in his heart."

How do you break a commandment?

How do you commit a sin?

How do you do a wrong thing?

Surely by breaking, by committing, by doing.

No, Jesus says to all that, it's not even necessary

that you actually DO it; you can commit the most heinous of sins just in your heart.

Jesus was harsh on anger, but even there the judgment required something to have been said. The anger had to find expression before it became something punishable. Here it doesn't. Here the crime, adultery, the ultimate betrayal, happens in the silence of the eye. The mind. The interior world of fantasy.

> If your right eye causes you to sin, gouge it out and throw it away. For it is better that you lose one of the parts of your body than for your whole body to be thrown into hell. And if your right hand causes you to sin, cut it off and throw it away. For it is better that you lose one of the parts of your body than for your whole body to go into hell! (Matthew 5:29–30)

Nothing has been said or done that anyone else can judge, so Jesus puts the impetus for punishment on us: you're the witness to your own crime, so punish it yourself. Cut off your hand. Gouge out your eye. Whatever caused you to sin, cut it off and throw it away. Better for you to enter life maimed and blind than to be thrown whole into the fires of enmity with God.

Stark. Clear. Jesus's meaning couldn't be more plain.

Right?

In Christian history some people have used this passage to demonize sexual attraction and paralyze people with unhealthy introspection and fear of themselves. Legend has it that the third-century Christian teacher Origen castrated himself (although even if that's true, the action was never condoned by any church authority). In a less extreme example, many conservative Christian leaders have tended to root their entire approach to male-female interaction in a way that presupposes the ultimate goal is to avoid anyone becoming attracted to anyone else, unless the attractees end up married. (If you thought you would end up married, and then you didn't, too bad for you.)

Bad applications aside, though, nearly all balanced Bible teachers throughout history would have said that Jesus did not intend that kind of interpretation. This is an example of hyperbole—exaggeration used for effect, to drive a point home.

It was never meant to be taken literally.

Really, Jesus? Are you the kind of God who exaggerates?

You—Mr. "Let Your Yes Be Yes and Your No Be No"?

Let's backtrack.

Is the idea of this passage to demonize sexuality?

It has been taught that Adam and Eve did you-know-what in the garden after the fall; that was the real original sin.

That's nonsense. Really, it is; read the Bible. Read Genesis 2. Read Ezekiel 18. Read the Song of Solomon.

Human sexuality is good and beautiful and created by God; human fruitfulness is good and beautiful and blessed by God; beauty and vitality and virility are gifts of God.

That is what the Scripture teaches without doubt.

Jesus is indelibly Jewish, with his roots in all of the aforementioned Old Testament passages and the values they promote. He is a Hebrew of Hebrews. He is not against sex.

And this teaching in Matthew 5 has nothing to do with feeling attraction toward someone. It has nothing to do with natural drives and desires. It really doesn't.

The key words are *adultery* and *to*.

First, *adultery*. This isn't the generic word for messing around with someone you aren't married to. It's the specific word for betrayal within marriage.

So this isn't about a young man looking at a young woman and finding her attractive and finding it hard to get her off his mind.

We don't have to be ashamed or afraid of ourselves.

This is specifically about a man looking at a married woman *to* lust after her.

There's the other key word: *to*. This man looks "to lust," Jesus says; in other words, he's looking with intention. He's looking beyond the point of attraction; he's deliberately feeding desire.

But she's married, or he is. Or both. Not to each other.

(I hope you can see the indictment of pornography here. "Looking to lust" is the whole point. And yes, that's a problem even without a marriage being involved, but we would need to discuss other Scriptures to really support that.)

So this isn't just objectification (which it is) or a dishonorable use of another human being (which it also is); it's also a betrayal of a marriage covenant.

There's a third party involved.

Your spouse has a claim to your body,[2] but to your thoughts too.

For Jesus, one senses this is a particularly big deal.

(And thou shalt love the Lord thy God with all thy heart, and with all thy soul, and with all thy mind, and with all thy strength … For this cause

---

[2] 1 Corinthians 7:3–4

shall a man leave his father and mother, and shall be joined unto his wife, and they two shall be one flesh. This is a great mystery: but I speak concerning Christ and the church.[3])

■■■■■

Sin begins in the mind, generally, then manifests itself in the flesh. What we think about we eventually do, we eventually become. Don't allow yourself to lust, we're taught, because you might eventually commit adultery.

Or just don't do it at all, because the moment you choose to lust after someone who does not rightfully belong to you, who in fact belongs to someone else, the deed is already done.

■■■■■

So punish yourself. "If your right eye causes you to sin, gouge it out and throw it away. For it is better that you lose one of the parts of your body than for your whole body to be thrown into Gehenna. And if your right hand causes you to sin, cut it off and throw it away. For it is better that you lose one of the parts of your body than for your whole body to go into Gehenna!"

You know your own guilt. You've caught your-

---
3 Mark 12:30, Ephesians 5:31–32 (KJV)

self in the crime. Punish it. Be ruthless. Cut off the source. Identify what part of you caused the sin—the eye, the hand—and cut if off, gouge it out. Away with it. Leave yourself as whole as you can be without sin.

Stark. Clear. Black-and-white.

And then when your left eye causes you to sin, gouge that out too. And when you sin with the stump of your hand, hack it off at the wrist, and then the elbow. When your foot carries you into a sinful place, saw right through the bone. Piece after piece, limb after limb, into the fire to spare the rest of you.

Jesus would rather have you disfigured and hideous than not at all.

Or is that not what he's saying?

Presumably the disciples sinned, with eyes and hands involved, and not one of them ever cut off a hand or gouged out an eye. (Peter cut off an ear, but not his own, and Jesus promptly put it back.)

Jesus never once reprimanded them for daring to walk around whole when they were clearly sinners.

Is Jesus talking straight, or is he talking slant?

Is the point here that your eye *doesn't* cause you to sin; that your hand *isn't* the problem; that the problem is deeper, in your heart and soul where you can't gouge it out, and since you'll never work your way into God's good graces by hacking things off, you'll have to come and be made new and whole entirely?

Justice won't get you where you need to go; you're going to need forgiveness.

■■■■■

Or is this, after all, hyperbole used for effect? Is the point not punishment but getting serious, zealous, about cutting ourselves off from sin?

Is the point here that the porn addict should throw away his cell phone and give up his Internet connection; that like Joseph in Potiphar's house, sometimes we need to run-not-walk away from the source of temptation without hanging around to see whether we can withstand?

Is the point that sin is truly awful, and eternity truly matters, and we need to stop making excuses and treat sin like our mortal enemy because it is?

■■■■■

Maybe the point is both.

Maybe neither.

Maybe Jesus is very slyly and subtly pointing to a completely different problem: the age-old tendency of human beings to throw one another under the bus.

In particular, historically speaking, for men to throw women under the bus.

The principles of fidelity and purity and chastity surely apply to men and women alike; but in Jesus's example it is a man lusting after a woman.

Some have used this passage to demonize sexuality; then they used it to demonize women.

If a man who wants to love God lusts after a woman, it is surely the woman's fault.

Her neckline is too low. Her skirt is too short. Her hair is too long, too loose, or too pretty. Her form is too feminine. Her face is too beautiful. Her voice is seductive.

So it's her fault.

You think I'm kidding, but history can attest: in many cultures, many places, many times, the answer to the problem of lust has been to control, shame, and ostracize women.

And if that didn't work, stone them.

Women cause men to sin, after all.

John 8: Jesus was in the temple when the Pharisees brought to him a woman caught in the act of adultery.

Just the woman.

Not the man.

You cannot catch ONE person in an act of adultery.

"Teacher," they said, "Moses taught us that such should be stoned. What do you say?"

Jesus told them to let the sinless one throw the first stone; then he, the Sinless One, released her from their trap.

In his culture, his time, men caught in compromised circumstances were far too quick to say, "She has caused me to sin; cut her off and throw her away, for it is better for me to enter life without her than for both of us to be thrown into hell together."

That's why Jesus turns to the subject of divorce—cut her off and throw her away—next.

It's an endless cycle.

Jesus will have none of it.

■■■■■

I don't know what Jesus is saying. Maybe some of this. Maybe all of it.

Maybe something else.

Jesus is considered the greatest moral teacher of all time, not necessarily the most straightforward.

From Jesus's words I draw several conclusions I can apply to my life.

>   1. That fidelity is precious, and it matters as much in my thoughts as in my actions.

2. That sin is heinous, even when it's "just" in the mind, and zeal can be required to fight it.

3. That the real problems are in my heart, not my hand or my eye or my DNA or my habits, and I need Jesus to fix them.

4. That it's not okay for me to blame anyone else.

Oh, and something else too—that women as a class can't and must not be blamed for the sins of men as a class.

I find that comforting.

That old pattern hasn't actually died out, and I've felt its pressures and its shaming too. I'm glad Jesus doesn't agree with it, even if you think I'm reaching with this interpretation. And of course it goes both ways: I can't blame any other group of people (men, terrorists, Democrats) for my sins.

Jesus never excuses any sin on the basis of it being some other person's fault.

He wants us honest.

We are the bride of Christ. He wants us faithful, He wants us real, He wants us whole.

It was also said, Whoever divorces his wife must give her a written notice of divorce. But I tell you, everyone who divorces his wife, except in a case of sexual immorality, causes her to commit adultery. And whoever marries a divorced woman commits adultery.

(Matthew 5:31–32)

27

Recalibrating Our Religion: Jesus on Divorce

Divorce is a huge and painful issue. I'm not, in this book, going to give marriage advice, attempt a clinical commentary on what is or is not allowable for Christians, or make blanket judgments of any kind. All of those things are beyond the scope of this book and frankly, beyond the realm of my personal authority.

Instead I want to attempt a recalibration in the way we think.

I would argue that's what Jesus is doing here too; every moral teaching in this part of the Sermon on the Mount is not a new law but a reorientation to an old one. He's not changing the law but changing the way we understand and relate to it.[1]

---

[1] I know that's controversial in itself. Some say that Jesus was changing the law here. But he wasn't. To change the law of Moses was a sin, and as a Jewish man "born under the law," Jesus could not change the law without making himself a sinner.

No Longer Two, But One

In the previous chapter, I said that Jesus's words on divorce are part of his words about lust, not a separate topic; and as we saw there, the crux of his teaching on lust isn't so much about reining in natural desires as it is about marital faithfulness—not in act only but also in the mind and in the heart.

In marriage, the Bible teaches, your body belongs to your spouse; in this sense, so do your thoughts.[2] You owe your spouse fidelity, not only in body but in mind and heart and soul. It is no more okay or harmless to look at porn within marriage or to follow other women with your eyes than it is to actually cheat on your wife. Ask any woman who's caught her husband doing this how deep the pain and betrayal go.

Love can't and shouldn't be compartmentalized. In a commitment as entire as marriage—"they are no longer two, but one flesh"[3]—love has to involve all of you.

I pointed out, too, that I see a possible connection between Jesus's hyperbolic "if your hand causes you to sin, cut it off and throw it away" and the tendency throughout history of human beings to throw one another under the bus. We would recoil in horror at the idea of actually dismembering ourselves, but many in our culture think nothing of cutting off and throwing away another person, even a spouse.

---

2 1 Corinthians 7:4
3 Matthew 19:6

That's where the link is: that's why Jesus goes to divorce here. I'll tip my hand: I *don't* believe Jesus was talking straight with all that "cut off your hand and gouge out your eye" business; I think he wanted his listeners to react with horror at the thought, and then he let them know that fundamentally, that is what divorce is.

If you would go to great lengths, any length, to preserve your right hand or your right eye, Jesus is saying to men who wanted easy excuses to offload their wives, *why wouldn't you do the same to preserve your marriage?*

The Bible's radical teaching is that marriage makes one entity out of two entities: that when a man and woman are joined in marriage, they are not two any longer but one. There are situations in which separation may have to be enjoined, just as there are situations in life where amputation is necessary to save a life. But such a solution must be recognized for the drastic and tragic step that it is.

Provision and Protection

In the Old Covenant, Moses permitted divorce and remarriage as a form of protection, especially for women. The cultural background is this: men, who had all the legal and actual power, would reject their wives and send them away, and those rejected women had nowhere to go. Since the entire economy revolved around households, a woman without a household had no means of providing for herself, no protection, and no home.

Historically such women have typically ended up in prostitution.

To protect rejected women, Moses ordered that any man who wanted to send his wife away had to write her a certificate of divorce. In other words, he had to give her papers that gave her a legal status and rights. With those papers, she could marry someone else, without fear of being stoned as an adulteress or labeled a prostitute. She could gain the protection and provision of being a wife in a husband's household again, because her first husband set her free to do so. The law also gave men who were genuinely wronged by unfaithful wives a humane way to be free of a marriage that was no longer really a marriage. Rather than calling the executioners, they could write a certificate of divorce.

In his teaching on divorce and remarriage, I don't believe that Jesus was snatching that protection away from the vulnerable. That would not be moral or loving, and it would be uncharacteristic of the ways in which the New Covenant typically develops and builds on the Old. So the point of this passage in Matthew is not to say that whereas in the past, divorce laws could be used to protect women and wronged spouses in general, from now on the vulnerable would have no protection and no rights.

Rather, Jesus was addressing men who were abusing the law. The law was given to protect, but instead, men were turning it into a license to reject their wives for any reason and whenever they wanted to.

Instead of dignifying women with this provision of Moses's, they were using it as a get-out-of-marriage-free card for themselves.

That was never its intent.

Jesus's words here are a smack upside the head, especially to Pharisees, who were waving the law of Moses around as a justification for forgetting all about Genesis 2 and the "one flesh" reality: *You're not fooling anyone,* Jesus is telling them; *that "right" you're waving around is a filthy rag.*

The law was given to protect the vulnerable from the consequences of something tragic and awful.

Marriage creates a new life; divorce is a living death. Stop treating it like a game.

That's the point.

What All of This Means

What do I take from all this, ultimately?

I'm not married, never have been. The topic of

consecrated singleness is one I can speak to with personal authority. Marriage is not.

But I can draw a few conclusions from Jesus that apply to me too.

First, that Christians ought to stand for the sanctity of marriage. Jesus treats the one-flesh union of husband and wife as incredibly sacred.

Second, that God cares about the vulnerable and looks out for their needs, and that although his standards are black and white, he provides for people who find themselves swimming in a grey world.

Third, that provision should never be turned into license. This doesn't just apply to marriage and divorce. Who hasn't heard of "greasy grace"? How many times have we taken Jesus's promise of forgiveness as license to sin? How often do we wave our get-out-of-jail-free cards in the air instead of exulting and glorifying in actual victory over sin?

Yes, we will be forgiven when we sin, but we are called to live in holiness. Yes, God is patient with us, but we're meant to live consecrated lives.

Jesus is more compassionate than anyone who ever lived. Compassionate enough to take our sins on himself and die with them on the cross in the ultimate act of deep, painful empathy. But he also has the highest standards of anyone who ever lived. Moral excellence—faithfulness, purity, self-sacrifice, radical fidelity—is the way of Christ.

Again, you have heard that it was said to our ancestors, You must not break your oath, but you must keep your oaths to the Lord. But I tell you, don't take an oath at all: either by heaven, because it is God's throne; or by the earth, because it is His footstool; or by Jerusalem, because it is the city of the great King.

Neither should you swear by your head, because you cannot make a single hair white or black. But let your word "yes" be "yes," and your "no" be "no." Anything more than this is from the evil one.

(Matthew 5:33–37)

28

Everything Sacred: Jesus on Telling the Truth

When Jesus used the repeated phrases "You have heard that it was said / But I tell you," he wasn't changing God's law—he was changing the way people used it. His teachings don't represent an actual change of morality, where something that used to be right is now wrong or vice versa, but a reorientation of our hearts toward the law of God.

The New Covenant promise, after all, is that we will be people with the law of God on the inside, people who are inwardly oriented toward righteousness and justice. This is a powerful and a wonderful thing.

This passage, on taking oaths, is very much in line with that promise.

To unpack it properly, we need to get to the core idea Jesus was addressing, which isn't so much oath-taking itself, but the well-known injunction in the Ten Commandments, "Thou shalt not bear false witness against thy neighbor."[1] Or to put it more bluntly, "Do not lie."

Kindergarten Promises

What is an oath, anyway? It's important to know that oath is not just a fancy word for a promise. Merriam-Webster offers two subdefinitions:

> (1): a solemn usually formal calling upon God or a god to witness to the truth of what one says or to witness that one sincerely intends to do what one says
>
> (2): a solemn attestation of the truth or inviolability of one's words

Both in English and in biblical parlance, an oath is different from a vow, which is a solemn promise to devote oneself to something—a marriage, say, or a specific religious action or lifestyle (the word "devote" comes from the Latin for "vow.") Jesus taught his followers never to take oaths, but early Christians were perfectly comfortable with vows.[2]

I was introduced to the idea of oath-taking (or "swearing") the same place most people are: on the kindergarten playground at recess. There, swearing-

---

[1] Exodus 20:16, KJV
[2] See Acts 18, where Paul took a traditional Jewish religious vow.

of-oaths is used exactly the same way it is in the adult world. "Close your eyes and open your mouth; it's not gross, I swear!"

The problem isn't so much the act of "swearing" as it is the implication that if I *wasn't* swearing, *if I wasn't taking an oath,* you couldn't necessarily trust what I say.

In kindergarten oath-taking is enjoined when it is clear that the speaker is not getting anywhere on the basis of integrity and trust alone, so something stronger is needed.

Invoking Accountability

In our modern world (maybe because of Jesus's words) we've left off the older, more key part of oath-taking, which was actually invoking some higher power, precious thing, or terrible consequence to keep you accountable to your word. We'll still say, as a joke, "I swear on my mother's grave," but most of us never actually *do* swear on precious or frightful things anymore.

In the ancient world, such swearing was the point.

Since I was likely to lie to you if it was to my benefit, I could only really establish my credibility by binding myself to something supernatural, essentially by calling down a curse upon my head if I broke my word.

Most of the time, one would swear by one's god. The idea is, "As my god hears me and will punish me for lying, I am telling the truth."

The Old Testament instructions concerning oath-taking were twofold: one, do not swear on any other god except Yahweh, your God; and two, keep your oaths.

By contrast, Jesus told his disciples not to swear oaths *at all*. This suggests several things.

Embracing Integrity

First, it suggests that the very idea of oath-taking is coming from a wrong place, because anyone should be able to trust *anything* that comes out of your mouth.

My parents actually would not allow us kids to use the phrase "I swear," largely for this reason. As soon as we have that phrase to fall back on, we decide that everything else we say somehow counts less. If we don't play the super-integrity card, we don't really need to have much integrity in our day-to-day interactions at all. I didn't pinky-swear, so you can't hold me to it.

Much like using the divorce law as license instead of as protection for the vulnerable, it's human nature to see "don't break your oaths" as permission to go ahead and bend, twist, or break everything else.

Jesus will have none of that. You ought to be trustworthy all the time. Your word should be your bond, in a sense; and if you must change something you've said, you must do it with humility and apology and repentance, not with a gleeful "But I didn't swear it!"

Christians should be the most honest and upfront people you will ever meet, and when we say yes or no, people should know they can trust us to mean it.

(This, by the way, is one of those little things Jesus taught that has power to create wholesale societal transformation, and has done so in various societies since. Think about it. One way to judge the value of a moral teaching is to ask not "Do I want to live like this?" but "What would happen if everyone in my society lived like this?")

The Power of Words

Second, Jesus implies there is power in invoking higher powers, and it's not wise to do so. "You cannot make a single hair white or black," he points out in reference to swearing on one's own head; i.e. on one's own life.

To bind yourself by things you cannot control, to swear by higher powers that you will do things you may find yourself unable to do, is foolish.

The Scriptures are unanimous about the power of words. "Death and life are in the power of the tongue," says Proverbs 18:21 (KJV). That words should have power is only natural; we live in a universe spoken into existence. Words are at the very base of everything; they define and energize reality. We should be careful with them.

We're Not in Charge

Third, we are not in control, and we should not talk like we are.

Everything Sacred

Fourth, Jesus does away with the scale of sacredness.

Here's the idea: I might be more comfortable breaking an oath sworn on Jerusalem than an oath sworn on God himself. Or if I'm a pagan, I might be more comfortable breaking an oath sworn on a lesser god than one sworn on a mightier god, because the lesser god might not notice or care or have as much power to thwack me for it. When we trade the requirement of absolute integrity at all times for weighing everything we say in terms of possible consequence, scales like this will always crop up.

Back to kindergarten: we would hear oaths like, "I promise I will catch you at the bottom of the slide, and if I don't you can have my peanut butter sandwich," and then when the promise was broken, the explanation was, "I don't like peanut butter anyway." That's the concept: you're only as trustworthy now as the potential consequence is severe or important to you.

But that means we're creating a value system where we weigh everything on a scale, and Jesus says the scale is false.

Do not swear by heaven, he says, because heaven is God's throne.

All right then; I'll swear by the earth—a lesser realm. No, says Jesus, that also belongs to God.

All right then; Jerusalem. No, that is God's too.

All right then; myself.

But no, Jesus says, because YOU are also God's, your life is not your own, you are not under your own control, nor do you have a right to throw your life away for a foolish oath.

We cannot measure our oaths on a scale of sacred to secular, because it all belongs to God. Everything is sacred.

Integrating Everything

To live and speak in the way Jesus calls us to means not just that we avoid tacking "I swear!" onto our speech but that we change the way we orient ourselves to life, to words, and to our world.

Integrity becomes important in itself and not just because of potential consequences. We stop measuring the world in terms of reward and punishment; we stop splicing our existence into "God's things" and "not God's things"; we honor the power and the meaning of words and are not careless with them.

In all these things we integrate our existence: our speech, our life, our values, and our worship come into a unity of honor and submission to God.

We leave behind our right to be anything other than completely sold out to God at all times—body, soul, heart, and mind.

29

Righteousness Redux: What Is the Point?

Since diving into the moral teachings of the Sermon on the Mount, we've detailed out Jesus's teaching on personal responsibility, on anger and contempt, on lust and fidelity and the sacredness of marriage, on honesty and oath-taking and seeing everything as sacred.

Every one of these reorientations toward the law of God is powerful and insightful and has the seeds of radical culture change within it.

But what is the point?

It's All About the Inside

These teachings reach back to Moses, delve the depths of our hearts, and lay out a way of life that is suited to the kingdom of God—a way of life that submits to God's authority in every part of ourselves.

And that ultimately is the point, and the point I don't want to lose sight of: that this isn't about learning more and harder rules, and working harder and more scrupulously to follow them; *rather, this is about becoming a reconstituted people, changed from the inside out, living a life that is holy and sacred and set apart because we love God and because we have received from him the greatest gifts imaginable.*

It's important in the midst of the moral teachings, where Jesus is so exacting, not to forget that this is not a list of things we must do to become acceptable to God but instead a way forward for us, a vision of what life can be when it is empowered by the Lord's Spirit, a higher and more life-giving way that is given to us *as a gift*.

It's All About the Gifts

We can't forget that this entire teaching began, not with a call to pull ourselves up by our bootstraps, but with a blessing on the spiritually impoverished, the grief-stricken, the struggling, and the starved—*and the promise to them, to us, is that God will give us his kingdom. He will draw near to us, he will give us an inheritance, and he will personally feed our hunger and our thirst.*

"Those who are persecuted for righteousness are blessed," Jesus finished that list, "for the kingdom of heaven is theirs."[1]

---
[1] Matthew 5:10

The Mystery of the Kingdom

For Jesus to tell thousands of people in his own day, and by extension hundreds of thousands and millions and eventually billions of people in the millennia to come, that a kingdom has been given to them is puzzling, because we do not perceive of kings as being all that plentiful.

Kingdoms can only rightfully be said to be given to rulers; plebs live in them, but the kingdom isn't *theirs*. We can understand the kingdom of God in terms of an empire, where Jesus is King of Kings, big King over little kings, but how many little kings can there really be room for?

A lot, if Jesus is to be believed.

This is part of the promise and the challenge of the Sermon's moral teachings. We are not used to believing we have as much authority over ourselves as Jesus indicates we do. We "can't help" being angry; we can't help lusting; we can't help it if we get backed into a corner and tell white lies. Most Christian teaching concurs: we're victims of original sin, unable to battle our base urges with anything like real success. That's why we need Jesus.

And that's true. The Bible is clear that none of us will get entirely clear of sin in this life.[2]

Yet with his description of "surpassing righteousness" in our actions and hearts, Jesus indi-

---
[2] See 1 John 1:8–10

cates that part of being given a kingdom is being given the authority to battle victoriously against our worst enemies, beginning with ourselves.

Worship leader Misty Edwards talks about the inner life of every human being as "an edgeless galaxy," a universe within a universe.[3] Looking out on a crowd of people, one is looking at countless universes, countless little spiritual realms in connection with each other and with God and yet each unique and discrete.

And maybe that's what some of this kingdom business is about: that each of us has a realm, and it's our job to bring our realm to Jesus and submit it to the rulership of heaven, and when we do he will give us a throne in our hearts and lives and empower us to sit on it well.

Pulling It All Together

When you think about it, that's one of the thrusts of this whole moral section: that we need to stop trying to control one another and instead focus our efforts on taking dominion over ourselves.

We must cease viewing ourselves as victims and begin to believe we have power and agency in our own lives, because in Christ, we do.

If you don't know where to start, begin back at

---

[3] As in the lyrics to her song "Invisible One," Little Bird (Forerunner Music, 2014).

zero. At poor in spirit, mourning, meek, and hungry. In that place receive the kingdom anew, and press forward again: to transformation, to authority, to life as a king under the blessing and authority of the King.

"Whoever practices and teaches these commands will be called great in the kingdom of heaven," Jesus said. And when he was resurrected (much later in the story), "Go into all the world and teach all nations, teaching them to observe everything I have commanded you."[4]

Grace does not just set us free from sin's consequence but from its power. That we might live above contempt, above anger, above lust, above fear, above covetousness, above dishonesty and finagling and always having an angle—this is not just a pipedream. This is surpassing righteousness, and it is the way of the kingdom.

It will transform our world as it transforms our lives.

---

4 Matthew 28:19–20

You have heard that it was said, An eye for an eye and a tooth for a tooth. But I tell you, don't resist an evildoer. On the contrary, if anyone slaps you on your right cheek, turn the other to him also. As for the one who wants to sue you and take away your shirt, let him have your coat as well. And if anyone forces you to go one mile, go with him two. Give to the one who asks you, and don't turn away from the one who wants to borrow from you.

(Matthew 5:38–42)

30

Justice According to Jesus, Part 1

Jesus spends three-fifths of his moral teachings on three of the great commands in the Ten Commandments: Thou shalt not murder, thou shalt not commit adultery, thou shalt not bear false witness.

He brings in the streams of oath-taking and divorce law to drive home the true nature of these three commands, because oath-taking and divorce law had been used as license to get around them. That is abuse of the law, Jesus says; go back to the heart, the core purpose, the clear vision. Don't look for loopholes, look for the best way.

It's interesting, by the way, that a discourse on law is broken into five sections. In biblical typology five is the number of grace. Perhaps this is a reminder that law itself *is* a grace—a gift from God meant to give us life.

Defining Justice

For the last two sections of this discussion Jesus leaves the Ten Commandments behind and instead draws out two of the more significant laws found elsewhere in the Old Covenant. These aren't arbitrary, and they treat of universal subjects: he didn't happen to talk about, say, the prohibition against mixing linen and cotton or the proper weight of temple spoons.

The first law he treats here defines our concept of justice. The second defines our concept of love.

Justice first.

> You have heard that it was said, An eye for an eye and a tooth for a tooth. But I tell you, don't resist an evildoer. On the contrary, if anyone slaps you on your right cheek, turn the other to him also. As for the one who wants to sue you and take away your shirt, let him have your coat as well. And if anyone forces you to go one mile, go with him two. Give to the one who asks you, and don't turn away from the one who wants to borrow from you. (Matthew 5:38–42)

It's really here that Jesus gets radical. In the first three-fifths of the discourse, as we've seen, Jesus didn't change laws, nor did he really say anything *new;* he reminded people of things they already knew and pulled away their excuses for breaking those laws.

He called them back to a higher vision, a better way: to a life that is actually lived righteously from the heart as opposed to a checklist approach where we keep our noses clean while our hearts are filthy.

(When I was a kid, my parents—more than once—illustrated the idea of "keeping the spirit of the law and not just the letter" in the context of housecleaning. No, if your responsibility is to clean the bathroom and today's chore is wipe down the sink but you ignored the overflowing garbage and the pile of towels on the floor, you did not actually fulfill your duty just because you wiped down the sink.)

Eyes, Teeth, and the Limits of Retribution

The Old Testament gave a fast and easy definition of justice: "An for an eye and a tooth for a tooth."[1]

That sounds harsh to modern ears, because we mostly deal with fines and community service rather than eyes and teeth, but in its context this was much like the divorce law—not so much a license as a limit.

People were already seeking out their own jus-

---

[1] Exodus 21:24

tice, and true to form they tended to overstate the damage done and demand outsized payback. When someone knocks out my tooth it's not just my smile that gets damaged but my pride, so I'll have his whole head, thank you very much.

In that kind of "justice system" the rewards go to the mighty, and it matters very much who you offended, not just what you did. The law of God sets a limit on that: judge damage fairly, repay it in accordance with the damage done, don't play favorites.

A tooth is worth a tooth, not a life or someone's freedom; an eye is worth an eye. End of story.

But we tend to see license where God is setting limits, don't we? Now this eye-for-eye thing becomes the whole way we measure justice. We take the whole vast idea of justice and judgment and boil it down to tit-for-tat retribution.

There is, of course, merit to this particular law.

But taken alone, it misses the big picture of justice by a long, long way.

Justice According to Jesus

God's justice, as written about by the prophets and revealed in the law, is not primarily retributive at all. It's primarily restorative. Jesus would demonstrate that fully and personally by going to the cross and making the full restoration of the entire human race possible, but it's there in the Old Testament from the very beginning. Justice, according to the law and the prophets, can be mercy; and mercy can be justice.

> This is what the LORD Almighty said: "Administer true justice; show mercy and compassion to one another." (Zechariah 7:9, NIV)

> Yet the LORD longs to be gracious to you; he rises to show you compassion. For the LORD is a God of justice. (Isaiah 30:18, NIV)

With the goal of restoration in mind, Jesus challenges his followers to react very differently to wrongdoing done against themselves. Don't respond with retribution at all, but with generosity and kindness. Your enemies won't know what to do with it.

Lots of people won't like it when we do this. We all want justice for ourselves, but most of us tie that very tightly with the demand that people who have hurt us get their just deserts. So tightly, some of us, that we can't actually imagine one without the other. How *can* we be restored, if the other person never has to give up an eye?

A Monkey Wrench Called Grace

In his call to nonviolent response and forgiveness, Jesus detaches justice from retribution. As we observed earlier, he's asking us to break the cycle of sin and punishment, to interrupt the whole thing and throw it off-kilter by offering forgiveness and generous grace.

The enemy doesn't know what to do with that.

We don't know what to do with that.

We want our grace to be deserved. (Ha, ha.)

But we can't so much have it both ways, can we? Not when we've all got eyes and teeth on our record.

But Can It Be Done?

I suspect that of all Jesus's teachings, this one is the hardest to practice and the least actually done. It's also one of the most explosively powerful. Sadly, it hasn't always been Christians who have taken it most seriously. Gandhi, whose practice of Sermon-on-the-Mount nonviolence freed India, wrote that "the Sermon on the Mount went straight to my heart ... The verses 'But I say unto you, that ye resist not evil: but whosoever shall smite thee on thy right cheek, turn to him the other also. And if any man take thy coat let him have thy cloak too,' delighted me beyond measure."[2] Earlier, he wrote, "Though

---

2 From his Autobiography, 1958. Quoted in M.K. Gandhi, What Jesus Means to Me (Ahmedabad, India: Navajivan Publishing House, 1959), compiled by R.K. Prabhu; 3.

I cannot claim to be a Christian in the sectarian sense, the example of Jesus' suffering is a factor in the composition of my undying faith in nonviolence which rules all my actions, worldly and temporal."[3]

Even today, progress in the area of human dignity and civil rights is threatened when this foundation of nonviolence and mercy is forgotten or abandoned, when the path to freedom becomes about retribution and revenge. We are in danger when we forget.

Revenge is a hunger that can never be satisfied. It must instead be laid to rest.

---

[3] A statement made in 1939, quoted in Gandhi, What Jesus Means to Me; 5.

You have heard that it was said, An eye for an eye and a tooth for a tooth. But I tell you, don't resist an evildoer. On the contrary, if anyone slaps you on your right cheek, turn the other to him also. As for the one who wants to sue you and take away your shirt, let him have your coat as well. And if anyone forces you to go one mile, go with him two. Give to the one who asks you, and don't turn away from the one who wants to borrow from you.

(Matthew 5:38–42)

31

Justice According to Jesus, Part 2

In the last chapter, we saw that the law's "eye for an eye and tooth for a tooth" was a limit on retribution rather than an ideal portrait of justice. Jesus's own definition of justice, given here, is restorative rather than retributive, and it works by love and grace, not by anger and tit-for-tat vengeance.

There is a retributive side to God's justice, and God is angry with sin. Jesus himself has made this very clear.

But where he can, God chooses to confront sin with love and grace first. There is a point of no return for sinners, but God's way—as seen so vividly in Jesus—begins with aggressive love, self-sacrificing embrace, and open invitation.

Only after all these have been spurned does the wrath of God come into play.

If you want justice, Jesus is saying here, don't

begin with revenge. Begin by doing everything in your power to overcome evil with generous, startling good.

One Caveat: This Isn't About Abuse

The idea in Jesus's teaching here is not that an abused person should remain with an abuser or enable them by, for example, keeping their crimes a secret. In fact, when reformers great and small have practiced nonviolence in history, it has had the effect of revealing and exposing injustice on a massive scale. Again, there *is* a retributive aspect to justice, and there is a time to enact it. Romans 13:4 tells us that government is given a sword by God in order to punish evildoers. Likewise, the restoration spoken of in Matthew 5:25 and Matthew 18 requires that the offender repent. If no repentance is forthcoming and a situation is dangerous, God is not asking you to stay in it. Those who would say God requires the vulnerable to stay in a dangerous situation are guilty of playing exactly the kind of game "an eye for an eye" was written to expose and combat.

Going the Extra Mile

As Jesus unpacks the idea of nonresistance, what's described is not passivity. It is active and subversive in the extreme. It actively turns a victim into an aggressor of love: wronged, you turn around and overwhelm an enemy with goodness.

Paul actually called this "heaping coals of burning fire" on an enemy's head. It's not about enabling unjust empires; it's about overthrowing them.

In practice that's what it does. It can be done on a grand scale, as in the Civil Rights movement, or on a smaller but no less powerful one—read Corrie Ten Boom's stories of prisoners in a Nazi concentration camp turning the tables on their captors by blessing and praying for them. It's like an enemy catching what he thinks is a deer in a net and finding out he's got a lion.

Practicing Aggressive Goodness

I might suggest, if we find we have enemies, that we get super practical about this and figure out how we can turn the tables on them by overwhelming them with generosity and help.

Imagine if we could love radical terrorists into the kingdom before they've even had a chance to terrorize. Or if we could so overwhelm the staff and patrons at an abortion clinic with care and love that their lives are changed. Imagine loving people in the media, in opposing political parties, or in the entertainment industry with so much goodness and genuine care that their stereotypes are challenged and they find they must reexamine their assumptions.

Let's bring it closer to home.

What if you stop resisting the church member who so irritates you and instead make a point of blessing them? What if when you're angry with someone in your family, you express practical love for them—in whatever shape that takes? What if when a friend hurts you, you turn around and bless them?

What would the world look like if we all practiced mercy?

G.K. Chesterton famously said that the Christian ideal has not been tried and found wanting, it has been found difficult and left untried.[1] Perhaps nowhere is that more true than here, in the principle of turning the other cheek.

We fear being made into victims and doormats. But this principle, practiced biblically, does just the opposite. It makes us more than conquerors in Christ.

---

[1] G.K. Chesterton, *What's Wrong with the World,* originally published in 1910. This quote comes from the public domain Kindle version, 2012, loc. 370.

You have heard that it was said,
Love your neighbor and hate your enemy.
But I tell you, love your enemies and pray
for those who persecute you, so that you
may be sons of your Father in heaven.
For He causes His sun to rise on the evil
and the good, and sends rain on the
righteous and the unrighteous.

For if you love those who love you, what
reward will you have? Don't even the tax
collectors do the same? And if you greet
only your brothers, what are you doing
out of the ordinary? Don't even the Gentiles do the same? Be perfect, therefore,
as your heavenly Father is perfect.

(Matthew 5:43–48)

32

How to Be Perfect: Loving Our Enemies and Becoming Like God

Jesus gives up the game with this one.

This is the last section of Jesus's moral teachings, his five short discussions of moral law. As we saw, in biblical typology, the number five is considered to represent grace. The law itself, rightly understood, is a gift of grace; it is grace that makes us righteous by faith; and in the end, to live the law the way Jesus tells us to results in grace upon grace: grace to those who anger us, grace in broken relationships, grace in commitments to others, grace in our dealings with ourselves, grace and truth all the way around.

Previously, I said that the last two commands Jesus deals with, rather than being two of the Ten Commandments, are more "big principle" kinds of laws, defining justice and love respectively. Jesus first shifts the discussion of justice from retribution to restoration, as we just saw. Next, he shifts the concept of love from something earned to something freely and unconditionally given.

Love as the Unifying Principle

Love is a big deal to Jesus. According to him, love is the unifying principle of the entire law. Asked what is the most important commandment, he responded that the greatest and first commandment is to love the Lord your God with all your heart, soul, mind, and strength; and "the second is like it: You shall love your neighbor as yourself."[1]

For Jesus, it all boils down to love. Love is why he came. He came to inspire our love for God, to fellowship with us, to give his life in love, to rescue his enemies in love, to teach us to love. Love is the whole point.

To quote Bob Jones, "There is only one question the Lord will ask you when you stand before Him in death, 'Did you learn to love?'"[2]

Beyond Loving Our Neighbor

"Love your neighbor as yourself" is a difficult

---

[1] Matthew 22:39

[2] Bob Jones was a leader in the charismatic movement whose legacy is mixed and rightly controversial. I reprint this quote because it's profound, and not as a blanket endorsement of Jones.

enough command to put into practice, although we can wrap our heads around it easily enough. It's not hard to see that it's good for us to love other people as much as we love ourselves, and to try to benefit them and do good toward them. No one really admires outright selfishness. We talk a big game in our culture about being "true to ourselves," but we all know that shouldn't be done at the expense of everyone else.

But "love your enemies" is another thing. We may instinctively know that community is good and neighbors should huddle together, but it's usually an outside enemy we're huddling against. We value community in part because of the world "out there," the people and groups and races and parties that are against us.

Some of this enmity is just perceived; some of it's real. Jesus doesn't say persecution is all in our heads. He was speaking to people who lived under a foreign empire, a dominant power that exercised sometimes brutal policies. When he was born, a local puppet king called Herod had all the infants in the region who were two years old and younger murdered. When the Jews tried to stage an uprising less than five years before the birth of Jesus, the Romans crucified hundreds of Jewish men and lined the roads with them, so they could gasp and writhe and die in public above their families and friends.

But at least the Romans respected Jewish religion. Regimes before them were culturally and religiously genocidal. A few generations ago, before Rome, Judea had suffered the rule of the Greek Antiochas IV Epiphanes, who made it his aim to stamp out their religion and culture and sacrificed a pig on their most sacred altar. Before Greece they had Persia, with Haman's famous attempt to massacre every Jew in seven provinces because one stubborn man named Mordecai wouldn't bow down to him. These were people who knew about enmity and persecution.

An Understandable Postscript

Somewhere along the way, in the long history of the Jews against foreign and violent oppressors, they had tacked a very understandable line onto the original law: "Love your neighbor, but hate your enemy." That latter part isn't in the law of Moses, but it had become pseudo-Scripture by Jesus's time, for obvious and justifiable reasons. In fact when enmity is real, when hatred and persecution are real, it can feel *wrong* not to hate your enemy. It becomes a duty, something the righteous *must* do so as to stand up for the truth, to preserve their identity and their personhood, to remain faithful.

But Jesus doesn't agree.

He tips his own hand here: he has, after all,

come to die for his enemies. He plans to carry out his own advice to "agree with your adversary quickly" to the furthest possible degree: he is going to seek reconciliation and restoration with people who don't want it or deserve it.

Unreasonable Love

This kind of love is completely unreasonable. Paul draws out the wonder of it:

> For while were still helpless, at the appointed moment, Christ died for the ungodly. For rarely will someone die for a just person—though for a good person perhaps someone might even dare to die.
>
> But God proves His own love for us in that while we were still sinners, Christ died for us! Much more then, since we have now been declared righteous by His blood, we will be saved through Him from wrath.
>
> For if, while we were enemies, we were reconciled to God through the death of His Son, then how much more, having been reconciled, will we be saved by His life! And not only that, but we also rejoice in God through our Lord Jesus Christ. We have now received this reconciliation through Him. (Romans 5:6–11)

The Nature of God-Love

God burns on his own fuel.

I was lighting a candle beside my bed one night, watching the wick catch and begin to burn, when I heard those words in my heart.

Here is the answer to why and how God loves so unreasonably—an insight into the divine nature that calls us to do the same.

When Moses encountered God on the mountaintop, he saw a bush on fire, but it was not consumed. The fire, then, wasn't using the bush as fuel; it was burning from some other source.

God burns on his own fuel.

I didn't really understand that, though I was awed by it, but the next day I was out walking and thinking about love, and relationships, and I suddenly got it (part of it, anyway): this is what it means that God's love is unconditional, that it's based in his nature and not in our response.

Human love needs to be fed by outside fuel. That's the premise of best-selling books like *The Five Love Languages:* everyone has a "love tank," and if it doesn't get filled with the proper fuel, it becomes very hard to feel loved or give love. We end up running on empty and burning out. To love someone who doesn't love you back (in a way you can receive and feel) is the hardest thing in the world.

But it's not hard for God, because while he wants our love, loves our love, asks for and receives our love, he doesn't need it. The love with which he loves us comes out of his own nature. It draws on an energy source that isn't us.

So he can love his enemies, though they do not love him back.

He can give endlessly, creating new life and rain and sunshine, though we don't return the giving.

He can go to the cross for people who have only barely begun to figure out who he is, much less love him with the kind of love he desires. His burning love can carry him that far.

He calls this being "perfect."

What Love Looks Like

Often we think of God's love in purely religious terms. God's love is expressed in the death of Jesus and the forgiveness of our sins, with the gift of eternal life tacked on to that. That is the sum total of how we understand God as loving us.

Yet Jesus declares the sun to be an expression of the love of God, and the rain. Sent indiscriminately to God's friends and enemies alike, because he loves them.

There is no one the love of God doesn't reach and no one who has not felt it, even basked in it, without necessarily recognizing what it was.

Sun and rain together give life and energy to everything that grows and lives on the earth, thus feeding us, watering us, giving us gentle breezes and thunderstorms, giving us waves and cloud formations and unspeakable beauty.

This is the love of God. For you and for me, and for our enemies.

Somewhere across the world a terrorist is waking up, drawing a breath, feeling sun on his face, and all this is a gift of love to him.

From God.

Somewhere a human trafficker is enjoying a drink of water or the taste of his favorite food, and this is God's gift to him, for he too is loved.

A despot in some faraway country, responsible for the ruin of hundreds of lives, is feeling the lift of his heart as a warm breeze blows across his face, bearing with it the scent of flowers and of rain, and this is the touch of grace, of love—perhaps the last such touch he will ever feel before a heart attack or assassination or old age or suicide takes him away.

God will judge his enemies. He will pour out his burning wrath upon them.

But first he will love them.

For he has always loved them.

Do this too, Jesus says, "so you may be sons of your Father in heaven." The word "sons" here emphasizes family resemblance, genetic propensity. Love your enemies, says Jesus, and you will look like God. Perhaps you will remind the world of him.

The Reward of Love

You could spend your life just loving those who love you back, those who fuel your tank; you could greet and honor only your own brothers and let the rest of the world stay outside. You could do that, but then where, Jesus wants to know, would be your reward?[3] You'll be doing what's only human, what everybody does—even the turncoats and outsiders themselves.

There's no reward in being exactly like everybody else.

Mediocrity doesn't win the day.

Middle-of-the-road doesn't look like God.

You can be like the herd, or you can step out and be like *God*, look like God, be perfect like God. There's a reward for that.

When Jesus talks about rewards, I believe they're both intrinsic and extrinsic. He doesn't say what the extrinsic reward of loving your enemies will be; we can assume this is where Pauline talk of

---
[3] Jesus is very unembarrassed about rewards. Ask him why you should do certain things, and he will say, "Because of the reward!"

crowns and victory wreaths comes in. But the intrinsic reward is perfection.

God measures perfection rather differently than we do.

He's not a perfectionist, just perfect.

To be "perfect" is to be whole, to be complete. Finished.

Isn't that what we all desire?

Isn't that the deepest yearning of all our hearts—to be *whole*? To be everything we're meant to be? To not be broken anymore but finished, entire, lacking nothing?

There's a road to that kind of perfection, Jesus says; it's attainable. It's love.

Start by loving your neighbor, like the law said, but keep going, keep pressing forward, love even your enemies and pray for them, because when you come and pray to God for your enemies, you're talking to someone who loves you and loves your enemies and burns on his own fuel.

And then you will be perfect too.

PART 3:

Trust at the Core: Jesus on Spiritual Disciplines

> BE CAREFUL NOT TO PRACTICE YOUR RIGHTEOUSNESS IN FRONT OF PEOPLE, TO BE SEEN BY THEM. OTHERWISE, YOU WILL HAVE NO REWARD FROM YOUR FATHER IN HEAVEN … AND YOUR FATHER WHO SEES IN SECRET WILL REWARD YOU.
>
> (Matthew 5:19–20)

33

Keeping Secrets and Finding Right Rewards: Jesus on Spiritual Disciplines

The words *disciple* and *discipline* share the same root. This shouldn't be a big surprise, but for some reason it took me years to notice it—and when I did, it hit me with a wave of revelation. The connection sheds a lot of light on just what it means to be a disciple of Jesus.

A disciple is a learner in a specific area, a "discipline." And a disciple is one who practices certain behaviors and habits, "disciplines," in order to achieve a set result.

In our case the area of study and of achievement is spiritual life, which for Jesus is the fountain and foundation of all of life. Everything begins in the spirit and works its way into the physical realm; it's been that way since God spoke the world into existence.

By the way, this is why a life lived "in the flesh"

is so deadly: when we're oriented toward the flesh instead of the Spirit, things begin in the body or physical realm and work themselves into our spiritual lives instead of the other way around. That's why "sorcery," a fairly spiritual activity, is called a "work of the flesh" in Galatians.[1] Or at least that's my take.

Spiritual Disciplines in the Sermon on the Mount

In the Sermon on the Mount, spiritual disciplines are right in the middle of the discussion. That shows their key importance to Jesus and his listeners. Jesus takes it for granted that his listeners, Jewish people with some interest in their religion, are already practicing these spiritual disciplines, but he shows how in many cases, they had lost the spiritual root and turned them into works of the flesh instead. He also gives them the key to recovering their real purpose and power.

This is a very relevant message for us today. We too are prone to turning innately spiritual things into works of the flesh.

The three disciplines Jesus discusses in this central section of the Sermon are giving to the poor, prayer, and fasting.

Giving to the poor had such a pivotal place in

---
[1] Galatians 5:20

the Jewish concept of righteousness that they actually called it "practicing your righteousness"; this is the wording Jesus uses when he starts his discussion in Matthew 6:1. We could use similar wording to describe prayer and fasting: they are "practicing your relationship" and "practicing your humility."

In the case of Jesus's listeners, though, many had turned these spiritual disciplines—practices meant to come from the spirit and achieve spiritual goals—into works of the flesh done to achieve a fleshly reward.

The Problem of Wrong Rewards

Here was the problem: God does and will reward these particular behaviors, but so will people. We're kidding ourselves if we think that godly behavior only gets us persecution and disdain from people; it's actually a very quick way to get yourself exalted in the eyes of people around you who share your faith and values. If you give and are seen giving; if you pray and are seen praying; if you fast and are seen to be fasting, people will put you on a pedestal. It's as true now as it was in Jesus's day.

And when we're given the option to go for an easy, cheap reward instead of a difficult, valuable one, very often we'll go for the easy reward.

As an example: I really struggle with self-control in the area of getting up in the morning. I want to get up early for multiple excellent reasons, not least among which are the pursuit of God and the sanity that comes with getting a jump on my day instead of my day getting a jump on me. But all too often, every morning when my alarm goes off, I hit snooze and go back to sleep.

Why? Well, when I hit snooze and get back under the covers where it's warm and cozy, I get a happy little dopamine hit.

The rewards of getting up early would be *so much better* as not even to compare. There would be personal growth, there would be sunrises, there would be happy dopamine hits and endorphin rushes. More of them and longer lasting.

But given the choice between all of that and a quick hit, I keep choosing the quick hit.

So it is with spiritual disciplines. *We get a choice of rewards.*

Do them continually, for the right reasons, in the right way, and grow spiritually, encounter God profoundly, and receive rewards that come from the heavenly realm.

Or get people to admire you and say nice, affirming things about what a great person you are.

Most of us will choose the latter by default.

Thankfully Jesus has come along to rescue us from our defaults.

Done in the right way, the spiritual disciplines he talks about become habits that empower our spiritual lives. They put us into contact with God and habitually grow and prune our lives. Done the wrong way, they become detrimental.

Thankfully, it's not that hard to do these things right.

The secret, Jesus says, to getting the right reward, is to do spiritual disciplines in secret.

Actually take steps to make sure no one sees you except God.

(You don't have to get ridiculous about this; it's the general principle that counts.)

So don't pray on street corners (a common thing in a religious society like Judea in Jesus's time); pray in your closet. Don't give publicly, with lots of fanfare; give quietly and secretly. Don't fast in a way that calls attention to yourself, fast privately.

When you do this, you'll discover something profound: that your Father is in secret, and he sees in secret.

The Father Who Is in Secret

To me, "your Father who is in secret" is one of those profound revelations that Jesus just casually drops, a line we're likely to breeze past without even letting sink in what's being said.

The Father is in secret.

When you stop and think about it for a moment, that's obvious. God chooses to be invisible. He chooses to work invisibly. He speaks silently. He gives to everyone but doesn't set himself up in the sky on a visible throne dishing out gifts and rewards where everyone will recognize him and worship appropriately.

God is at once obvious[2] and hidden. He is in secret.

When we do godly things, then, Jesus beckons us to join the Father in secret. To find the hidden place where God is and meet him there, to join him in his work.

God isn't standing on the stage; he's sitting incognito at the corner table in the coffee shop, and you can go and huddle with him there and talk.

So God is in secret, and he sees in secret. That's the second thing Jesus constantly points out. If you want to do spiritual disciplines right, you have to do them for the right set of eyes.

The Audience of One

In her excellent book *What Is the Point?*, Misty Edwards writes about the power of living life "for an audience of One," of doing everything for one set of

---

2 Romans 1:20

eyes alone. This, she says, is the whole key to living a life that pleases God. It's the hardest thing we can do and yet the most powerful: "When we have the confidence that [Jesus] is attentive and remembers even the smallest words spoken and rewards the smallest reach toward Him, this is faith."[3]

In Jesus's words, doing things before the eyes of men makes us into hypocrites and idolators; doing things for the eyes of God alone leads us into encounter and reward from the God of heaven himself.

A Note About Practicalities

It's worth mentioning that Jesus isn't talking about taking your faith underground and making it impossible to tell that you're a Christian.

Obviously, people were aware that Jesus prayed, and occasionally he did it publicly and even for the sake of those who were listening. He also preached and taught in public. So Jesus isn't teaching that faith should be kept private in that sense. Rather, he's warning against doing religious actions for the wrong reasons, and in this case, the best way to combat the wrong reasons is to do the actions differently—in a way that thwarts our wrong motivations and gets us zeroed in on the right ones.

---

3 Misty Edwards, What Is the Point?: Discovering Life's Deeper Meaning and Purpose (Lake Mary, FL: Charisma House, 2012), 44.

The fact is, there is no reward for prayer in a closet except the rewards you find in secret—encounter with God, personal transformation, answers to prayer. Giving secretly doesn't do anything for your reputation or your status among believers, but it may do a lot for your ability to truly love and care for others, as well as benefiting those others in deeper ways because they don't become beholden to you. Instead of gaining power over them, you set them free—but that's not the kind of reward our flesh typically craves.

It's easy to become very self-condemning and frustrated when we fall into fleshly motivations and patterns, but Jesus is teaching us that overcoming those powerful motivations may sometimes be as easy as changing the way we carry something out in practice.

You can cheat your flesh and get back to the spirit that way, and it's not even very hard.

So whenever you give to the poor, don't sound a trumpet before you, as the hypocrites do in the synagogues and on the streets, to be applauded by people. I assure you: They've got their reward! But when you give to the poor, don't let your left hand know what your right hand is doing, so that your giving may be in secret. And your Father who sees in secret will reward you.

(Matthew 6:2–4)

34

The Spiritual Discipline of Giving to the Poor

Jesus doesn't start his discussion of spiritual disciplines by trying to convince people to do them. He treats them as a given: these are things his listeners are already doing. We can see this clearly in the first discipline.

In verse 1, Jesus actually called giving to the poor "practicing your righteousness." If you don't over-theologize *righteousness*, this seems like a natural connection. There's a deep understanding in all of us human beings that giving to those who lack is a *right* thing to do, a good thing, even a duty.

In the Bible, giving to the poor has a long history. It was commanded and systematized in the law of Moses on many levels. Deuteronomy 15 is one example:

> If there is a poor person among you, one of your brothers within any of your gates in the

> land the LORD your God is giving you, you must not be hardhearted or tightfisted toward your poor brother. Instead, you are to open your hand to him and freely loan him enough for whatever need he has ...
>
> Give to him, and don't have a stingy heart when you give, and because of this the LORD your God will bless you in all your work and in everything you do. For there will never cease to be poor people in the land; that is why I am commanding you, "You must willingly open your hand to your afflicted and poor brother in your land." (Deuteronomy 15:7–8, 10–11)

The Bible actually draws a straight line between one's generosity toward the poor and one's own prosperity. Because God is watching and rewards such "righteousness," when you give to the poor, "you will be blessed in all your work and in everything you do."

But it is the book of Job that draws the clearest picture of this type of righteousness. Job is considered by many to be the oldest book of the Bible, existent probably as an oral poem even before the book of Genesis was written.

When we first meet Job, he is renowned for two things: his fabulous wealth and his righteousness. God himself extolls Job as a "a man of perfect integrity, who fears God and turns away from evil" (Job 1:8). But what does it mean to say that Job was a righteous man? If we dig a little deeper, we find that his righteousness is described in terms of devout commitment to God and of his service to the poor and needy.

Here is Job's description of his own life in Job 29 and 31. It is worth reading in full:

> I rescued the poor man who cried out for help,
> and the fatherless child who had no one to support him.
> The dying man blessed me,
> and I made the widow's heart rejoice ...
> I was eyes to the blind
> and feet to the lame.
> I was a father to the needy,
> and I examined the case of the stranger [the foreigner or outsider].
> I shattered the fangs of the unjust
> and snatched the prey from his teeth.
>
> ...
>
> If I have dismissed the case of my male or female servants
> when they made a complaint against me,
> what could I do when God stands up to judge? ...
> Did not the One who made me in the womb also make them?
> Did not the same God form us both in the womb?
> If I have refused the wishes of the poor

> or let the widow's eyes go blind,
> if I have eaten my few crumbs alone
> without letting the fatherless eat any of it—
> for from my youth, I raised him as his father,
> and since the day I was born I guided the widow—
> if I have seen anyone dying for lack of clothing
> or a needy person without a cloak,
> if he did not bless me while warming himself with
> the fleece from my sheep,
> if I ever cast my vote against a fatherless child,
> when I saw that I had support in the city gate,
> then let my shoulder blade fall from my back,
> and my arm be pulled from its socket.
> For disaster from God terrifies me,
> and because of His majesty I could not do these things.
>
> (Job 29:12–13, 15–17; Job 31:13–23)

More Than a Dollar Figure

I love Job's description of a righteous life because it highlights that what is going on here is not just about giving money.

Job does not mention a dollar figure or boast of how much he has given up in order to care for the poor. The idea isn't that money is bad and so we should try to get rid of it; God makes it fairly clear that his will is for his people to prosper, and that often means financial prosperity as well as other kinds. The Bible speaks of *loaning* to the poor (without exorbitant interest) as much or more as it does outright *giving* to them; the idea is to help others become prosperous. Rather, Job speaks of fathering orphaned children and inviting them to eat at his own table; of promising dying men that he will look after their wives; of using his position of influence to advocate for the disadvantaged in government. And he speaks of the worldview that drives all this: that the same God who made him in the womb also made those who serve in his household as slaves.

The fact of creation makes us all equals. We did not make ourselves.

Boiled down, then, the act of giving to the poor is simply an expression of the greatest commandment and its natural outgrowth: Love the Lord your God, and love your neighbor as yourself.

Love, Not Money

Put simply, biblical giving to the poor is about extending our lives to others. The call to do this can be demanding and difficult. So, often, we default to doing something else instead—giving money. But these are not the same thing. In fact, giving money can sometimes end up hurting people, and when it does, I would argue that we shouldn't do it.[1]

---

[1] In our modern, increasingly capitalistic, globalized world, this is an issue we need to explore seriously. The book When Helping Hurts is a great starting point. For a thought-provoking discussion in a missions-specific context, try *We Are Not the Hero: A Missionary's Guide to Sharing Christ, Not a Culture of Dependency* by my friend Jean Johnson.

Giving to the poor is not about throwing money at them so they'll go away and we'll feel better. It is about entering into the life and needs of another person, sharing the burden, and giving what we can—whether that's a loan or a gift, practical help, counsel, friendship, a coat, a pair of shoes, a job, or a word of encouragement.

Of course, you can't really know what someone else needs unless you're willing to get to know them, to extend yourself personally in some way. It takes humility and the willingness to become very uncomfortable, very vulnerable. It might even mean discovering your own poverty.[2]

Jesus, we are told, left the riches of heaven to come to earth.[3] He did not write us a celestial check to solve our problems; rather, he identified with us in order to love us well.

We are called to give to the poor in much the same way, which isn't to say that we are all called to take a vow of poverty, but that we are called to extend ourselves to others.

To the poor, whoever the poor may be.

Out of our riches, whatever our riches may be.

Rejecting the Easy Way Out

Jesus called his contemporaries on the carpet for

---

[2] A great book on entering into the lives of the poor—and letting them into ours—is *Junkyard Wisdom* by Roy Goble.
[3] 2 Corinthians 8:9

taking the easy way out: they gave money to the poor, publicly and loudly, so they could reap the rewards of being seen and applauded by everybody else.

Not only does this *not* create identification with the poor, it actually widens the divide. Rather than Job's "are we not equals?", such behavior loudly proclaims to the whole world that we are *not* equal to the poor, we are better.

It hurts us too, because we're robbed of both relationship with the poor (by identifying with them in their humanness) and of relationship with God (by identifying with him in his giving and voluntary sacrifice).

We get a cheap reward and lose the whole, transformational point.

But we don't have to do this. We can reject the easy way out and go back to giving the way God intends it.

It will make us uncomfortable, but it might just be worth it.

It might just change our lives.

The Call of Jesus to Authentic Faith

Characteristic of Jesus's teaching on spiritual disciplines is his constant calling out of a crowd he calls "the hypocrites": "So whenever you give to the poor, don't sound a trumpet before you as the hypocrites do ... Whenever you pray, you must not be like the hypocrites ... Whenever you fast, don't be sad-faced like the hypocrites" (Matthew 6:2, 5, 16).

Ironically, people often dismiss Christianity on the grounds that "Christians are hypocrites." Some (not all) are, just as some (not all) of the religious Jews of Jesus's day were. But the problem isn't with Christianity itself. Jesus called out hypocrisy in his earliest teachings and made it clear that it had nothing to do with the way of life he taught. The problem is with our propensity to perform.

As Christian speaker Graham Cooke puts it, much of modern-day faith is much too "PC"—not "politically correct," but "performance Christianity." Jesus calls us not to perform but to live fully and authentically before God. In the original Greek, the word *hypocrite* meant "actor"—a hypocrite was literally someone who performed on a stage for the applause and appreciation of an audience, often while wearing masks. It was Jesus who first used the word to lambaste people who were living their whole religious lives as a performance, even as he called us back to authentic religion and relationship with God.

So when it comes to spiritual disciplines, the first thing Jesus tells us is to get off the stage. Don't be a hypocrite. Don't perform.

Instead, seek God in the most quiet, private, personal places. Bring God into the intimate parts of your life and do things just for him, just because you know he's watching and present, just because you want to encounter him.

This becomes very clear when Jesus turns to the discipline of prayer. Don't pray like the hypocrites do, on a stage for everyone to see and hear. Instead, go into the most private room in your own house, and shut the door, and pray there, where your "Father is in secret."[4]

As human beings we seem to be wired to please and impress one another, and so the performance trap is incredibly easy to fall into. As someone who grew up in a Christian milieu, I understand the pressure that comes on us to put on the mask and just keep performing, living our lives to gain the praise or avoid the condemnation of others, no matter what's going on internally.

When Jesus tells us not to be like the hypocrites but to seek God out personally and privately, he's giving us permission to ignore that pressure and be real—to seek God before we worry about anyone else's impressions or judgments.

He's letting us get off the stage. He's telling us we don't have to perform anymore.

---

4 Matthew 6:6

Reality Sets Us Free

Jesus's whole teaching on spiritual disciplines can be summed up like this: You can let things be real.

You can be who you are in the presence of God. You can come messy, you can come broken, you can come passionate, you can come hungry, you can come apathetic. You can just come—to GOD, not to the star machine. Not to the performance Christianity pressure cooker.

The best place to overcome hypocrisy is in our private spiritual lives, in prayer and fasting and acts of generosity. These things shape and reshape our hearts.

Are Christians hypocrites? Yes, sometimes. We all succumb to the pressure to follow a script and dance for the crowd sometimes; we all get out of touch with reality. Jesus knows how exhausting and miserable the PC life is.

So he gives us permission to leave it behind.

Whenever you pray, you must not be like the hypocrites, because they love to pray standing in the synagogues and on the street corners to be seen by people. I assure you: They've got their reward! But when you pray, go into your private room, shut your door, and pray to your Father who is in secret. And your Father who sees in secret will reward you. When you pray, don't babble like the idolaters, since they imagine they'll be heard for their many words. Don't be like them, because your Father knows the things you need before you ask Him.

(Matthew 6:5–8)

35

"Your Father Knows": Why It Matters Who You Pray To

I grew up on the KJV, so I knew "babble" in this passage as "vain repetition": empty parroting, just saying words to say them.

We've all known people who do this, maybe even do it ourselves—before a meal, say, or when repeating liturgical prayers.[1] Being a conscientious child I worried about this somewhat. Repeating the Lord's Prayer seemed especially suspect, which is funny when you think about it. (After all, Jesus said, "Pray like this ...")

But the point here is actually less about the action of repetition and more about the misunderstanding behind it.

---

[1] Liturgical prayers are not a problem in and of themselves; in fact, they can be incredibly powerful and formative. It's "vain" or "empty" repetition of them that is the problem—not the repetition itself, nor the prayer itself.

Babbling Your Prayers

The Bible's most stark example of babbling prayers is probably that of the priests of Baal in 1 Kings 18. In this story the prophet Elijah challenged the priests of a foreign god, Baal, to a showdown on Mount Carmel. He set up an altar with a sacrifice on it. The challenge was this: "You call on Baal to send down fire from heaven and burn up the sacrifice, and then I will call on Yahweh to do the same thing."

The priests of Baal prayed, danced, wailed, and cut themselves around that altar all day, from morning until evening. Baal remained unresponsive, and Elijah passed the time catcalling—Maybe your god is asleep; maybe he's stepped out for a bit; maybe he's using the bathroom. Pray harder!

Finally the priests of Baal gave up. Elijah stepped forward, drenched the altar with water, and simply prayed, "Answer me, LORD! Answer me so that this people will know that You, Yahweh, are God and that You have turned their hearts back."[2]

Immediately, fire fell from heaven and consumed not only the sacrifice but even the stones of the altar.

Prayer Is Not a Burden

The priests of Baal repeated their prayers in vain, because no one was listening. Their prayers bur-

---

2 1 Kings 18:37

dened them, exhausted them, and even wounded them. In the end they were disgraced.

Can you relate?

Honestly, as a Christian there have been times when I felt like prayer was too much of a burden to carry. It was heavy, exhausting, frustrating, wounding. In the end I felt like no one was listening, and I was embarrassed at the effort I'd put forth.

Why was prayer this way for me?

I had picked up ideas, attitudes, and methods of prayer from old revivalists and from my own works-oriented soul. I tried to do them in my own strength, and it was a recipe for spiritual burnout.

I'm not saying everything I did was wrong, but sometimes we pick up burdens that aren't meant for us. A revivalist two hundred years ago may have had a grace to spend six hours on his knees that you currently don't have, because he had a calling to do it that you don't share.

Please don't get me wrong: if God calls you to spend six hours on your knees, do it. The grace and power will be there. And seeking God is always good. Jesus calls us to do this and to keep on doing it.[3] Seasons of "push" are normal before a breakthrough.

But … and this is a big "but" … picking up other people's burdens and trying to carry them in our

---

3 Matthew 7:7

own strength is not the way this works.

If prayer continually feels to you like an all-day-long self-flogging session, something is wrong.

And Jesus highlights what in this passage.

You're Praying to Your Father

Jesus said the idolators of his day thought they would be heard "for their many words"—that their efforts were the key.

Instead, Jesus says the key is who you're praying to: "Your Father knows the things you need before you ask Him."

This is the key: *you are praying to your Father.* Your Father already knows your needs, because he pays attention and he loves you. Your Father already has plans underway to meet them. Your Father wants to meet with you in secret.

Prayer is not about heroic effort and striving. If you'll notice, Jesus's model prayer is seven lines long. It can be prayed in under a minute. And it's powerful. Prayer is about communing with our Father.

Years ago my frustration with prayer came to a head. I had trained myself to pray long, exhausting, convoluted prayers, and I couldn't do it anymore. At this time the Spirit pointed the Lord's Prayer out to me: he pointed out that it was short, simple, and extremely nonburdensome.

So I just started praying it.

As I did, I meditated on its words. And then I started praying off of it—thoughts and prayers that spun out from the centerpiece of Jesus's prayer.

Today, I can spend hours in prayer. But it's not exhausting at all. Actually, it's life-giving, freeing, and even enjoyable.

Why?

Because I've figured out that I'm praying to my Father.

Your Father Knows

It's important as well that we know our Father's character when we pray. Jesus points out one aspect of it here: your Father already knows your needs. That means you don't need to give him long explanations or help him come up with a plan to meet them. When it's rooted in relationship, prayer becomes about expressing trust, seeking wisdom, and receiving from God.

I have found that prayer becomes easier and more wonderful the clearer I get on who my Father is. The more I understand his nature and character, the more I love to come and meet with him in secret.

Every wrong concept I have of God is a weight holding my prayers down. As those concepts change and untruths fall away, my prayers become lighter and increasingly filled with life.

The idolators of Jesus's day worshipped statues and carvings, things they had created and imbued with personality. By contrast, we worship the living God who is our Father, and who reveals himself to us through the Scriptures and through the Spirit.

The more clearly we see our Father, the better we can pray.

At my church one year we spent four evenings in prayer together to start the new year. Our lead pastor, Marc Brûlé, coined a phrase that became a theme for us: "The power of prayer is not in the one praying, but in the One hearing."

And to that I say, amen.

Therefore, you should pray like this:
Our Father in heaven,
Your name be honored as holy.
Your kingdom come.
Your will be done
on earth as it is in heaven.
Give us today our daily bread.
And forgive us our debts,
as we also have forgiven our debtors.
And do not bring us into temptation,
but deliver us from the evil one.
[For Yours is the kingdom and the power
and the glory forever. Amen.]
(Matthew 6:9–13)

36

"Pray Like This": How to Pray the Pattern in the Lord's Prayer

Jesus, as we've seen, criticized "vain repetition" or empty babbling: praying like the prophets of Baal, in a desperate show of works meant to get the attention of an indifferent God.

Jesus is clearly against that kind of praying. What sometimes gets confused with it, but Jesus is *not* against, is liturgical prayer—the use of prewritten, preset, or prepatterned prayers.

Liturgical prayers are regularly employed in all high church settings and usually held in suspicion by evangelicals. But Jesus himself gives us the most famous of liturgical prayers in Matthew 6:9–13, and I have personally found tremendous benefit in praying it, verbatim, when I'm alone with God and when I'm in groups.

In fact, I pray the Lord's Prayer nearly every morning. It's the cornerstone of my personal devotional life.

The Pattern in the Prayer

Praying the Lord's Prayer word for word, nearly every day as I said, is like an anchor for my thoughts, immediately bringing them into focus. It's an anchor for my soul, as well, directing my feelings upward toward my Father in heaven. And it ensures that I pray at least one thing of great value every morning!

But the Lord's Prayer is also impactful when we use it not just as liturgy, saying the precise wording Jesus gave us, but also as a pattern.

The Lord's Prayer (or "Our Father") lays out a pattern for the way we pray as well as the words we pray. It's like a ladder, leading up to heaven and bringing heaven down to us—much like the vision Jacob saw at Bethel in Genesis 28, a vision Jesus explicitly connected to himself in John 1:51.

"Our Father in Heaven"

The first rung of the ladder (top or bottom, I don't know—you decide!) focuses our thoughts on God himself. Prayer is about God, after all, approaching God and connecting with God.

However, this isn't some disconnected adoration wherein "it's all about God and it's not about us." That's a false dichotomy. Jesus actually connects us immediately to God: this is a *relational* prayer—"Our Father in heaven."

Of all the lines in the prayer, this one has probably opened up the greatest amount of revelation to me. To begin every day recognizing and confessing that God is my Father has been life-changing.

"Your Name Be Honored as Holy"

I usually add the word "let" when I pray this line: *"Let your name* be honored as holy." This is the first request in the prayer, and it's a God-focused request: let the name of God, the name of Yahweh, of Jesus, be honored as holy.

I take this line inward: Let your name be honored as holy in my life. Let your name be honored in the deepest part of my heart. Let your name be honored in my choices and my actions. Let it be honored, sanctified, revered in my thoughts.

And then I take it outward: Let your name be honored as holy in my church, in my community, in my nation, in our world. Let the transformational power of your holiness be enacted throughout the world. Let it be honored in my government, in my culture.

"Your Kingdom Come, Your Will Be Done on Earth as It Is in Heaven"

I generally treat these requests as a single unit, and again, I add the request: "Let your kingdom come, let your will be done."

Like the prayer of holiness, I take this both inward and outward. In many ways, this is a request for the outward manifestation of the inner attitude in the first request—that we might revere and honor the name of God.

There is so much that could be said about this request (and I will be writing in more depth about each line of the prayer), but I want to focus here on the pattern.

Notice what this opening emphasis of the prayer says about our needs. Some might say these requests aren't "about us" at all, that they're "not about our needs but about God's glory," but again I think that's a false dichotomy.

Actually, these opening requests express the ultimate need of mankind. We are praying for God to give us exactly what we need on the most minute and the most cosmic scale, understanding that those things are intimately connected. My innermost, most personal needs are intimately connected to the need for the entire universe to align with the Creator.

Praying this every day, connecting our own souls to this transcendent purpose, is truly transformative.

"Give Us Today Our Daily Bread"

Or, as it can also be translated, "our bread for tomorrow." In a world without artificial preservatives, bread needed to be baked and obtained on a daily basis, so the emphasis here is on immediate physical need. This is the part of the prayer where I come down from the high of holiness, kingdom, and the worldwide will of God to ask my Father for money to pay the bills, food for dinner, energy and focus for today's work—stuff like that.

It's helpful to be really detailed about this: check in with yourself to see what felt needs are pressing on you today and intentionally, specifically ask God to meet them.

"And Forgive Us Our Debts, as We Also Have Forgiven Our Debtors"

In Matthew 6:14–15, Jesus makes forgiveness something of a prerequisite for getting our prayers answered—so it's interesting to me that this line doesn't come first in the Lord's Prayer. We aren't required to "clear the air" before we pray: instead, we connect to identity, purpose, and provision, and *then* ask God for forgiveness.

Don't get me wrong: I believe the best time to ask God for forgiveness and cleansing is the exact moment you realize you need it. But I see in the pattern of the Lord's Prayer a lot of grace, and God empowering us with purpose and identity to be able to forgive. He doesn't withhold the kingdom until we forgive; he gives us the kingdom so that we can.

This again is a great daily discipline, and one to be really specific and intentional about. Check in with yourself: Are you holding judgments against anyone? Holding a debt over someone's head? Who is it? What is the debt? Whatever it is, choose to release it. At the same time, do you need to be freed from any debt yourself? Receive God's forgiveness for it. And if you need to make things right with another person, take the first steps to do so.

"And Do Not Bring Us into Temptation, But Deliver Us from the Evil One"

The idea of "temptation" here is not just temptation to sin. It also includes the concept of trouble or trial, which the evil one brings into our lives for the purpose of tripping us up in our walk with God and causing us to sin against him. (Think Job.)

I love this line in the prayer, although I find it challenges me deeply because it flies in the face of my deeply ingrained fatalism. I tend to believe there's no avoiding trouble. Apparently there is, as

Jesus tells us directly to pray that we will be delivered from the evil one and not led into temptation.

Again, don't get me wrong: Jesus also said that in this world we will have trouble. Suffering is part of life here, and it's part of God's purposes for us. That's clear throughout the Bible. But at the same time, let's not underestimate the power of prayer or fail to use an access point for protection that Jesus himself has given us.

"For Yours Is the Kingdom and the Power and the Glory Forever"

Okay, so there's a good chance Jesus didn't actually say this at the end of his prayer. Most textual scholars agree that it was added in the margin by some copyist somewhere down the line and eventually got pulled into the text itself.

But I still use it. It's a beautiful end point, a beautiful benediction, a beautiful recalibration of our minds and hearts toward God. And besides, it *is* Scripture: it's a direct (although truncated) quote from David's prayer in 1 Chronicles 29:11–13. So sometimes I just pray the whole thing:

> Yours, LORD, is the greatness and the power and the glory and the splendor and the majesty, for everything in the heavens and on earth belongs to You. Yours, LORD, is the

kingdom, and You are exalted as head over all. Riches and honor come from You, and You are the ruler of everything. Power and might are in Your hand, and it is in Your hand to make great and to give strength to all. Now therefore, our God, we give You thanks and praise Your glorious name.

Pray Like This

If you don't already "pray like this," I would encourage you to give the pattern in Jesus's prayer a try. Pray it every day, as you start your morning. It doesn't take long, and it isn't burdensome. Let each line of the prayer resonate in your heart, and follow it in any direction it takes you.

Our Father in heaven ...
(Matthew 6:9)

37

How to Find Yourself in the Words "Our Father"

In North American culture, we're a bit flippant about names. We tend to use first names for almost everyone, without a lot of regard for relationship or age or role. But even we haven't managed to erase the importance of names.

What you call someone is deeply significant.

What's in a Name?

The way you address someone identifies your position relative to them and their position relative to you.

For example, I call my father "Dad." My friends don't call him that; they don't have the same position in his life, so they don't have the right to use that name. To them he's "Jay" or "Mr. Thomson."

My mother calls my dad by his first name, which

I don't have the position to do, and she also uses other names for him that no one else does or can.

In the same way, you address your boss, or a police officer, or a prime minister in a way relative to your position, and vice versa.

Jesus opens the Lord's Prayer with the words "Our Father."

So right off, he positions us relative to God and God relative to us.

In a world where it's pretty common to feel lost, Jesus tells us right where we are. He finds us in relation to a fixed point—God, our Father in heaven.

God My Origin

The Bible is incredibly layered, and the words "our Father" can be looked at in myriad ways, all of them wondrous and revelatory.

But for me lately, the idea of God as my *origin* has been especially significant.

That's what the words "our Father" mean, after all. By using these words, Jesus points to God as our source, our origin, our progenitor. God is our first cause.

My life came from God, and so did my essential nature—my character as a human being. We're told in Genesis 1 and 2 that God created humankind, male and female, in his own image.[1] What does this strange and wonderful statement mean?

While it means many things, ultimately it means we can know ourselves only by knowing God, and to some degree, we can only know God as we come to know ourselves.

In his *Confessions,* St. Augustine of Hippo wrote, "Men go abroad to admire the heights of mountains, the mighty waves of the sea, the broad tides of rivers, the compass of the ocean, and the circuits of the stars, yet pass over the mystery of themselves without a thought."

GOD MY PROVIDER

What caused this truth to hit me so hard was my awareness of how relentlessly needy I am. And my needs don't end with physical ones. Oh no, give me food and water and a roof over my head, and I still remain a great need with skin on.

I need love. I need purpose. I need affirmation and identity in something transcendent.

My own tendency is to see my needs as an imposition on God—as something problematic that it would be good to shed.

But if I see God as my source, my origin, my Father, then I realize something: God isn't just the

---

[1] Genesis 1:27

meeter of my needs, he is also the source of them.

I need love because God is love, because he loves, and because he wants my love. Purpose and identity are found in God. My creative nature is found in God. My deep desire for authentic, intimate relationship comes from God.

My needs aren't impositions, they're drivers—pointers, hungers, leading back to the source.

Follow the river of the soul to its headwaters, and you'll find God and know yourself for the first time.

Lost and Found

We feel generally lost as human beings because we are. We are wandering around the face of the earth without a clue who we are, where we came from, or where we're going. We try to answer the question of who we are in various ways—religious ways and scientific ways and local, personal ways. But eventually, if we'll still the noise long enough, we all find ourselves out under the stars at some point, staring up and feeling frighteningly small, and knowing with every atom of our beings that *there is something more.*

So Jesus says "The Son of Man has come to seek and save the lost."[2]

---

[2] Luke 19:10

The New Testament calls Jesus the "archégos" of life and of salvation.[3] The Greek word means origin, beginning, source, author, pioneer. Jesus, God-made-man, is all of this, the source both of our original natural life and of our second birth, our regeneration as children of God.

So don't hide from your needs. Don't try to cover them up or be ashamed of them. Instead, get quiet and really look at them, and see what they tell you about who you are and where you came from.

And then say the words "My Father." And try the name "his child" on for size.

After I thought about masks in relation to hypocrisy, it struck me that many pagan religions around the world require people to put on masks in order to participate in the supernatural.

With Jesus it's just the opposite.

With Jesus you are only allowed to participate in the supernatural if you take the mask off.

If you are real about who you are, so that you can find out who God is.

Here I Am

The very beginning of Jesus's prayer requires us to show up as children of God and acknowledge him as the source not only of our needs but of our own

---

[3] Acts 3:15, Hebrews 2:10

selves. It positions us before him with the role and rights of children, looking to the only One who can really tell us who we are.

"Our Father in heaven." It is worth getting alone with these words, getting quiet with them, and taking the time to think deeply and marvel at what it means that God is our Father. Let us not pass over the mystery of ourselves, or miss the chance to express gratitude and worship to the One who gave us life.

"Our Father" is not the beginning of a stale recitation. It's the beginning of a journey—back to the beginning, and all the way forward to the end.

Your name be honored as holy.

(Matthew 6:9)

38

Honoring the Other: What Holiness Means

"Holy" is a slippery word, hard to grasp but possessing an unmistakable power. In Jesus's prayer we turn it into a request: Let your Name, God, be honored as holy—let it be "hallowed," as older English has it, in the world and in our lives.

What does that mean?

Your Name Be Honored as "Other"

In one of the Bible's most awe-inspiring scenes, the prophet Isaiah sees a vision of God in the heavenlies:

> In the year that King Uzziah died, I saw the Lord seated on a high and lofty throne, and His robe filled the temple. Seraphim were standing above Him; each one had six wings: with two he covered his face, with two he

covered his feet, and with two he flew. And one called to another:

> Holy, holy, holy is the LORD of Hosts;
> His glory fills the whole earth.

The foundations of the doorways shook at the sound of their voices, and the temple was filled with smoke. (Isaiah 6:1–4)

In Hebrew the word for "holy" is *kadosh;* in Greek *hagios*. Latin uses *sanctus* to translate it, so in English we have a variety of related words: *holy, sanctified, sacred, consecrated,* and *saint*.

All of these words share the basic meaning of "set apart" or "other."

Holiness implies transcendence. When Moses encountered God in the burning bush and asked to know God's name, God replied "I AM THAT I AM."

This is a holy name. It has no reliance on anything else; it is not creation-bound.

When I give someone my name I reveal a thousand points of connection with the created world: I am Rachel (a Hebrew name, many thousands of years old, that means "Lamb of God" and connects with Jewish history through the matriarch of Israel); Starr (a family name, connecting me to past generations in my own family); Thomson (a Scottish last name deriving from the English "son of Thomas"—itself a name with many connections to history and places and generations).

The name of God has no such connections. He is who he is.

He is holy.

God Is a Holy Spirit

Because of its transcendence, holiness also implies purity. This is how we use the word when we implore one another to live holy lives. We understand that to live a set-apart life means to live a life that is pure, that is clean and uncontaminated on some fundamental spiritual level.

In the Old Testament, God instructed the Levitical priests, who were themselves specially holy (consecrated) to the Lord to "make a distinction between the holy and the profane, and between the unclean and the clean."[1] Generally speaking, that which was "unclean" was usually connected to death, corruption, or sexual impurity in some way. This is true even in the dietary laws, where most of the animals considered unclean are carnivores or scavengers.

Throughout the New Testament, Jesus encountered evil spirits that possessed people and caused disease, infirmity, and madness. They are interest-

---

1 Leviticus 10:10, NASB

ingly called "unclean spirits"—unholy spirits. Pagan gods were also seen as unholy spirit beings, the worship of whom specifically included unclean or unholy sexual and spiritual practices.

By contrast, the Spirit of God is a holy spirit; in fact, he is called *the* Holy Spirit.

Isaiah responded to his vision of God's holiness by crying out:

> Woe is me for I am ruined
> because I am a man of unclean lips
> and live among a people of unclean lips
> and because my eyes have seen the King,
> the LORD of Hosts.
> (Isaiah 6:5)

But God does not leave Isaiah in this acute awareness of his own sin and impurity. Instead, God himself takes steps to change the situation:

> Then one of the seraphim flew to me, and in his hand was a glowing coal that he had taken from the altar with tongs. He touched my mouth with it and said:
>
> Now that this has touched your lips,
> your wickedness is removed
> and your sin is atoned for.
> (Isaiah 6:6–7)

We Are a Holy People

In the same way, we are atoned for by Christ's sacrifice and made holy, chosen for the Lord. This is not our doing; it's a gift of God.

Marriage provides a powerful picture of what this means. Married people are set apart for one another; they have a sacred bond that would be profaned if shared with anyone else.

The Bible links or at least parallels sexuality and spirituality many times. Idolatry is consistently compared in Scripture to adultery. As God's people, we have been made "holy"—set apart for him. We are "married" to God in a covenant that must be held sacred and kept pure. This is what it means to be a "saint" or "holy one."

1 Peter 2:9 reminds us:

> But you are a chosen race, a royal priesthood,
> a holy nation, a people for His possession,
> so that you may proclaim the praises
> of the One who called you out of darkness
> into His marvelous light.

When we speak of holiness, then, what we should not have in mind is a list of rules for their own sake. What we *should* have in mind is a life of total commitment and consecration, of being fully set apart.

God has called us to be his holy people, so he has set us apart from the profane and the common and made us pure, equipped for his purposes, and filled with his praise.

We were not born like this. Peter is clear that we were once in darkness; we were unclean, unholy. But God has chosen us to share in his transcendence as a people who belong specially to him.

That is not just a change of behavior; it is a change of identity.

Making God's Name Holy

What then does it mean to make God's name holy, as we pray in the Lord's Prayer?

Earlier, we looked at finding ourselves in the fatherhood of God. Here, in the second line of the prayer, we embrace God as he is—holy and other—and commit to honoring him as he is.

When we pray that God's name will be honored as holy, we give up our right to make God in our own image. We give up our right to live for ourselves, recognizing that his holiness calls for our own holiness. ("For it is written, Be holy, because I am holy."[2])

We also pray that God's Name (his reputation or the known part of himself) will be honored as holy

---

[2] 1 Peter 1:16

not just in our own lives but all over the world.

This is not a selfish desire on God's part. There is a direct connection between our honoring of God's transcendence and purity and the degree to which we can live the lives we were born to live. This is true for us and for every other human being on the planet. When we learn to "walk by the Spirit,"[3] we learn to live truly free and fulfilled.

Isaiah's vision ends where he could not have imagined: not only does God not destroy him or dismiss him as unclean, not only does God step in and purify him, but he is then given the opportunity to join God in his mission.

In the Lord's Prayer, we are given the same opportunity. Made pure and set apart by the action and will of God, we have the chance to lift our whole world to a higher, purer life.

> Then I heard the voice of the Lord saying:
> Who should I send?
> Who will go for Us?
> I said:
> Here I am. Send me.
> (Isaiah 6:8)

Lord, let your Name be honored as holy.

---

[3] Galatians 5:16

Your kingdom come.
(Matthew 6:10)

39

Kingdom Come, Part 1: A Brief History of the Kingdom of God

As a writer and speaker I frequently hear from Christians who express frustration with Christianity as they know it. We are grateful for forgiveness and the promise of heaven (what most of us understand as "the gospel"), yet we sense there's something more.

There is. Something *much more*.

If you feel trapped inside a paradigm that isn't big enough to take in all of the Bible, let alone all of life; and if you chafe at the sense that there must be a bigger picture but you just can't find it, *you're not alone*. Lots of people feel this way, for good reason: in the last several hundred years, we have reduced the gospel of the kingdom that Jesus preached to the gospel of personal forgiveness and going to heaven.

The one encompasses the other, but they are not the same thing.

From the very start, the kingdom of God is central to Jesus's life and message. It's also central to the prayer he taught us: "Your kingdom come, Your will be done on earth as it is in heaven." This is the heart of it all.

What Is the Kingdom of God?

Simply put, the kingdom is the rule of God.

Great, you may think, that's (not very) helpful. God is in charge: Why is that good news? And why do we have to pray for it? Isn't that just a given? God is in charge, God will judge everybody, that's why we need forgiveness—aren't we just right back where we started?

To get a clearer picture of what all this means, we need to break the concept of God's rule down a little further. The question isn't whether God rules, but how.

In the Bible, the kingdom of God is the rule of God in and through willing "imagers" of God. The kingdom was originally set up in Eden, with Adam and Eve as regents under God. They were given "dominion" (kingship) over the earth, not autonomously but as God's agents, tasked with extending *his* rule throughout the earthly realm. In this situation, heaven and earth were essentially one.

God ruled and Man ruled, and these two things were the same.

Trouble in Paradise

But Adam and Eve broke faith with God and tried to establish themselves independently of him. When they did this, the God-through-man rule over the earth—with the many benefits that come from cooperation with the Life-giver and Father of lights—was lost. Now God ruled and Man ruled, but not together. They struggled against each other, Spirit against flesh, in a situation of disharmony. Other spiritual powers (i.e. demonic powers) came in and began to exert their rule over humanity and the earthly realm as well.

If the original kingdom of God in Eden was like an empire in which the "little kings" and subjects both loved and willingly served the "High King" or emperor, now earth was a fractured empire in which the little kings were in rebellion, and even though the High King still ultimately reigned, the fractured empire could not fully receive the benefits of that reign because of its own rebellion.

God, however, planned to reinstate his rule. So he called a man named Abraham and created a nation from his descendants. He delivered this nation from slavery, gave them his law, and covenanted with them to become their king.

> The LORD came from Sinai and appeared to them from Seir ... So He became king in Je-

shurun [Israel] when the leaders of the people gathered with the tribes of Israel. (Deuteronomy 33:2, 5)

Just as Eden was a place of incredible fruitfulness and blessing as humanity walked with God, so God intended that his rule would bring incredible fruitfulness and blessing to Israel, and through them, to all the nations of the earth.

Eventually the rule of God, seen clearly in his human regents in Israel, would draw all of the nations to voluntarily worship Yahweh as High King.

Once again, a people on earth lived under the rule of God, with all of the blessings and benefits that come through his kingdom. But once again there was a problem: the people rebelled. They chose other gods, violated the covenant, and rejected God's rule over them.

Rejection and Reinstatement

This rebellion came to a head after the period of the judges, when the people of Israel demanded that rather than ruling them through his chosen judges, Yahweh give them a king like the other nations. Samuel, the last of the judges, understood what was happening as the rejection of God's kingship. God himself agreed:

> Listen to the people and everything they say to you. They have not rejected you; they have rejected Me as their king. (1 Samuel 8:7)

The kingdom of God on earth has always been about God's reign being administered through willing imagers, human beings who receive authority from God and exercise it in accordance with his will and character.

That's why God doesn't just establish his kingdom by wiping out rebellious mankind; that isn't the plan.

The kingdom can't be said to have come on earth until the vision of Eden is restored: human beings walking with God and having dominion under him to be fruitful, multiply, and shape a heavenly society on the earth.

The next significant step in kingdom history came after the disastrous first king of Israel (Saul) had been deposed by God and a new king, a second king, was chosen. This king was David, and because he was loyal to Yahweh and a man after God's own heart, the kingdom of God would be reinstated in and through his rule.

David's throne was the kingdom of God on earth. In Scripture, this was most clearly expressed when it came time for that throne to pass to Solomon. God said to David:

> Furthermore, I declare to you that the LORD Himself will build a house for you. When your time comes to be with your fathers, I will raise up after you your descendant, who is one of your own sons, and I will establish his kingdom. He will build a house for Me, and I will establish his throne forever. I will be a father to him, and he will be a son to Me. I will not take away My faithful love from him as I took it from the one who was before you. *I will appoint him over My house and My kingdom forever,* and his throne will be established forever. (1 Chronicles 17:10–14, emphasis mine)

God told David that he would adopt Solomon (whose name means "Peace") as his son. He also told David to give Solomon a second name: *Jedidiah*, which, like *David*, means "beloved."

From Golden Age to Exile

The reigns of David and Solomon were the golden age of Israel. The blessings of the covenant were most fully seen in their day: the people of Israel won victory over all their enemies and prospered to an almost unbelievable degree. The rule of God through his chosen kings did indeed bring life and blessing.

One of the most prophetically significant events

during this time was the visit of the queen of Sheba, who came to hear Solomon's legendary wisdom. This was the mission of Israel being carried out: the rule of God was seen as so good and so right that the Gentile nations voluntarily came to seek and worship him.

But it didn't last. Solomon fell into idolatry in his later years, and his son, Rehoboam, rebelled against God and lost the kingdom. The tribes of Israel fractured into two separate nations, called Judah and Israel. While Judah was sometimes faithful to God, Israel never was.

Both nations ended up in complete apostasy and were sent into exile. The kingdom of God on earth had ceased to exist.

The Beloved King

But God had not abandoned his plans for Adam (humankind), Israel (his chosen people), or David (his beloved king). Quite the contrary. God would keep his promise to establish David's throne "forever." Though the kingship would lapse for a time, it would be restored.

No prophet states this more clearly than Isaiah, the same prophet who warned Judah of its coming exile into Babylon. The familiar "Christmas prophecy" of Isaiah 9 is in fact about the kingdom:

> For a child will be born for us,
> A son will be given to us,
> And the government will be on His shoulders.
> He will be named Wonderful Counselor, Mighty God,
> Eternal Father, Prince of Peace.
> The dominion will be vast,
> and its prosperity will never end.
> He will reign on the throne of David
> and over his kingdom ... from now on and forever.
> (Isaiah 9:6–7)

This is only one of many prophecies about the restored throne of David. Though it was a mystery at the time, looking back now we can see how Jesus was both a human descendant of David back on the throne and Yahweh himself taking back direct kingship.

As the God-man, Jesus is the kingdom of heaven come to earth.

At Jesus's baptism, a voice from heaven thundered, "You are my beloved son" (Mark 1:11). This was not only a statement of affection, but against the backdrop of David and Solomon (both called God's "beloved"), it was a declaration that *"This is the king."* [1]

From the moment he began his ministry, Jesus's declaration was that the kingdom had come.

---

[1] Thanks to Michael Heiser for this insight as well.

In the context of the Old Testament, the message could not be clearer: the rule of God was being resumed through his beloved son and king, bringing with it blessings and abundance and victory over God's enemies.

But if you'll remember, the kingdom was always about co-reigning, about willing imagers being given dominion and extending it in partnership with God. This destiny is at play here too: not only is Jesus bringing the kingdom, *he's giving it to us.*

Your kingdom come.
(Matthew 6:10)

40

Kingdom Come, Part 2: Why Do We Pray "Your Kingdom Come"?

To recap: we have just traced the history of the kingdom of God (the rule or reign of God) on earth, as it existed originally in Eden and then as it took shape in ancient Israel, only to be lost through the period of the exile. Finally, as prophesied, the heir to David's throne arrived. Jesus was born into the line of kings in direct fulfillment of prophecy. Jesus is the Beloved King, the "Root and Branch of Jesse"[1] whose rule will fill all the earth with the personal knowledge of God, as the waters cover the sea.

This was Jesus's message, his "gospel," from the very beginning.

> From then on Jesus began to preach, "Repent, because the kingdom of heaven has come near!" (Matthew 4:17)

---

[1] Isaiah 11:10, 1

The Kingdom Given to Us

The Sermon on the Mount is the first extended teaching we get from Jesus in the gospel of Matthew. It basically tells us what Jesus was preaching when he preached "the gospel of the kingdom."[2] For modern readers, it comes as a surprising twist that Jesus doesn't just preach "God's on the throne; everybody bow or else!" Instead he talks about the kingdom being *given to us*. In Jesus's wording, the kingdom is something we can "inherit" (or not); something we choose to enter (or not); something that must be sought and discovered (or not); *something that is planted inside of us*.

Jesus is generous in his giving of the kingdom. We qualify to receive the kingdom if we have nothing:

> Blessed are the poor in spirit, for the kingdom of heaven is theirs. (Matthew 5:3)

That makes the kingdom open to anyone who will receive it. You can't earn it; it's a gift. The only thing that will keep you out is choosing not to come in—which is usually the result, in some sense or other, of pride.

---

[2] As a related point, the terms "kingdom of God" and "kingdom of heaven" are synonymous. Matthew favors "kingdom of heaven," which refers to the spirit realm where God exists and from which he rules. It's a term his Jewish audience would have understood. The other gospel writers, who write to more Gentile audiences, favor "kingdom of God." But they are the same thing.

But why? Why is God offering us such a gift? Why is God giving us his kingdom—not simply as subjects, but as rulers in some sense? That's what it means to be given a kingdom, after all—but how does that even make sense? Don't we need to get mankind *off* the throne and God back on? Aren't the two locked in eternal competition? Why in the world would Jesus show up, bringing the kingdom—and then give it to a bunch of spiritually impoverished, made-of-dust human beings?

The answer lies way back in Genesis.

Given Dominion

We first see the kingdom of God on earth in Genesis 1:26–31, where Adam and Eve are created in God's image and then given rule over the earth and all of its creatures and resources. There's no sense that God is giving up his rule here, or that they are in competition with him. Rather, Adam and Eve possess a delegated dominion—they are God's representatives, his ruling agents, who are responsible to bring heaven to earth.

God, it turns out, isn't into dictatorial rule. He likes to share.

But of course, we know the rest of the story: Adam and Eve broke faith with God. There was a kingdom split: earth became a rogue territory, a divided, warring mess.

But God always had a plan to reestablish his rule. The key is that he never gave up the original plan: *the rule of God on earth was always supposed to be manifested in and through human beings.*

God doesn't need to use people to accomplish his purposes. But he wants to.

This is where ancient ideas like "free will" become so important. We are the way we are—free agents with the ability to choose, to create, to enact—because that's how God wants us.

God isn't a puppet master, and he's not after our puppet strings. He's after mature children who are shaped in his character, who love his will, and who purposely, freely manifest the character and will of God in the world.

That's what we were created to do.

That's the message of the whole New Testament. That's what "your will be done on earth as it is in heaven" means.

But I'm getting ahead of myself.

The Kingdom of God Is Within You

After the fall and before Jesus came, the best picture of the kingdom of God on earth was the kingdom of David and his son Solomon. Theirs was a kingdom of incredible prosperity, wisdom, and might. During David's reign, Israel's enemies were conquered one by one; during Solomon's reign, the kingdom was at peace. As we saw, Solomon's name means "Peace"; he is a type of the "Prince of Peace" to come—Jesus.

Jesus's disciples expected him to restore the Davidic kingdom, in accordance with the prophecies of Isaiah and others. And he did. But not in the way they thought he would.

Instead, he taught them that the kingdom of God was already with them—"among" them or "within" them (Luke 17:21). He said the kingdom of God belonged to those who were like children, to those who were poor in spirit and would receive it.

And he called his followers "the church." This is an incredible term. The Greek word translated "church" is *ekklesia*. Literally it means a governing assembly of citizens—something like a town council. To be a church is to be an assembly of kingdom citizens, citizens who have some dominion—authority—within that kingdom.

That Jesus spent so much time in the Sermon on the Mount teaching on spiritual disciplines tells me that the primary realm where we're given dominion is our own inner lives. Dominion doesn't mean taking control, lording over others, or conquering by military means. It does mean imaging God, becoming spiritual people, becoming holy, and stewarding the resources and responsibilities God gives us in a way that brings his blessings and manifest presence into the world.

Why Do We Have to Ask?

Jesus was clear that the kingdom of God came when he did. Yet he teaches us to ask for it to come: "Your kingdom come," or more accurately, "Let your kingdom come," or "May your kingdom come."

Why do we have to ask?

I see two answers to this question.

The first, incredibly, ties into the history we've covered above. God originally gave dominion over the earth to mankind. So when it comes to reinstating his own rule, he waits for us to request it—essentially, to give him permission. He is still honoring the dominion given to us in Genesis 1.

Don't get me wrong: there will come a time when judgment is convened, and God will not ask permission to judge. This isn't about us being more powerful than God or having something we can hold over him.

It's about his nature, about his choice to honor us, about his love.

Love is patient and kind. Love is not jealous or boastful or proud or rude. It does not demand its own way. It is not irritable, and it keeps no record of being wronged. It does not rejoice about injustice but rejoices whenever the truth wins out. Love never gives up, never loses faith, is always hopeful, and endures through every circumstance.[3]

---

[3] 1 Corinthians 13:4–7, NLT

The second answer has to do with timing.

Already, Not Yet

The kingdom of God has come—but it's not fully here. It's among us, but it's not fully realized. It's present, but it's still, in some sense, invisible. It's actively transforming the world we live in, but it has yet to be revealed.

The kingdom of God is an already-but-not-yet kingdom. There is a fuller realization of it still coming, and we'll enter that fuller realization after the day of judgment and the resurrection. But right now, we *have* received the kingdom. It's here—in seed form.

Everything the kingdom will be is already with us. The growth of the kingdom is already transforming the world, like the growth of a crop transforms a field. Much is still invisible, rooting and germinating under the ground. But it's here.

As Jesus will later teach, we are the soil.

We have received a kingdom. But we also pray: Let your kingdom come.

Let it grow. Let it transform us. We give permission. *We ask.*

We want the gift, Lord. Your kingdom come.

Your will be done on earth as it is in heaven.

(Matthew 6:10)

41

The Will of God and the War for Life: Why Praying "Your Will Be Done" Is an Act of Warfare

The second half of Matthew 6:10 parallels or fleshes out the first half. First we ask for the kingdom of God to come, then we pray more deeply into what that *means*.

On the surface, "let your will be done" is a pretty simple request. Yet, few things seem to trip us up as much as the "will of God"—understanding it, finding it, fulfilling it.

We tie ourselves into knots, paralyzed by the idea of a "perfect will of God" that we just can't seem to find, and fearing that if we live our lives "outside" of that will, we're going to wreck everything—not so much because our hearts are wrong, but because we're clumsy.

I suggest this is not at all what Jesus is teaching here. Rather than restricting our lives, the will of God frees them.

On my fireplace mantelpiece, there's a little plaque that was given to my roommate and me when we bought our (very big) house. It quotes Psalm 18:19 from the KJV: "He brought me forth also into a large place; he delivered me, because he delighted in me."

Our friend didn't know it, but this is actually one of my life verses. And one of the key areas where I've experienced its truth is in this whole idea of "the will of God."

The Will of God Is Good

First off, it's really, really key to understand that the will of God is *good*.

Why am I even bothering to say that?

Because I think most Christians don't believe it. I certainly didn't. For years, most of my associations with "God's will" were predominately negative.

Several years ago, some friends and I wrote a course called "Time to Align" in which we addressed this issue. One of its key lessons is called "The Good Will of God," and we opened it with the following story:

In early 2016 we spent a month in New Zealand. We did women's and youth events, prison outreach, and overcomers' groups, and we set up a ministry tour for the next year. Of course, New Zealand is *beautiful*. It was hot, but who can complain when you're surrounded by breathtaking beauty, Pacific skies, and a wealthy, modern society?

So the jokes started coming. "Boy, you're really suffering for Jesus!"

We posted pictures on Facebook of hiking a gorgeous coastal mountain. And the comments: "Hoo boy, look at you suffering for Jesus!"

We make these jokes because as Christians, we think that serving God for real would mean preaching in a dump in the middle of a Third World country and dying of typhoid fever (unless you manage to get martyred first. Major brownie points if you do!).

For many people, a subconscious belief underlies statements like this, and it's not funny at all.

The belief is that if you surrender your life completely to God, he's going to hand you an iron-bound rule book and a one-way ticket to a war zone. He will take your freedom and your life away from you and give you a life you really don't want ...

Is this what keeps us from selling out 100% to Jesus—that we think he wants us to suffer, to be miserable, to live in this tiny little box with a bunch of rules and nothing else, rather than understanding that he wants us to be full of life, receiving and transmitting his love everywhere we go?

There is suffering involved in following God. This is true because our world is broken and at war with God. And God can and does transform our suffering, making it beautiful in its own right and giving us, as Isaiah promised, "beauty for ashes, the oil of joy for mourning."[1] He can even make us into the kind of people who seek out places of difficulty and learn to rejoice in them as we serve him. But fundamentally, notwithstanding hardship and suffering, the will of God for our lives is good.

God's will, as he has expressed it over and over in the Scriptures, is that we prosper and be at peace. His will is that we be fruitful, multiply, and exercise dominion over the earth. It is that we experience righteousness, peace, and joy through the fellowship of his Spirit indwelling us. It is that we love him and that we be loved by him. This is abundant, eternal life. This is what we are asking for when we pray "your will be done."

The will of God is not a narrow, only-one-choice-is-the-right-choice, prescribed and predestined box in which we must fit ourselves. It's a wide country, a beautiful, abundant, and light-filled way of life.

At times it will involve specific steps and instructions; at other times it is simply about doing justly, loving mercy, and walking humbly with our God.[2]

---

[1] Isaiah 61:3, NKJV
[2] Micah 6:8

And at times it *will* involve great suffering. Yet, even then, the will of God is never about suffering for its own sake, but about suffering for the sake of intimate fellowship with Jesus and ultimately, entering into his glory.[3]

WE ARE AT WAR

In the last two chapters, we talked about the kingdom of God in history and in the present.

The historical kingdom of David and Solomon contains a key to understanding our present. In typological terms, we're in the first half of the kingdom establishment, the era of David—which is the era of war. The era of Solomon, of peace, is still coming.

This is why the will of God must be sought and prayed for, and why we must also fight for it. Jesus has taken the throne, but much of the world is still in darkness or active rebellion against him. Other spiritual powers are actively battling against the kingdom of God.

> For He must reign until He puts all His enemies under His feet. (1 Corinthians 15:25)

Our enemies are not flesh and blood. They are spiritual forces: what Ephesians 6:12 calls "the

---
[3] Romans 8:17

world powers of this darkness ... the spiritual forces of evil in the heavens."

As God's earthly kingdom council (aka his "church"), it's our job to represent him, to know his will, and to carry out his will. Because the will of God is good, that's a marvelous and wonderful task! We are called to flood the dark world with light. But we can't do it on our own, and we will face opposition.

This is why we pray.

In Psalm 121:1–2, David wrote these beautiful and familiar words:

> I lift up my eyes to the mountains—where does my help come from? My help comes from the LORD, the Maker of heaven and earth. (NIV)

In the ancient world, mountains were understood as places where the heavens met earth. The gods lived in the mountains, and they would use mountains to descend from heaven to earth. David's psalm declares that Yahweh, the One God who is Maker of heaven and earth, is his help, and he will come down to aid him in the time of need.

Jesus's prayer is much the same. "Your will be done on earth as it is in heaven" is a call for supernatural help. We are accepting God's will as good and best, proclaiming that we desire it, and asking that help will descend to us.

Earth is our realm. It was given to us in the very beginning. It has suffered, and still suffers, under the twisting and corruption of everything that runs counter to the will of God.

As children of the kingdom, we can ask for things to change. We want life abundant, not only for ourselves but for this entire realm in which we have dominion.

The enemy won't like your prayer. It's an act of warfare. A line in the sand.

So ask.

"Your kingdom come, your will be done on earth as it is in heaven."

Give us today our daily bread.

(Matthew 6:11)

42

The Power of Embracing Our Need: Meeting God in the Prayer of Daily Dependence

At this point in Jesus's model prayer, our focus seems to take an abrupt shift. Everything thus far has been high-minded, downright celestial in scope:

> Our Father in heaven,
> Your name be honored as holy.
> Your kingdom come.
> Your will be done
> on earth as it is in heaven.

And here we come crashing back down to earth. We've been on this incredible journey of identity, finding our source in the heavenly Father, realizing his holiness (his great "otherness") and ours, partnering with God to bring the kingdom to earth.

And now here we are: needing to eat.

Needing food, like a dog or an ant or a horse

needs food, and knowing that without it—and without it provided daily, regularly—we will die.

Humanity, we are a riddle indeed. Made in God's image. Cosmic in our destiny. And yet determined and sustained by calories, by nutrients, by a good balance of carbohydrates and protein and fat.

The Humility of Being Human

To be human is, or should be, incredibly humbling. We think of ourselves as independent and strong, nearly autonomous sometimes. But our bodies will begin to shut down within a single day if we don't eat.

If that doesn't put things into perspective for us, nothing will.

We are indeed greater wonders than we realize. But at bottom, we are created beings. We are just as much created beings as rocks and trees and the neighbor's cat are created beings, and we are just as dependent on the whole ecosystem of weather and life and death and balance as they are.

Which means that we are ultimately completely, totally, fully, devastatingly dependent on God.

Jesus said it best: "Without me you can do nothing."[1]

Nothing. Not breathe. Not think. Not hold our own cells together.

Nothing.

---
1 John 15:5

The Prayer of Dependence

Daily praying "give us today our daily bread" reminds of us this. It's supposed to. It's the ultimate perspective we so desperately need.

We need God. We aren't him. We are embarrassingly needy. And at the same time, God means to work out his purposes, his will, and his glory in us.

Right in the middle of Jesus's prayer, heaven meets earth. The cosmic will of God takes form in this: that we should be fed every day.

The kingdom is built in our place of need. God's will takes care of us, in the most humble and basic and foundational of ways.

The point of Jesus's prayer, I want to be careful to say, is not scarcity. This is sometimes read as though we are asking, "Do not give us anything except the bare minimum each and every day." That's not in keeping with the Bible's vision of abundance, as the Sermon on the Mount itself will point out.[2] The point is daily, faithfully connecting our need to God's willingness to provide. It's daily, faithfully recognizing our smallness and God's love for us. It's expressing our dependence.

It's worship.

And this should go without saying, but … it's asking. Prayer is action. Prayer causes things to happen. Prayer is an exercise of faith, and faith "is

---

[2] Speaking of how God clothes the grass with splendor, Jesus asks in Matthew 6:30, "won't He do much more for you—you of little faith?"

the substance of things hoped for."[3] So in a very real sense, prayer is connected to provision.

("You do not have," James tells us in his typically blunt way, "because you do not ask."[4] So ask.)

Asking Every Day

The Greek term for "daily bread" means exactly that: fresh bread, bread that just got baked this morning and that we can pick up from the market to eat this afternoon. In any culture where meals tend to come from the local market or the backyard or the field exactly when you need them, it's a very immediate and relatable term.

In our culture, where we buy hundreds of dollars' worth of food at once and stick it in the freezer, the term loses some of its power. So does the whole concept. When you have a little money in savings, an RRSP, a biweekly paycheck, and a pantry stocked with food, the "daily bread" thing may feel overly conceptual.

But the reality is we are no less needy because of all this. We're just less in touch with how urgently dependent we actually are.

So I recommend practicing this part of the prayer every day. And not just by repeating the line "give us this day our daily bread."

---

[3] Hebrews 11:1, KJV
[4] James 4:2

Personally, I ask the Lord for:

- Food for today.
- Money for the specific bills that are due.
- Provision to carry out specific projects or meet specific needs in my business or ministry.
- Money to give where I see a particular need.

And then I expand it. It's not just bread or money I need. I need energy for a meeting this afternoon. I need clarity for a piece I'm writing. I need emotional healing from an encounter or memory. I need physical health. I need courage to jump off my latest faith cliff. I need to hear from the Lord. I need help with my attitude.

Our culture shames us for expressing need. God does the opposite: he invites us to express it.

This is the reality of being human: we are endlessly needy.

This is the reality of being God: he wants to meet our needs.

So ask. Invite him into your life in this way, specifically, daily expressing requests and gratitude every time you talk to him.

James has another comment for us when we're willing to live this way: "God resists the proud, but gives grace to the humble ... Draw near to God, and He will draw near to you."[5]

---
[5] James 4:6, 8

And forgive us our debts,
as we also have forgiven our debtors.

(Matthew 6:12)

43

The Centerpiece Prayer: Why "Forgive Us Our Debts" Is the Central Step in the Lord's Prayer

Right on the heels of asking for provision—that God will meet our needs—Jesus teaches us to ask that our debts may be forgiven, and he adds the only note of conditionality in the Lord's Prayer: if God will answer this prayer (and the clear implication is that he will), we will likewise forgive everyone in debt to us.

He highlights this again right after the prayer, in verses 14–15.

Jesus talks about forgiveness a lot, so in the course of this series I've already written on it several times. Here, I want to take a step back and see forgiveness in light of what we've studied for the last few chapters: the reality of the kingdom of God and our place in it.

The Centerpiece Prayer

If the Lord's Prayer is a ladder to heaven, opening up the way for heaven to come down and for us to go up, "forgive us our debts" is not the first step.

I find this fascinating because I would naturally expect that it would be: that I cannot expect any communion with God until I forgive and have been forgiven.

First John 1:9 (NKJV) offers familiar advice: "If we confess our sins, he is faithful and just to forgive us our sins, and to cleanse us from all unrighteousness." The best time to confess your sin is the moment you recognize it as sin. Unconfessed sin breaks our fellowship with God.

And yet here is Jesus, not requiring us to begin with this step. Instead he begins with a great deal of context: of focus on God, on his holiness, on his kingdom, and on the doing of his will, here on earth as in heaven.

Then we take one step more and ask that God will meet our needs. In this we confess our deep and endless neediness and simultaneously recognize that God, by his very nature, is a Giver and Provider.

It's only then that we arrive here: at the centerpiece.

Again, in Western literary and oral forms we tend to place the important points at the beginning and at the end, with the middle being more a supporting text. Ancient Eastern literature is different: you will commonly find the main point right smack in the middle.

As here.

The Lord's Prayer is all about communion with heaven, and it is forgiveness that makes that possible.

THE LANGUAGE OF DEBT

The language of debt makes it clear why this is so, and why forgiveness is so central to the whole of the gospel and to our lives. We must receive forgiveness, and likewise we must give it, or we will never enter the unhindered fellowship with God that is the gospel of the kingdom.

Of course sin can be spoken of in other ways. Luke's version of the Lord's Prayer has "sins," and William Tyndale brought "trespasses" into the prayer, a more aggressive idea than debt). We can speak of lawlessness, wrongdoing, evil, and iniquity. All these things are connected. The Greek word we translate "sin" is *hamartia,* literally "mark-missing." As Paul puts it in Romans 3:23 (KJV), "all have sinned and *come short* of the glory of God."

But *debt* emphasizes the way in which all of this creates bondage.

Debt is a very real burden. In one of his practical passages Paul urged believers not to borrow money,[1] and Proverbs says, "the borrower is slave to the lender."[2] Debt means we are no longer free. Debt has a tendency to grow, and it hampers our ability to invest in the future or move forward into new things. I know people who couldn't go to the mission field because they needed to pay off school debts, who felt they couldn't get married or change careers or make other life changes because they were so bound to pay off credit cards or student loans.

Debt keeps us tied to the past: we cannot move into the new until the old is paid off.

Debt makes us vulnerable as well. It's one thing to hit bumps and snags in life when it's just you, but when you've got major bills due? When collectors will start calling, and then your car might be repossessed, and then you've lost your house? When the government can start taking money right out of your bank account because you've defaulted on your taxes?

Debt multiplies tragedy and places us in real bondage.

The big idea here is that sin means we owe something. There's a tab being kept, and sooner or later it will grow to the point where we can call nothing our own, where we cannot be free of the past, and

---

[1] Romans 13:8
[2] Proverbs 22:7

where we cannot do anything to better our own situations. Our whole lives will become about paying the debt off—but it's hopeless.

We can't do it. Pride says we can. Humility (which is truth) says we have to be rescued, because we can't do this on our own.

In the ancient world debtors ended up in slavery, literally paying off their debts with their own lives. Even until very recently, debtors went to prison, and their children would carry on the bondage, with their lives mortgaged to getting their parents out of jail.

The Way Out

This is the moral situation of the world. We are in debt. In some very real sense, sin ties us to the past and creates a situation in which we owe. The idea of "making atonement for our sins" is easily romanticized, but the truth is we can't do it. Sinners who try to atone for themselves will find they are never able to come to the end of their debt—to feel that they have truly paid it off.

We saw earlier that as human beings, we were given dominion—kingship—over the earth. This is why it matters so much what we do. We are both powerful and responsible. Our actions matter. That is why we are held accountable and why the debt incurred is so big.

This is also why it matters when others sin against us. The debts created are real and weighty. When we do not forgive others, we hold them in a real kind of bondage. I don't entirely understand how this works. But I know that in a moral and spiritual sense, it's true.

So God has an offer. He will get us out debt: not by suggesting an aggressive payment plan, or lowering interest rates, or helping us liquidate assets we didn't know we had.

He is offering to write our debts off. To give us a clean slate—a new beginning.

As his gift.

The catch is that if we accept this gift, we must extend it to others. When we are in debt ourselves, we are not free to forgive debts. We have to call in everything owed to us so that we can apply it to our own debts. But if we accept freedom, in God's economy, we must share it.

We no longer have a need to collect. We have to release our right to do so.

The Year of Release

In ancient Israel, God instituted a once-every-fifty-year celebration called the Year of Jubilee. For forty-nine years, the Israelite economy went on as normal. Debts were incurred and collected. Land changed hands, passing out of its ancestral ownership, as people sold it to pay off lenders. People who could not pay off their debts became slaves.

But every fifty years, the situation reversed. A national clean slate was declared. All debts were written off. Land went back to its original owners. Slaves were set free.

Jesus came preaching a message of Jubilee, quoting from Isaiah: "The Spirit of the Lord GOD is on Me ... to proclaim liberty to the captives and freedom to the prisoners ... to proclaim the year of the LORD's favor."[3] Many commentators recognize that the year of the Lord's favor which Jesus came to preach is the Jubilee, the year of release: the time in which debts are released and everyone is free.

Free to start over. Free to buy, to sell, to prosper, to grow.

And free to forgive.

We cannot atone for our sins. We can't pay off the debt we owe. It grows, and it creates a vicious cycle from which we can't escape. If we want to bring heaven to earth, if we want to see the kingdom of God come, there is only one way for us to do it.

By receiving forgiveness, and then by giving it.

---

3 Isaiah 61:1–2

AND DO NOT BRING US INTO TEMPTATION ...
(Matthew 6:13)

44

"Lead Us Not Into Temptation": The Prayer You Didn't Know God Wanted You to Pray

Most of the Lord's Prayer makes good sense to me. Sure, sometimes I choke a little bit on "give us this day our daily bread" (isn't it selfish to pray that God will meet my needs? Shouldn't I just trust him and not have to ask? Should we be asking God for material things at all?), but not often. It's this penultimate bit—"lead us not into trouble"—that throws me off, because it directly counters the way I naturally think about the spiritual life. My natural assumption is that God *wants* us to go through a lot of difficult things so we can grow. So rather than ask for deliverance from such difficulty, shouldn't we be running headlong into it?

I'm not the only one who thinks this way. Several years ago, I was in the Philippines on a ministry compound when I heard a sermon from a visiting American preacher. He said that we should ask God to send trouble our way, because it will build our character, make us stronger in faith, and conform us to the image of Christ. Jesus *wasn't* afraid of suffering, he said, and neither should we be. In fact, we should embrace difficulty and trouble for all the blessings they bring.

Now. Jesus wasn't afraid of suffering, and neither should we be. And if we embrace hardship like good soldiers of Christ, God will in fact brings lots of good out of it. All of Christian history attests to this fact.

But—despite my natural affinity for his point of view—I couldn't get behind the preacher's exhortation. As I listened to him tell us to pray for temptation and trials to come into our lives, I realized he was telling people to pray *the exact opposite of what Jesus told us to pray.*

Everything that preacher said about trouble and suffering fit my worldview just fine. I have no instinctive respect for the idea that you can or should use prayer like a "get out of jail free" card. But that's essentially what Jesus said we should do.

Temptation, Trial, and Trouble

About now you might be protesting that Jesus didn't say we should pray against troubles; he said we should pray against *temptation*. And of course the KJV and some other translations use "temptation" here. The problem is that most of us think of temptation almost exclusively in terms of temptation to sin (or cheat on our diet) and not in terms of difficulty and troubles that test us, which is a more biblical understanding of the word.

James tells us bluntly that God doesn't tempt anyone to sin, yet Jesus was "led by the Spirit" into the wilderness to be "tempted" by the devil.[1] So there's more to temptation, in this biblical sense, than being provoked to do something bad.

Actually, there's a direct biblical connection between the ideas of trouble, trial, and temptation to sin. The story of Job provides a helpful example. Job lived a full, blessed, and prosperous life, until he was blindsided by a mountain of trouble. Loss, bereavement, and illness all hit him at once.

Job didn't know it, but the trouble was actually a *trial*. A spiritual accuser had stood up in heaven and declared that Job's faith in God was a sham and would crumble the minute it was tested. While Job wallowed in grief and pain, the whole heavenly realm (full of beings both good and evil) was watching.

Trial doesn't come without temptation. In pretty much every case, when we go through hardship in life, Satan is angling for a particular result—that our sufferings will cause us to give up on God. He

---

[1] Matthew 4:1

wants us to stop trusting, stop worshiping, stop believing, and declare God a liar.

Job didn't do that. He hurt, and he didn't understand, and he asked a lot of hard questions and voiced a lot of long complaints. But he kept his faith. He passed the test.

When troubles hit our lives, God promises to work good through them. But we need to be aware that someone else also has a purpose in the difficulties we face. We have a spiritual enemy who wants us to turn against God, and he will do what he can to make that happen.

"We are not ignorant of the enemy's schemes,"[2] Paul wrote. We can't afford to be ignorant either.

Led into Temptation

Being led into trouble, trial, and temptation is no small matter. Not everyone comes out of such tests unscathed. Not only that, but trials take a lot of time, energy, and focus, draining these things away from other, more positive pursuits in our lives. So while, again, trials and testing will come, we shouldn't go looking for them. To do so is a form of hubris—a manifestation of pride and presumption on our part.

Jesus knew these risks better than anyone. He warned his followers that while he had come to give

---

[2] 2 Corinthians 2:11

abundant life, there was a thief out to "steal, kill, and destroy."[3] God will at times lead us into trials, even as he led Jesus into them, and if we ever find ourselves in a trial, the thing to do is what Jesus did—cling to God, stand on faith, root ourselves in the Scriptures, and surrender ourselves as fully as possible to God while refusing to give the devil an inch. But it is because the devil is a player in all of this, and he really wants us to give up those inches, that we are actually taught by Jesus to pray for protection from temptation. In his book *Understanding "Our Father,"* Catholic author Scott Hahn writes, "We pray for deliverance from Satan because we know that we cannot defeat him in a game of one-on-one; nor do we trust to the weakness of our faith. We gladly pray the prayer of realists, the prayer of weaklings; for that is what we are. 'Lead us not into temptation, but deliver us from evil.'"

The enemy would like to keep us in a constant state of trouble, trial, and temptation. His goal is that we will fall. And if God allows trials in your life, you can know several things clearly: that God wills for you to overcome, and will empower you to do so; that your life matters, or the enemy wouldn't bother; and that when you come out of the trial with your faith intact, it will accomplish something significant for the kingdom of God.

But it's not the will of God that our trials be

---
[3] John 10:10

never-ending. It's not his will that the enemy be given free rein to jerk us around and bring destruction into our lives. That's why we exercise our right to influence the permissions of heaven through our prayers.

Better Things

It's important for us to learn healthy, biblical attitudes toward suffering, and those attitudes include acceptance, surrender, and even rejoicing in grief and pain. But Jesus's prayer keeps us from tilting into an unhealthy expectation of only-bad-all-the-time. Like any good father, God wants better things for our lives than constant, unending battle.

If God allows us to suffer, he also promises us comfort, restoration, and victory. The entire Bible assures us that God is *good* and that his will for his people is good. And we don't have to write a special definition of *good*, in which good becomes evil and vice versa, to believe that.

If you are blessed: Ask that God will not lead you into temptation.

If you are in trouble, and therefore tempted: Declare your loyalty to God and ask him to give you victory and lead you out.

Expect goodness. Expect deliverance. Expect that trials will be limited both in time and in scope (as Job's was, and Jesus's). *Pray* that it will be so.

And ask God what better things he has for you today. Make the most of those times when you are *not* undergoing trial, when you're free, happy, blessed, prosperous, and having fun; and make the most of those times when you are.

We don't have to expect the worst. We don't have to pray that we'll suffer and have a hard time. We can pray, "Lead us not into temptation."

It is God's good pleasure to answer that prayer.

... BUT DELIVER US FROM THE EVIL ONE.

(Matthew 6:13)

45

"Deliver Us from the Evil One": What the Devil Has to Do With It

As we just saw, God supports and even solicits our requests to be delivered from trial, trouble, and temptation. That tells us something important: that God himself isn't the source of our trials, or at least most of them. Someone else is.

This is one of those verses that can be translated two different ways. In some translations we read "deliver us from evil." In others we read "deliver us from the evil one." They are essentially the same thing.

We Have an Enemy

The Bible *could* tell the story of the world as being purely about man and God. It could describe this universe as a closed moral system, in which the major factors are man's sin and God's righteousness, free will and justice, human depravity and the glory of God. And sometimes the Bible gets represented as though this is the story it tells.

But it isn't.

From Genesis to Revelation, the Bible acknowledges the presence of another player, or rather, many such players: "For our battle is not against flesh and blood, but against the rulers, against the authorities, against the world powers of this darkness, against the spiritual forces of evil in the heavens."[1]

In its various forms, this other spiritual power has played an active and significant role in our history from the start. Mankind fell because Eve believed a lie, but she wasn't the liar. Nor, of course, was God. Something else came into the garden and directly countered the word of God: If you eat from the tree, he told her, "you will not surely die."[2]

Eve made the choice to believe the liar. In this first test of faith, she did not prevail.

The New Testament is clear about the very real danger this enemy brings. Peter tells us that he roams about like a roaring lion, seeking whom he may devour.[3] Paul warns against the enemy's "schemes" and "devices" and prophesies that he will make inroads in the church through false teaching

---

[1] Ephesians 6:12
[2] Genesis 3:4, NKJV
[3] 1 Peter 5:8

and demonic doctrine.[4] Jesus pictures him as a thief who comes to steal, kill, and destroy.[5]

It's interesting that Jesus doesn't see the sheep, human beings, as actually *following* the enemy. In fact he says, "They will never follow a stranger; instead they will run away from him."[6] We were created and designed to follow only one Shepherd. The thief's activity is to lure the sheep out and scatter them where they can be massacred, stolen, and destroyed.

Revelation 12:10 calls our enemy "the accuser of the brethren," bringing to mind the scenes in Job where a spiritual accuser provoked the series of attacks that put Job's faith to a severe test. In fact, the name "Satan" was originally just a title; it means "adversary."

What Is Evil?

The exact nature of evil is a matter of theological and philosophical debate. Is evil a presence, a thing in its own right; or an absence—the lack of something good? Social science might ask if evil comes from nature or nurture, if it's a product of our DNA or of our influences or of our choices.

I don't believe the answer is simple. But I do believe the Bible is clear about several things:

---

4 2 Corinthians 2:11; 1 Timothy 4:1
5 John 10:10
6 John 10:5

- Evil is not original. The Bible does not teach a dualistic universe in which there is a "Good God" and a "Bad God," a yin and yang that always go together and must remain in balance. Only God, who is good, is eternal, immortal, and original. He is the First Cause, the Unmoved Mover. The Bible also teaches that God cannot be seen as the creator of evil in its moral sense. God does not sin nor cause others to sin. This being true, evil cannot be seen as a creation in its own right, but rather as the perversion of something good.

- Evil is not creative. Just as evil is the perversion of something originally created as good, so evil cannot create—it can only pervert and corrupt. Evil doesn't create apples; it rots or poisons them. Lies twist and pervert truth. Sin twists and perverts God-given instincts and abilities. Rebellion and witchcraft warp and ruin human souls.

- Evil is corrupting and leads to death. Just as goodness in the Bible is connected to life, blessing, and the ability to bring forth life, evil is connected to death and to the processes that lead to it—rot, corruption, and decay.

In this last sense, we don't always have to see evil as specifically moral in nature. When the Bible says in Isaiah 45:7 that God "creates evil," for example, it doesn't mean that God causes someone to do wrong, but that he chooses to bring about the defeat and downfall of something or someone. Such defeat is an evil—a form of death and downfall—for the person experiencing it, but God will bring it about for reasons of justice. Circumstances may also be "evil" in that they are destructive, troubling, or sorrowful. In this way, poverty is evil. Natural disasters are evil.

When a person is evil, however, the evil is moral in nature because it involves choice. In the same way, the evil of "the evil one," the created being we now know as Satan or the devil, is moral and personal because it is the result of choice.

Because of his connection with rot, decay, curses, and perversion, Satan has been given "the power of death."[7] The end result of everything he has set in motion—including the transformation of his own character—is destruction.

Deliver Us from Evil

What all this means is that there's something of a double meaning in the prayer Jesus taught us. Just as "lead us not into temptation" is both a prayer to remain free of trouble generally and also a prayer to be protected from trial and testing provoked by

---

7 Hebrews 2:14

the enemy specifically, "deliver us from evil"—those things that are rotting, corrupting, and dying—is likewise a prayer to be delivered "from the evil one."

There is a recognition in the wording that we are under attack and need to be rescued.

The real key in all of this is that God *wants* us to pray this.

All of the Lord's Prayer is an outworking of its heaven-to-earth connection; every request is a way of bringing God's kingdom rule into our own lives. We are given the power to do this, to bring heaven down, in our prayers.

- We do it by honoring God's holiness.
- We do it by submitting our will to his will.
- We do it by asking for provision.
- We do it by receiving forgiveness and promising to forgive.
- And we do it by asking for rescue, for deliverance, from evil.

There is power in request. Our asking brings the power and resources of heaven to bear on the earth. And these things are *meant* to come to bear. We are in a battle; we need God's help. Prayer is one way—perhaps *the* way—victory over the enemy is won.

The practical takeaway? If you are under attack, don't just say "Ah well, God's will be done" and surrender your will to the Lord. It isn't the Lord doing the attacking. Yield to God in every way possible, of course. But also: ask God to deliver you from evil, and from the evil one.

If you can't bring yourself to ask for your own sake, do it for the kingdom's sake. Do it because the ground of your life is being contested by an enemy, and it belongs to God. And do it for obedience's sake.

After all: this is what Jesus told us to pray.

For Yours is the kingdom and the power and the glory forever. Amen.

(Matthew 6:13)

46

Praising the King of Heaven: The Controversial Doxology

This powerful doxology finishes off the Lord's Prayer with a shout of praise—a triumphant declaration that God is King forever and ever. At the end of a prayer that is all about human agents establishing the kingdom on earth through their trust and reliance on God, there couldn't be a more appropriate close.

Careful readers of the Old Testament may also find the doxology familiar. It didn't originate in the New Testament, and its origin makes it that much more meaningful.

A Question of Accuracy

There's a bit of controversy around the end of the Lord's Prayer, for one reason: these are the only words in the prayer that Jesus may not have said.

In most Bible versions, you'll find them either missing, bracketed, or footnoted to that effect.

The reason there's a question is that in the oldest manuscripts we have for the gospel of Matthew, this benediction isn't there. In later manuscripts, it is.

There are several possible explanations for the discrepancy. One of those certainly is that Jesus said the words, but the particular old manuscripts we have didn't include them for whatever reason, while others did, in a straight line all the way to the Bibles we have now.

("Newer" manuscripts are handwritten copies of "older" manuscripts that wore out and fell apart from use, so they constitute a sort of paper trail. And scribes did their best to copy accurately.)

But the general consensus is that Jesus didn't say the words; rather, they were added by a scribe in the margins as praise to God, and as more scribes copied the manuscript out by hand, eventually the margin note got incorporated into the text itself.

There are a few places where this happens in the Bible, though not usually so extensively. Something a scribe may have added—a "gloss," i.e. an explanation or clarification—eventually got added into the body of the text.

(In no case does this create a significant change of doctrine or meaning. Charges that "we can't know what the Bible originally said" because there are so many discrepancies in the manuscripts are totally misleading, because they ignore the nature of the differences. In the highest percentage of cases, these are things like one manuscript saying "Jesus" where another says "Christ." Every change of any import is marked in nearly every major translation, with alternate translations given in the footnotes. You can trust what your Bible says.[1])

But whether Jesus said these words at this time or he didn't, they are Scripture, and they're extremely appropriate as a benediction to the Lord's Prayer.

If a scribe added them, he chose his words of praise very deliberately.

They are in fact a direct quote from 1 Chronicles 29:11–13, and they were originally given in the context of the kingdom of God coming to earth.

The Kingdom of the High King

"For yours is the kingdom, the power, and the glory" is an abridged version of the prayer in 1 Chronicles. The full doxology reads:

---

[1] Those interested in this topic might want to check out the free training available at BiblicalTraining.org. I love the series called *"Why We Trust Our Bible"* and highly recommend it.

> Yours, LORD, is the greatness and the power and the glory and the splendor and the majesty, for everything in the heavens and on earth belongs to You. Yours, LORD, is the kingdom, and You are exalted as head over all. Riches and honor come from You, and You are the ruler of everything. Power and might are in Your hand, and it is in Your hand to make great and to give strength to all. Now therefore, our God, we give You thanks and praise Your glorious name.

The one who spoke these words was David, and he did so at a time when his son Solomon was about to take the throne. David understood his own role perhaps better than any other Israelite king (including Solomon) ever did. He knew that God himself had been Israel's king and that his own appointment to the throne came straight from God. Though he may not have known it early on, by the end of his life he understood that his rule was "the kingdom of God" on earth and that he ruled Israel not as ultimate potentate but as a lesser king under the King of Heaven. He understood that he was a shepherd of Israel, stewarding the sheep on behalf of the One whose subjects and possessions they truly were.

David understood that his throne was a throne of the kingdom of God and that his progeny were destined to sit on that throne forever—in the heavenly realm and into eternity. This destiny was fulfilled in Jesus, a physical descendant of David, many generations later.

David's prayer acknowledges God as good, as the one who blesses, provides for, protects, and prospers his people. It includes lines that would make many Christians uncomfortable, leaning too much toward "prosperity gospel" or "worldly" physical blessings. Yet the Bible presents the kingdom of God as manifesting itself in just these ways.

From Genesis on, in fact, the kingdom is about human flourishing in right relationship with God. We can't cut God out of culture, economy, wealth, government, art, or anything else that makes up human life and expression without losing some of the Bible's vision for us. And contrary to popular perception, Jesus didn't do so. He came to plant his kingdom in seed form, and he fully expected it to grow into a full harvest—affecting every part of human life and society. The import of Jesus's kingdom being "not of this world"[2] wasn't that it wouldn't *affect* this world. It was that because its power and authority didn't come from this world, it wouldn't operate in a top-down, violent, empire-building way. Instead, it would grow from the inside out, changing hearts first and society second.

That is in fact how the kingdom does grow. Whenever Christians have turned to militaristic

---

2 John 18:36

means of "enforcing" the kingdom of God, we have instead opened doors to the enemy and undermined our own mission. Hundreds of years later we're still trying to pick up these pieces. When Christians focus on the preaching of truth, the practice of love, and the work of inside-out, transformational discipleship, whole nations are blessed and changed. But I digress.

The Best Possible Benediction

The Lord's Prayer is a kingdom prayer from beginning to end. It acknowledges God as holy High King. It acknowledges our own part in bringing God's kingdom by submitting the dominion we were given on earth to his rule, and it highlights our need to unite our will to God's will. It specifically connects the doing of God's will with our needs, our forgiveness, and our deliverance.

And finally, here, it turns everything back to God and acknowledges him as Ruler, Savior, Originator, Strength—King.

"For yours is the kingdom, the power, and the glory" is the best possible benediction. Because it is true, the Lord's Prayer will be answered in every detail. Heaven *will* invade earth. The kingdom *will* fully come. That is why we pray.

Whenever you fast, don't be sad-faced like the hypocrites. For they make their faces unattractive so their fasting is obvious to people. I assure you: They've got their reward! But when you fast, put oil on your head, and wash your face, so that you don't show your fasting to people but to your Father who is in secret. And your Father who sees in secret will reward you.

(Matthew 6:16–18)

47

Secret Sorrow and Private Fasting: How Jesus Meets Us in Our Brokenness

I have to confess: fasting has long been something of a mystery to me. The church context in which I grew up recognized fasting as a sort of prayer intensifier; it was typically used in a context where one really needed something from God or really wanted to draw closer to him (or both). But the rationale wasn't really explained.

On that front, the Bible doesn't help much. Jesus's teaching in Matthew 6 is a case in point: he assumes fasting, treats it as a given, rather than explaining it. Clearly, God-fearing Jews in his day practiced fasting on a regular basis.

But why? And should we do the same? And either way ... how does Jesus's teaching here apply to our lives today?

Why Fasting?

Fasting from food (and sometimes drink) is an ancient practice. It has been connected to religious life as long as religious life has existed.

All over the world, people of different religions even today treat fasting as a spiritual discipline. It's considered a way to elevate the spirit and discipline the body—to learn self-control and reorient oneself to reality in a healthier, more spiritual way.

For Christians, it's usually connected to times of intensified prayer. Fasting seems to clear the air, and the self-sacrifice involved helps us get serious about our prayers and lock our focus more pointedly on God. Some view fasting as a form of worship. It's also often connected to intercession, on a national, church, or personal level.

In the Old Testament, fasting is likewise connected to prayer. But there's a further element that's often overlooked: in the Bible, fasting was usually connected to times of intense mourning. Many times, fasting was a way of expressing sorrow over sin. It voluntarily mimicked the effects of extreme sorrow, when one is so grieved that one can't even eat.

This is why in the Old Testament, fasting is usually accompanied by other outward expressions of public repentance and mourning, like tearing one's clothes or hair, wearing sackcloth, sitting in ashes, and public weeping and wailing.

Understanding *that* background highlights something about Jesus's teaching on fasting: it's strange.

Public mourning, weeping, and repentance were the whole point of Old Testament fasting. By telling people to *hide* their fasting, to move it from a public to a personal level and to actually make it look like nothing was wrong, Jesus seems to turn the whole practice on its head.

Fasting for Show

While individuals did fast in the Old Testament, when we encounter fasting in the Bible it is usually corporate. The nation of Israel fasted to express repentance on more than one occasion (see Nehemiah 9 for a good example). Esther called a corporate fast before she went into the presence of the king, risking a death sentence, to intercede for her people.

God responded to fasting with grace and forgiveness—but he was also good at smelling a rat. At times these displays of national "repentance" were just a display. Just as God had no use for sacrifices made without obedience or loyalty to him,[1] so he didn't care much for fasts without real repentance.

Isaiah 58 is the classic passage on this topic. Here's a sample:

---
[1] See Amos 5:18–27

> Will the fast I choose be like this:
> A day for a person to deny himself,
> to bow his head like a reed,
> and to spread out sackcloth and ashes?
> Will you call this a fast
> and a day acceptable to the LORD?
> Isn't the fast I choose:
> To break the chains of wickedness,
> to untie the ropes of the yoke,
> to set the oppressed free,
> and to tear off every yoke?
> (Isaiah 58:5–6)

Secret Sorrow and the God Who Sees

In Jesus's day, it's clear that fasting had become a regular personal practice among those who considered themselves especially religious. But like prayer and almsgiving, it had fallen prey to a common pitfall: the practice had become about people, and being seen by people, instead of actually reaching out to and communing with God.

Jesus's advice is given to circumvent that problem. If no one knows you're fasting, you don't have to worry that you'll fast for the wrong reasons. You're free to fast before God alone.

The most significant parts of this teaching, to me, are the phrases "your Father who is in secret" and "your Father who sees in secret."

For us it's normal to think of religion or spirituality as personal, individual things, but in the ancient world it wasn't so. In the ancient world religion and spirituality were cultural, corporate identities and practices, as much a part of your DNA as your language or the clothes you wore.

By urging us to practice fasting—a particularly corporate and communal expression of worship—*privately,* Jesus urges us to make worship, prayer, and seeking God an intensely personal and individual thing.[2]

In the process, the content of our prayers changes too. In public, corporate fasting, you repent over the sins of your nation. You seek God for societal shifts, for rain, for peace. You wail and weep and throw dust and ashes in the air so that everyone will see how much your grief should impact them too.

But our lives are just as wrung by personal sorrows. We grieve and mourn things other people don't know about, things they *can't* know about. Even if we try to share certain things, there is a depth of pain, a depth of loss, a depth of regret, a depth of need that no one else can share or understand.

---

[2] This is not to say that there is no more corporate application for spiritual practices; all in all, Western culture arguably views the gospel and spirituality as *too* individualistic. Most of us desperately need to recover the communal dimensions of our faith. Yet, the individual/personal dimension remains critical in Jesus's way of knowing and following God.

That is where God will meet us. Seek your Father in secret, Jesus says, because he is in secret, and he *sees* in secret. God knows the depths of our hearts. He searches us out. He sees it all. And he invites us to come to him, to share with him, and to encounter him in our most broken places.

The fast that God has chosen is to break the chains of wickedness, to untie the ropes, to set the oppressed free, and to tear off every yoke. These are the things we are meant to do when we repent—the things turning to God will accomplish in our society. But they are also the things God promises to do, for us and in us, when we go to him with our grief.

Ultimately, what Jesus teaches us here is bigger than guidelines for fasting. It's about personal faith, secret sorrow, and the God who sees—and who promises that when we come to him, he will not let us down.

Don't collect for yourselves treasures on earth, where moth and rust destroy and where thieves break in and steal. But collect for yourselves treasures in heaven, where neither moth nor rust destroys, and where thieves don't break in and steal. For where your treasure is, there your heart will be also.

(Matthew 6:19–21)

48

Laying Up Treasure in Invisible Places: How to Live Life Jesus's Way

In September of 2014 my heart suddenly stopped beating in a parking lot. I never expected cardiac arrest to become a part of my personal story, but there it is. I was thirty-one years old.

Near-death experiences afford one an interesting chance to get up a little higher than the usual altitude and evaluate life. When things are so suddenly nearly over, you can get a clearer perspective on those things—on the stuff of your life, such as it has been.

When I woke up in the hospital sometime after the parking lot, without any memory of what had happened but unmistakably filled with grace, I was mostly aware of this: I had no regrets at all.

A little background is probably in order at this point. I do not live a conventional life. I never have. At thirty-one, I didn't wake up into a life that would be normal for most people.

Before I expound on that, I want to make the point that the details of my life are not important. The specific choices I made or didn't make are irrelevant. You could do the exact opposite of all of them and still be laying up treasures in heaven. In all honesty, I don't really recommend my path. (Unless of course you know God is calling you to it. Then jump in; the water's fine.)

In my early thirties, I had no formal education at all. I didn't have a stable career or a normal job. I've never had either. I had freelance clients in a self-taught field, and I worked when I wasn't on the road with a performing arts ministry I started with one of my closest friends seven years earlier. That ministry had no funding, no organizational backing, and no accomplishments of clear and obvious consequence. We just traveled around and shared our hearts with people through the arts and through speaking.

I'm not married, and I don't date. I have become a homeowner since, but in September of 2014 I lived in a bedroom with some relatives. The sum total of my personal assets were a Dodge Neon with nearly 300,000 kilometers on it, half a dresser's worth of clothes, some hiking gear, a guitar, and enough books to fill four or five bookshelves.

Again, let me be clear: I'm not recommending my lifestyle, nor am I knocking anyone who has a job, a degree, a spouse, children, and/or material blessings.

All of those things are good gifts from God—wonderful gifts from our Father. They make the world go around. They build the kingdom of God. *The details don't matter.* Our relationship to them does.

On the outside, my life didn't (and probably still doesn't) make a lot of sense. I've been blessed with really supportive family and friends—I am incredibly rich in relationships—but even they have not always understood some of the things I've chosen to do or not do.

And sometimes I have wondered if I'm actually a little crazy. Or in denial about a lot of really important things in life. Or just lazy.

But I woke up with no regrets. Zero. Of course I've done things I wish I hadn't done—I'm a sinner. But I'm forgiven, and that's not what I'm talking about when I speak of regret. I'm talking about the general trajectory of my life, the path I'd been following, the way I had built everything in my life around what was truly important to me.

Which was Jesus.

Some of my life decisions, I have made with fear and trembling. With a lot of doubt. Sometimes I've wondered if I'm self-deceived.

But I didn't regret any of them, after I died and came back. I was relieved to discover that.

How to Live with No Regrets

This chapter took me a long time to write, because Jesus says things that sound so simple but then turn out to be really hard to grasp. "Collect treasures in heaven." Okay ... how? What does that even mean?

I flopped around on this question for weeks. Does it mean "soul-winning"—leading people to Jesus so they'll be in heaven when you get there? I've often heard that interpretation. Does it mean valuing relationships with people?—they are eternal, after all, and pretty much nothing else on this earth is.

Then I made the connection to my hospital story, and I thought, *I can share that*. Because it's about treasure in heaven, even if I don't have all the answers. It's treasure in heaven that means we can live a weird, insecure, nonconformist life, and have no regrets. And *just as much,* it's treasure in heaven that means we can live a more mainstream, financially secure, workaday life, and have no regrets there either.

It's all about your heart—where it is, what matters to you, who you love.

It's about treasuring Jesus. But I'm getting ahead of myself.

It's pretty obvious that as Christians, we need to reject materialism. That's not the same thing as rejecting *material*—good luck with that if you try it, and anyway, God likes material. He made the whole world out of it and gave it to us as a gift. But we're not supposed to give our hearts to stuff. If we do, our hearts end up rotting and rusting and getting stolen and broken just like the stuff itself.

That's fairly obvious. But how do we go beyond that and store up treasure in heaven?

By now, you probably know that I don't think we should read "heaven" as referring merely to the afterlife. I believe that when the Bible uses the word *heaven*, it is referring to the spiritual realm: the invisible, intangible, at-base-of-everything realm where God reigns and where we are currently citizens, seated in heavenly places with Christ.[1]

So to collect treasure in heaven is to value and treasure spiritual things, holy things, eternal things. It is to make our decisions and order our lives by that value system. Most of all, it is to treasure God himself.

When we do, the wood, hay, and stubble of our lives somehow turns to gold, silver, and precious stones. Love for God infuses absolutely everything

---

[1] Philippians 3:21, Ephesians 2:6

with meaning—and it puts material things into their place, as gifts, never to be confused with the Giver.

Living Like Jesus

This is how Jesus lived. He treasured his Father above all things. He lived on every word his Father spoke, in the Scriptures and by the Spirit. Within his love for the Father, he loved his people, his sheep—his disciples and the masses alike.

He enjoyed creation. He ate and drank with gusto. He bossed the wind and walked on waves. He consecrated bread and wine, and in the resurrection he brought heaven and earth into one. But always, his treasures were heavenly.

I awoke from sudden cardiac death without regrets because as odd as my life has been, I've tried to live it treasuring Jesus.

Can I be vulnerable here? I experienced a sense of disappointment and even grief when I realized how close I'd been to the "other side." I felt like I had been living my life in a conversation, one full of questions, and I'd been just moments away from waking into all the answers—into the company I love the most and everything I have spent a lifetime seeking.

I think maybe, just maybe, that's what laying up treasure in heaven means.

I don't usually get this personal in my writing on Matthew, and I am not saying any of this to make a big deal out of myself. I say it because I want you to know: *what Jesus says is true.*

If you give your heart to material things, it will be lost to you.

If you store your heart up in heaven, in Jesus himself, you will find it. You will discover greater depths of love and joy at every turn. And you will live, in the final analysis, without regret.

Your heart can never be lost if Jesus holds it.

The eye is the lamp of the body. If your eye is good, your whole body will be full of light. But if your eye is bad, your whole body will be full of darkness. So if the light within you is darkness—
how deep is that darkness!

(Matthew 6:22–23)

49

Free and Full of Light: What Jesus Taught about Scarcity, Generosity, and Abundance

Not many Scriptures are preached out of context as much as this one, maybe because it's just not plain to English speakers in the modern world what Jesus was talking about. For years I thought he was talking about media consumption: the "garbage in, garbage out" principle. Not so. Squarely in the middle of Jesus's discussion of treasures in heaven, treasures on earth, and serving two masters, this passage is about money.

More specifically, it's about two conflicting mindsets that shape how we think about money: scarcity and abundance.

BOUNTIFUL EYES AND MISSING HEARTS

It was actually Proverbs that helped me put this together. I suddenly realized that Jesus was using a fairly common Hebrew idiom, brought out by the literal leanings of the KJV:

> He that hath a bountiful eye shall be blessed; for he giveth of his bread to the poor. (Proverbs 22:9, KJV)

> Eat thou not the bread of him that hath an evil eye, neither desire thou his dainty meats: for as he thinketh in his heart, so is he: Eat and drink, saith he to thee; but his heart is not with thee. The morsel which thou hast eaten shalt thou vomit up, and lose thy sweet words. (Proverbs 23:6–8, KJV)

One who has a bountiful, or good, eye lives in a world of abundance. He isn't afraid to share his bread with the poor; he's moved with compassion and secured by trust in the Father who provides. He gives and receives blessing without being ruled by it; his heart is free to be with God and with other people.

His whole body is full of light.

A mindset of abundance, which only grows as it is shared, is in fact a mindset based in truth. The truth is, we live in a world of abundance. This was true in Solomon's time and in Jesus's time, and it has perhaps never been more true than now.

One who has an evil, or bad, eye lives in a world of scarcity. He is ruled by fear. He can't give generously; his heart is missing from the transaction, as it is preoccupied with getting and keeping. His heart is weighed down by earthly treasures that rot and rust.

He is also driven, hurried, unable to rest. Because he does not believe in abundant blessing and a giving Father, all of life is a race to find security and wealth before someone else takes it first. "He that hasteth to be rich hath an evil eye, and considereth not that poverty shall come upon him."[1]

The Lie of Scarcity

A scarcity mindset is a trap, now as then. It keeps us locked in fear, in comparison, in envy and covetousness. It tells us "There is not enough." Therefore, we're all in competition with one another for the little that there is.

It's not just money, although that's where scarcity thinking is most obvious. It bleeds into the rest of our lives too.

There's not enough love.

There's not enough recognition.

There's not enough ability to succeed.

We live in fear of running out.

---
[1] Proverbs 28:22, KJV

It's a false fear, a lie.

The truth: God has placed us on an abundant planet, in an abundant universe. Although we can, at times, create scarcity through greed and faulty systems, fundamentally abundance is always there. We can tap back into it.

There is enough.

Poverty in the world is not the result of too few resources. It's the result of mismanagement of resources, of ignorance, of bad decisions, or sometimes of what we'd call plain bad luck.

To be clear: I'm not blaming the impoverished themselves. Some people are poor because of their own choices. But the world's poorest people aren't poor because of their own bad decisions; they're poor because of systemic problems.

The Bible always calls for one response to poverty: compassion, and sharing out of our own abundance.

But that's the key.

We have to *see* the abundance. We have to choose to live in it, and to give out of it. We have to choose to be full of light.

Holistic Affluence

There is no greater call to holistic living than this

one: "Love the Lord your God with all your heart, with all your soul, with all your mind, and with all your strength."[2]

We can't do this if our hearts are fractured. Jesus knows that. He knows that if our hearts are busy collecting treasures and sharing in their rust, rot, and corrosion, then our hearts are not fully with him.

If we fear that trusting God will leave us impoverished and unable to survive, we will take part of our hearts away from him so we can focus on securing our futures. That is the way of finite beings. We have needs. If we don't believe God can and will meet them (and most often that he already has), we will set out to meet them for ourselves. Please note that I'm not suggesting we shouldn't work for a living; as we'll see in more detail below, work is the most common way God provides for us. But that's the key: we work to receive provision from God, not to create it ex nihilo.

This is the Bible's whole teaching on prosperity in a nutshell: God gives abundantly. He wills that we prosper. But we must do so through trusting in his abundance, and not through greed, fear, or miserliness.

To live as children of light means to believe that there is enough.

---

[2] Mark 12:30

I love Merriam-Webster's second definition of *affluence:* "an abundant flow or supply: profusion."

In the kingdom, we are all affluent. We are recipients of God's abundant flow of provision.

Practically Speaking ...

Work is an integral part of human life. It has been since the garden of Eden. It's God's primary way of giving us access to abundance; it's also a primary way we find satisfaction and confidence in life. Work is a gift.

Jesus is not teaching that truly spiritual people don't work, or that living by faith means camping out by your mailbox waiting for mysterious checks to arrive rather than doing anything to access wealth. We do indeed reap what we sow. In work and finances, as in other areas of life.

So the practical difference between a "good eye" and an "evil eye" isn't found in working or not working; it's found in mindset. A mindset of abundance, a mindset that says "God will provide," "there is enough," "I am not my own source," "my efforts can be multiplied and so can my giving"—this mindset opens up possibilities. It is flexible, elastic, able to change. It embraces good risks. It gives and shares. It goes to work with a good will and confidence that our efforts will bring forth fruit.

This is a fundamentally different mindset from one of scarcity, which says there is only so much, and so we must grit our teeth and do whatever it takes to get it and then keep it.

Scarcity will stop us from taking needful risks. Scarcity will prevent us from sowing at all. (How can we possibly afford to sow seed, when a famine or a blight might destroy it? Better to hoard.) Scarcity will bring stress, narrow thinking, and cut-throat actions.

Scarcity fills our whole bodies, our whole selves, with darkness.

Jesus teaches a better way.

Today, there is enough. You can give without fear, explore without being afraid that you will run out.

You can be free and full of light.

No one can be a slave of two masters, since either he will hate one and love the other, or be devoted to one and despise the other. You cannot be slaves of God and of money.

(Matthew 6:24)

50

Money Can Be a Good Thing—But It's Always a Terrible Master

We know the story: a rich young man came to Jesus and asked what he should do to be saved. Jesus told him to sell everything he had, give the money to the poor, and follow him.[1] That story, taken together with Jesus's teaching in Matthew 6:24, for many creates a simplistic narrative: See, money is a bad thing. We must give it up to follow Jesus.

The tricky part, of course, is that we can't actually do that in most cases.

For most of us, the more we try to give up money, the more we find our lives revolving around it, because money is how we survive in the world. This is why so many missions-minded young people, having given up their jobs in order to devote themselves to ministry, find themselves spending a far larger chunk of time than they want to fundraising

---

[1] Matthew 19:16–22

and courting donors. Even Jesus and his disciples used money to buy food and drink, to pay their way as they traveled, and to give to the poor. While some will find themselves called to give up money or material possessions in order to follow Jesus, that isn't the normative call of most Christians—and it's not really what the story in Matthew 19 is intended to illustrate.

But the story of the rich young ruler is a perfect illustration of what Jesus is telling us here: money is a terrible master.

Everyone has a master, Jesus is saying. That is the nature of mankind. We don't live unto ourselves. We're always serving something else—something bigger than ourselves, or something smaller.

For most of us there are two choices: God or money.

God is a wonderful master. The best there is.

Money is a terrible alternative.

Slaves to Lesser Things

Man is the pinnacle of God's creation. For a human being to be enslaved to money—what a ludicrous and horrifying thing that is!

This might be Satan's most effective plot to demean and demoralize mankind: to enslave us to something so much lesser, so much beneath us.

To teach us to measure our worth in dollars.

Money is a wonderful servant, but it is a terrible status symbol. It is a wonderful servant, but a terrible dictator. It can accomplish marvelous things—when it does our bidding, and God's.

But when we switch that around, when we do *its* bidding, and even try to make God do its bidding, then the world is standing on its head, and nothing is what it should be.

This is Jesus's point. He revisits it, again and again, all through this section of the Sermon on the Mount.

It is not, *Oh, money is evil.* Money is nothing but a symbol by which we exchange value. Prosperity, abundance, time, resources, and value all come from God; money is just a way we measure them. Money also, especially in our age of paper currency, is an expression of trust. It is a kind of faith: evidence of things hoped for, a physical expression of something unseen. This is more and more true as the things we value and pay for are themselves intangible—knowledge, technology, expertise—as opposed to tangible things like silver or gold.

But if we make an idol of money, if we see it as our provider, as our life's goal and purpose, as The Thing that dictates and directs our lives, then our hearts can't be with God and we can't be whole.

That's why Jesus invited the rich young ruler to

sell all he had before he came and followed him.

It wasn't because his riches were a bad thing in and of themselves.

It was because he was enslaved to them.

Jesus was inviting him to come and be free.

Time to Make a Trade

We know that this interpretation of the story is valid because of the young man's response, and because the story is unique. The rich young man is the only person Jesus told to do this. In his case, Jesus looked at someone enslaved to the wrong master and invited him to make a trade.

The young man didn't do it. He "went away grieving."[2]

Jesus calls us to the ultimate holism in the way we live. Again: *Love the Lord your God with all your heart, soul, mind, and strength.*

If money is your master, Jesus says, you can't do this. You can't actually serve two masters. We were not created to be divided, we were created to be whole. So we will drift all toward one thing or all toward the other.

You will love one, hate the other. Despise one, be devoted to the other.

---

[2] Matthew 19:22

Devoted to God

By contrast with a slavish subservience to money, to be devoted to God is to be devoted to the highest thing there is. Ours is an "upward call in Christ."[3]

Devotion to God will always raise our minds, our hearts, and our spirits. It will exalt our actions. We will become better, purer, more beautiful human beings as we love God.

Devotion to God raises our vision to the heights and depths of all that is good and right and truly human, because it flows from what is divine.

Devotion to money, by contrast, is lowering. It demeans and flattens us.

God calls us to be holy and courageous; money calls us to compromise and cringing, to being controlled by fear.

God calls us to be generous, with all our whole lives as with our money; money, as a master, drives us to be stingy, fearful, greedy, grasping.

God is a God of abundance. Money—when it rules—is always about scarcity.

When it doesn't rule, when it's a servant, it can be a tool for righteousness.

That's why tithing, and regular giving and spontaneous generosity, are such powerful spiritual disciplines. They remind us who's boss.

---

[3] Philippians 3:14, ESV

They keep us moving in the right direction: up and out, not down and in.

Making the Trade

Switching masters, if money has been running your life, is easier said than done.

Jesus offers a lot of good pointers. There's his advice to the rich young ruler: Pry your fingers off your idol and give it away. Let it do some good in the world for a change.

Then follow Jesus.

That's the crux of the matter, really: *follow* Jesus.

From now on, if you're going to earn money, do it by serving God.

(Which doesn't mean "go into full-time ministry." It means, "whatever your hand finds to do, do it with your might, as to the Lord and not to men, for you serve the Lord Christ."[4] It's a heart thing.)

Then make a regular habit of letting it go. Practice radical generosity. Money can't control your life if you're heaven-bent on using it to worship God and bless other people.

Ask new questions when you go to earn. Don't ask, "How much money will this make?" Ask, "How much value will it create?" Don't ask, "Will there be

---

[4] Ecclesiastes 9:10, Colossians 3:23–24 (NKJV)

enough?" Ask, "How can I tap into the abundance God has made available?"

Don't meditate on money. This is a continual challenge for me, as a business owner. But I'm learning it can be done. You do it by bringing God into every part of the equation. When you budget, factor in the Lord's blessings. When you create a plan to earn (be it "start a new business" or "get out of bed and go to work today"), thank God that you're receiving his daily bread. His blessings.

Ask him how he wants to use it.

He's the boss.

He's our master—our good, kind, loving, creative, and sometimes playful master.

Tithe. Tithing may not be 100% biblical in the way we practice it today, but it's a good idea nevertheless.

There are three biblical responses to money. None of them are guilt. They are gratitude, joy, and generosity.

Receive money with thanks. Enjoy it. Give it away.

God is such an alchemist, he can bring goodness, life, and blessing even out of silver and gold.

This is why I tell you: Don't worry about your life, what you will eat or what you will drink; or about your body, what you will wear. Isn't life more than food and the body more than clothing? Look at the birds of the sky: They don't sow or reap or gather into barns, yet your heavenly Father feeds them. Aren't you worth more than they?

(Matthew 6:25–26)

51

Right Places, Right Times: What Looking at the Birds Teaches Us about Provision

As she told me in conversation one day, my friend Sheila watched a nature documentary about penguins. This is a bad idea for anyone who wants to retain magical, fuzzy feelings about the natural world.

I saw one recently too: there were all these penguins living on an island near Antarctica or somewhere, and every day they would go plunging off these sheer, sharp cliffs to get into the ocean to fish. The waves were so wild and powerful that a high percentage of penguins would get dashed back up against the rocks.

The filmmakers took lots of footage of bloodied, gashed-up penguins hobbling around on what were probably broken legs, and dead penguins bobbing in the water, never to go home to their poor, starving chicks.

"Nature is horrible!" Sheila announced to me. "It's cruel! It's terrible!" She paused. "It does make you wonder what Jesus meant with all his talk about how God takes care of the birds."

Birdwatching for Spiritual Profit

Jesus's admonition to look at the birds is advice I take literally. When I'm getting really worked up about provision, I go outside and watch birds. Preferably on the water, at the lake near my house. Or sometimes just pecking around the lawn.

I don't go watch nature documentaries. Jesus didn't say, "Look at the penguins on that God-forsaken rock in Antarctica."

But actually, even those penguins with their life-and-death struggle can teach us something about worry and provision.

Because they don't have to be on that rock. Not too far away is the entire continent of Antarctica, where there's a much smaller chance of getting dashed to pieces on your way home from work.

The penguins on that island are there because, paradoxically, it's a paradise for them. It's so harsh and horrible that no predators come or live there—not a single one.

Yes, feeding is a challenge. But the water is full of abundance. God provides, even for them.

The island isn't so God-forsaken after all.

Ours is a cursed world. Paul tells us that all of creation is subject to futility, trapped in the bondage of corruption, groaning and waiting to be set free when we are.[1] The whole natural world will enter "the glorious freedom of the children of God" when we do.

The gospel isn't just for people; it's for penguins too.

God provides for birds. He provides for us as well. On this basis, Jesus says, don't worry.

"Don't Worry" Does Not Equal "Don't Work"

I know I've harped on this a few times, but it bears repeating again. Christians are super weird about money. I have known people who literally quit their jobs, went home, and spent their days watching TV and waiting for welfare checks because they said they were obeying Jesus's command in this passage.

Jesus said don't *worry*. He didn't say don't *work*.

If you go outside and watch the birds (which I recommend, because it's relaxing and enlightening both), you'll notice that they do in fact work for their food.

They don't do what people in Jesus's time did. They don't sow, or reap, or gather wheat into barns.

---
[1] Romans 8:18–22

Nor do they do what we do in our time: they don't go to work, spend eight hours doing whatever it is we're tasked to do, and collect a paycheck every two weeks.

But birds do work. They go to the right place, at the right time, and they find and eat what God has placed there for them.

They don't seem to worry about it. They just go and do and receive.

Receiving What Is There for You

For birds, this is instinctive. They receive what God has placed in the world for *them*. They don't seem to consider themselves responsible to place the seeds there, or the worms, or the fish, or the frogs.

They don't think they have to manage the universe for this to work.

They just show up and collect.

They work with their own design too, I notice. Swans and ducks and herons and plovers collect on the water. Swallows snatch flies out of the air. Scarlet macaws crack nuts with their powerful beaks. Secretary birds stalk through grass so long it can hide lions, towering above it on their long, spindly legs, ready to snatch up snakes or lizards or mice or stamp them to death first.

Secretary birds even eat cobras, which makes them kind of awesome.

Don't we do the same? Come, do, collect. Receive.

Worry tells us we're in charge. It tells us we're in control, or more to the point, we should be in control but we aren't.

When we worry, we convince ourselves that making seeds turn into wheat is our job—as opposed to receiving what God has given us, being faithful and diligent about it (to till, to fertilize, to plant, to water), and then receiving the miracle that comes from heaven.

Wheat is a miracle. Fish are a miracle. Paychecks are a miracle.

Isn't your life more than all that? Jesus asks. Do we think God will create us, the greatest marvels walking, and then forget to feed us? Forget to do the miracles necessary to keep us eating and clothed and functioning day by day?

Need is a great reality, but so is the love of God, and his love is both generous and paying attention.

A bird that never leaves its nest will, presumably, starve. But one that goes, does, and receives will find there is food enough. Miracles enough.

And worry doesn't make a single one of them happen.

CAN ANY OF YOU ADD A SINGLE CUBIT
TO HIS HEIGHT BY WORRYING?

(Matthew 6:27)

52

Provision, Responsibility, and The Waste of Worry

Jesus starts teaching about money by telling us not to collect stuff, but to lay up treasure in heaven instead. It lasts and it's better, and you never have to worry that someone's going to break in and carry it off.

That's the way of invisible, intangible treasures: like air, they give life abundantly, without fear.

But he shifts quickly to talk about worry, and it's here he really focuses. Because we do. We worry. We worry incessantly, mostly about things we can't control anyway.

Like the birds, we get up in the morning and go to work, but unlike the birds, we worry that maybe even so, provision won't be there this time.

God's love, the value he places us on our lives, won't be enough.

Cubits and Realities

Human value. That's the rationale Jesus offers for our right to live carefree: "Aren't you worth more than birds? Isn't your life more than food? Isn't your body more than clothing? Won't God do more for you than he does for the grass—oh you of little faith?"

"But," I reply back.

But, somewhere in this world, someone is starving. For somebody, God, you are falling down on the job. Someone's clothes are full of holes, or are basically just holes with a few threads attaching them here and there.

Someone is going to die today.

Okay, true enough. In this world where sin and death are realities, so too are poverty and lack.

Should we therefore worry?

Jesus gives us a linchpin for his whole argument, an aha that sets us free, in verse 27: "Can any of you add a single cubit to his height by worrying?"

(In the ancient world, a cubit was a measure of length, taken from elbow to fingertip on a grown man. So not exact, but likely about eighteen inches. Some people had bigger cubits than others.)

Worry, you see, makes us feel like we're being responsible. If we meditate on all that could go wrong, if we stew in fear, if we remind everyone at all times that we can't expect everything to go well, we feel like we are being grown-ups.

Realistic. Careful.

The trouble is that worry accomplishes nothing, and stops a lot of things.

There are, in life, whole swaths of things that are out of our control. We can't make ourselves grow eighteen inches. We can't pull the sun closer to the earth, or push it further away. We can't even make our own hearts beat. They just go on doing it, until they don't.

Worry thinks about all these things we can't control. It meditates upon them. It exalts them.

And in doing so it drains our energy. It drains our hope, our optimism. It steals creativity and life. It zeroes in on scarcity and ignores the abundance all around us.

We can't make ourselves grow eighteen inches, but we *can* learn to breathe more deeply and expand our lungs. If we act (not if we worry), we can lose weight, add muscle, become more flexible.

If we act (not worry), we can combat poverty, lift up the downtrodden, change laws, enable commerce, dignify the homeless, mentor kids.

If we act (not worry), we can grow more into Christlikeness, we can serve God with our whole hearts, we can store up treasures in heaven.

Worry just saps and drains all of that, spending our energy on things we can't control and so sabotaging things we can.

Or, to draw a finer point, sabotaging things we can influence. I believe human beings have staggeringly powerful influence; I don't believe we have control.

Every step out, every attempt to *do,* requires that God meet us in the middle. He is generally and generously willing to do so.

Who among you can cause a meal to materialize on your table? But who among you can work a good day for it?

Who among you can force God to meet with you? But who among you can invite him?

Who among you can harry and worry and badger a seed into growing? But who among you can water it, feed it, wait?

Freedom from anxiety comes from these truths:

- That more fundamental than need is love, and God proclaims that we are valued more highly than anything else in creation.
- That God has created a world of abundance, where in order to receive we are mostly just responsible to show up.

- That we control nothing but influence everything, and so we can and do live in a world of tremendous grace and of tremendous responsibility too—and God blesses our attempts to take that responsibility seriously.

Ours Is Now

A little later Jesus wraps all this up with aphoristic sagacity: "Therefore don't worry about tomorrow, for tomorrow will worry about itself. Each day has enough trouble of its own."[1]

That it does. Leave the worrying to the day itself, then. Ours is this moment to act. To pray. To trust. To put off worrying for one more day that turns into forever.

In the meantime, what we will have accomplished without worry is enough.

---

[1] Matthew 6:34

And why do you worry about clothes? Learn how the wildflowers of the field grow: they don't labor or spin thread. Yet I tell you that not even Solomon in all his splendor was adorned like one of these! If that's how God clothes the grass of the field, which is here today and thrown into the furnace tomorrow, won't He do much more for you—you of little faith?

(Matthew 6:28–30)

53

"Won't God Do More for You?" How Jesus Confronts Our Low Expectations of God

A few years back I sat on a grassy knoll outside a hotel in some sunnier and drier part of the world than Ontario ... if my memory serves me right it was Kansas City in the spring, Eastertime.

I was on the cusp of making a faith leap in my work, or at least I thought I was. In reality it took me years more to make the leap. But at least I was talking to God about it.

(Half the time. The other half the time I just talked to myself.)

I took inventory of my life. The freedoms my work had brought me. The money in my bank account. The vacations I got to take and the nice things I could do for people.

In my mind, I budgeted. If I do this thing—if I

take this jump, obey God into this void—I can cut back here, and there. I'll stop eating out. Drive a clunker. I don't really care about clothes.

The Lord interrupted. "Why," he asked me, "do you think I will take worse care of you than you would take of yourself?"

Why indeed.

Look at the grass. The wildflowers. Look at lilac bushes and rose vines and purple-laden crab apple trees. Breathe deep of their fragrance. Be astounded at their fragile, profligate beauty.

Not even Solomon in all his splendor, Jesus says—Solomon, the king whose reign most typifies the kingdom of God in the Old Testament, whose reign was gold-paved streets and cedar halls and love songs and free-flung wisdom—not even Solomon in all his splendor was dressed so beautifully as the grass.

Won't he do much more for you—you of little faith?

Won't He Do More for You?

I've pondered that question for years.

Why are my expectations of God so measly and miserly?

Why do I think he's stingy?

Why do I assume that following God means cutting corners, especially where things like my health, my well-being, and my basic needs are concerned?

We equate ministry with poverty, and that's not entirely without merit. Historically, people who have embraced voluntary poverty for the sake of Christ have done great things, cutting ties of dependence on the world's systems and status symbols and enjoying the deep riches of trust and simplicity. Jesus did tell people to give up all they had and follow him, and he certainly didn't walk around flashing purple robes and gold rings. He told us not to lay up treasures on earth. And yet, here in Matthew 6, he challenges the way in which we automatically equate serving God with poverty and lack. He points out that God dresses the grass with extravagance, and he will certainly do far more for us.

I don't know how all these things dovetail. I can't draw you the Venn diagram where sacrifice and abundance and devotion and provision all meet.

I suspect seasons are involved. I suspect there are treasures not readily apparent to the eye, clothing radiant and splendid that isn't tangible but is no less real than Solomon's. At times there truly is no greater wealth than what we receive when we give up everything and follow, even in a lifelong embrace of simplicity and nonmaterialism.

But I also think our expectations of God are generally really low, even insulting.

God Isn't Frugal

Unless you are an aficionado of the prosperity gospel, you probably think of God and money as existing on a frugality spectrum. God is frugal toward us and expects us to be the same way—toward ourselves and each other.

Except that he isn't.

There's nothing frugal about the way God lavishes his grace on us. Nothing frugal or measured, nothing cautious or budgeted, about his love.

I don't think his provision is frugal either.

(Have you noticed sunlight?)

I think we use his provision badly. We're good at choking it out, or not seeing it for what it is. Or of equating provision entirely with money, when it is so much more. But that isn't God's fault, now is it?

Again, there are three biblical responses to God's provision. Gratitude. Generosity. Joy.

God clothes the grass more splendidly than Solomon.

Won't he do much more for you?

So don't worry, saying, "What will
we eat?" or "What will we drink?" or
"What will we wear?" For the idolaters
eagerly seek all these things, and your
heavenly Father knows that you need
them. But seek first the kingdom of God
and His righteousness, and all these
things will be provided for you.

(Matthew 6:31–33)

54

Trust at the Core: Why Jesus Lived in a Different World than We Do

Jesus lived in a different world than most of us because the Father was at the center of it.

The fatherhood of God was the number one fact in his day-to-day existence. Not need. Not lack. Not scrambling around looking for purpose or self-esteem or something to do so he wouldn't be bored.

For him, the whole world revolved (and revolves) around this fact: God is Father.

The Father knows. He sees. He's listening. He loves. He honors you. He thinks you're worth more than grass and birds. He's powerful. He cares. He does stuff when you ask him to.

Simple beliefs.

Life-changing, though.

When Trust Is at the Core

The idolaters didn't believe they had a loving father, so they invented gods and made deals with demons. They obsessed over their needs. They obsessed over power.

They obsessed over all the stuff we obsess over when trust is not at the very core of how we live.

It's interesting to me that even in the other great world religions, the most honored thinkers and leaders have been those who largely eschewed idolatry in favor of trust. Trust in the universe, trust in process, trust in the forces of life and death themselves.

They danced along the edge of truth, I think. Sometimes their devotees are better than we are at calming down and centering—turning off the clamor of noise and need and tuning into the inward, invisible things where life is truly located.

But Jesus gives us something much better than an impersonal universe, a life force, or an energy: he gives us a Father.

And he tells us pivotal, important things about what kind of Father this is, and what he prioritizes and thinks and does.

This Father loves. This Father creates. This Father sees. This Father knows. This Father will meet with you in secret, share his heart with you, and give you what you need.

He knows you so well, he knew your needs before you even expressed them.

Seek First the Kingdom

Knowing that frees us up for something better than the pursuit of sustenance and a hardscrabble existence: it frees us up to seek the kingdom.

We feel that we can't seek the kingdom because we have to provide for ourselves, we have to get our ducks in a row, we have to take care of things, we have to worry.

But if we don't have to do that, then we're free.

It's not necessarily a change in our circumstances that Jesus has in mind when he tells us to seek first the kingdom. Paul gives pretty good advice to new converts in 1 Corinthians 7:24: Whatever your life state was when God called you, stay in it. Don't rush to make some massive circumstantial change; find out how to meet and serve God and seek his kingdom where you are.

He might move you. Even probably will. But there's usually something to learn where you are first.

In the midst of a massive transition in my life, I told the Lord I wanted to change my career because I wanted freedom to seek him.

He spoke to my heart and said, "You will never be more free to seek me with your whole heart than you are right now."

I wrestled with that. I knew he was in fact calling me to make a change, and that it did have something to do with spending more time in the Word, in study, in prayer.

My work at the time was all-consuming mentally, exhausting physically. I knew I needed more head space.

But if my heart wasn't fully God's there, it wouldn't be fully God's when I got my head somewhere better.

If your heart isn't fully God's where you are physically, it won't be more fully God's if you move.

That's the principle.

One Master, All the Way

Earlier, Jesus told us that we can't serve two masters. We'll love one and hate the other; be devoted to one and despise the other.

Some of us try to shift masters, but we still want to hold on to the old one with a few fingers, because after all, that's where we've got all worries banked.

We end up halfhearted in our work and halfhearted toward God, trying to walk a line and mostly falling off.

The worries aren't necessary, Jesus says. They're not necessary because you have a Father. You can be a child.

So you're free.

Free to seek.

Free to serve.

Free to be a bird, or a beautifully adorned stem of grass: to show up, to do, to receive.

You are free to lay your head down at night tired and aching but resting in the kingdom.

You are free to smile up at the Father and know he's smiling back.

PART 4:

Seeking the Kingdom: A Spirituality for the Humble and Hungry

So don't worry, saying, "What will we eat?" or "What will we drink?" or "What will we wear?" For the idolaters eagerly seek all these things, and your heavenly Father knows that you need them. But seek first the kingdom of God and His righteousness, and all these things will be provided for you. Therefore don't worry about tomorrow, because tomorrow will worry about itself. Each day has enough trouble of its own.

(Matthew 6:31–34)

55

Seeing, Seeking, and Asking Questions: How to Find the Kingdom of God

I am meditating on the connection between the words *seek* and *see; sought* and *saw.* We seek to see. At the end of our lives, what we have seen will be what we sought.

And what we didn't see, we didn't seek.

Are our lives really this simple? This connected—A leads to Z; seeking leads to sight?

I think they are. Jesus at least seems to believe so.

And so where we set our sights will define our horizons.

■■■■■

Our seeking distills into questions.

Here is what the Gentiles seek: "Where will we live? What will we eat? What will we wear?"

Need-focused and earthbound questions. They are also cyclical and do not tend to grow. No sooner is "What will I eat?" answered than it has to be asked again, and in the same way: "Now what will I eat?"

We seek to see. To "see": to set our eyes upon, to know for ourselves. To understand and more than that, to experience.

When I ask the question, "What will I eat?" I don't so much want someone to give me the verbal answer "You will eat meat and potatoes for dinner," or even to understand on an intellectual level what "meat and potatoes" means; I want to experience actual meat, and actual potatoes, physical and tangible. To set my eyes on them, "see" them, and actually eat them, actually experience them.

If we "seek answers," this is the kind of answers we seek.

Experiential knowing. Mystical experience, direct contact. Open vision. Sight.

■■■■■

If we want better answers, we should ask better questions.

I am writing this beside the lake. It is a warm, calm, and beautiful day in late May, here in southern Ontario where I live. Nevertheless it has been a hard day for me. I'm not sure why. I asked myself why it was hard—I sought to know.

I chased my thoughts around in circles for a while, looking for answers. Found a few. Knew them on a deeper level. Wasn't satisfied or helped for all that.

So I changed my question and asked, "Why is this a good day? Why am I having a good day today?"

I found a *lot* of answers. Better answers to better questions. Since one of those answers was "because it's a beautiful, sunny day," I decided to throw in the towel on my original plans (which had been sidelined by all that tail-chasing anyway) and come to the lake.

Then I thought I'd bring my typing keyboard and my Bible with me, so I did, and I'm writing by the water. Finding better things.

Food and water and roofs and clothing are good things.

But the kingdom of God is better. The righteousness of God is better. God himself is better.

If I seek these better things, I start by asking better questions.

Not "What will I eat?" but "Who is God?"

Not "What will I wear?" but "Where is God working right now? If I look closely, where can I see him?"

Not "Where will I sleep?" but "What is the love of God like?"

Jesus indicates we are playing a game that has limits. We are finite. We cannot actually ask, and seek out answers to, all of the questions.

Only some of them.

So pick the best ones.

We don't have the time or the emotional energy or the mental capital to chase the kingdom and to chase our needs, so Jesus says go for the better chase, undertake the better hunt, and your Father will look after the needs.

What we seek to see we will see, know, understand, experience.

There's an alchemy in seeking, because asking better questions doesn't necessarily mean different actions, but it does mean a different experience. Brother Lawrence called this "practicing the presence of God." He washed dishes to experience God, and he did experience God. While others just experienced dishes.

I can eat bread and find God, while others eat bread and just find bread.

Bread and wine, communion in the body of Christ—or just bread and wine, crumbs and alcohol.

Snacks or sacraments.

It depends on what you're seeking.

> Do not judge, so that you won't be judged. For with the judgment you use, you will be judged, and with the measure you use, it will be measured to you.
>
> (Matthew 7:1–2)

56

Jesus on Judgment: What "Do Not Judge" Does and Does Not Mean

Of everything Jesus taught, I wrestle with this passage maybe the most.

It's just so darn hard for me to obey, partly because I don't understand it, partly because I don't want to do it.

I have an analytical mind and a discerning spirit, and both of those good things lead me to want to judge. I also wrestle with the human desire to compare and to feel superior, and I think maybe *that* is the real reason I find this command so hard to carry out.

Understanding Jesus on Judgment

Understanding first.

What does Jesus mean by these words? And what does he not mean?

It's a common complaint among Christians that non-Christians, people who have never in their lives cracked open a Bible and who treat the names of God as shorthand for the declaration of a foul mood, can nevertheless quote this verse. "The Bible says don't judge."

That's true, it does. And yet our natural response is to rise up in righteous indignation and protest, "But that's not what it *means!*"

Okay then. What *does* it mean?

Discernment vs Judgment

I draw a distinction, because I think the Bible draws a distinction, between noticing-understanding-discerning and the act of judgment.

It wasn't, for example, judgmental of Paul to notice the servant girl following him and Silas through the streets of Philippi, screaming out, "These men are servants of the Most High God!"[1]

He couldn't *not* notice that, just like we can't not notice the way someone dresses, speaks, acts, carries on, lives their life.

And it wasn't judgmental of him to understand how her actions were affecting the crowds and hindering his ministry (or not).

Paul also discerned, spiritually, the cause of her

---
[1] This story is found in Acts 16:16–18.

behavior: she was possessed by a demon.

And eventually, being fed up (which also doesn't seem to be the same thing as "judging"), he cast the demon out.

In general, all of Jesus's disciples felt free to notice, to understand, and to discern, and they acted on what they noticed, whether by calling one another out on hypocrisy (Paul again, publicly chastising Peter in Antioch in Galatians 2) or calling the entire city of Jerusalem to repent for their complicity in the crucifixion of Jesus (Peter this time, in Acts 2).

Jesus's "do not judge" did not hamstring their ability to act as prophetic voices to their nation or to one another, nor did it stop them from announcing the superiority of their faith over paganism, nor did it stop them from forming a community that was distinct from the world around them.

So "judgment" isn't any of that. Jesus apparently did not mean that we cannot see, understand, discern, and speak out. Elsewhere he said, "Stop judging according to outward appearances; rather judge according to righteous judgment."[2]

But "do not judge" is strong language, and rather than trying to find loopholes out of that, we would be well served to take Jesus seriously and to change the general posture of our hearts and minds toward each other.

---

2 John 7:24

Judgment is natural. Leaving it behind is hard. But if we are going to be people of grace, it's essential that we learn how.

Knowing Where to Quit

Perhaps the key to carrying out Jesus's command here is knowing where to quit. Another way to say that might be *knowing the limits of our jurisdiction,* or even more, *recognizing the limits of our understanding.*

My friend and coauthor Mercy Hope uses the analogy of crime to explain this. As a civilian you can see someone committing a crime and recognize what you are seeing. You can call the police. You can even personally intervene to stop it. The police, with their higher jurisdiction, may even put the person under arrest. But either as a citizen or as a police officer, you do not judge, and the law prohibits you from doing so. The judgment must happen in a court of law, through due process, and can only be passed by an individual fully qualified and appointed to do so.

Why is this so? Our justice system recognizes that just because we see something bad happening does not mean we understand the whole story. What we see may turn out to be something very different under the surface. A crime has many components, including motive and forethought and the presence of accomplices.

It may be better, or far worse, than we initially believed it to be.

There's another interesting story in Acts 5, where a man named Ananias decided to lie to the apostles and through them to the Holy Spirit, and after Peter discerned the lie and accused Ananias of it, Ananias dropped dead.

But it's interesting to see what Peter did and didn't do in this situation. He recognized the lie for what it was, discerned the role of the enemy ("why has Satan filled your heart?" he asked), and announced the sin.

He didn't carry out the judgment. Ananias was stricken by God himself, not by Peter. But more interestingly to me, he didn't answer his own question.

Why *had* Satan filled Ananias's heart?

That remained a mystery. Peter didn't even venture a guess.

There are things we can see, understand, discern. But along with them there are always other things, things we can't see, understand, or discern. Truly righteous judgment must deal with these other things.

The limits of our knowledge mean we are not qualified to judge.

Doing What Jesus Said

As easy as it is for us to pull the "it doesn't mean that; we can still call sin sin" card when people accuse of us of transgressing Jesus's command by judging them, I am concerned that it's *too* easy.

Maybe we fall back on that objection because we are judging, and we shouldn't be, and we don't want to face what's in our own hearts.

There have been times in my life I have judged, been convicted of it, and fought for the right to keep judging. I could so plainly see what was going on! How was I supposed to not judge that?

Thankfully, Jesus is pretty clear about this. A commitment to nonjudgment doesn't mean checking our brains, shutting down our discernment, and accepting that everything is fine.

It means not placing ourselves in the judge's seat. It means not picking up the gavel, not passing sentence, not seating ourselves on the throne of God and pretending we can see all.

In a biblical worldview, ultimate judgment is a fact. It will come, and it will come exactly when it is supposed to, with God (not us) as the judge.

Here's the thing: God alone knows why Satan filled Ananias's heart. God alone knows exactly what led this man down that road, what factors and temptations and past history and wounds and hardness all led to his lie.

And while Ananias suffered a fairly swift consequence for it, in the final judgment, we may find God is more lenient—or more harsh—than we expected.

Not Judging Is a Choice

On some level, seeing, understanding, and discerning are all instinctive and automatic. We do them intuitively.

The same is not true of judgment. We choose to judge others, so we can also choose not to.

We can choose to recognize the limits of our understanding. We can choose to say, "I don't occupy the judgment seat, and I don't want to." We can choose to walk in humility and love toward one another, rather than lifting ourselves up as judge and jury.

We can choose to love mercy, and to love one another more than we love our own views and the conviction of our own rightness.

I think ultimately, that's what Jesus is saying here. Judgment is inevitable. It will come to all. Let it be God who brings it, not us; let it come in the fullness of time, not prematurely.

Let us love one another while we can, and in the process, what we see clearly now may be changed, and transformed—from the final word on a person's life to a stepping-stone along the way of grace.

Do not judge, so that you won't be judged. For with the judgment you use, you will be judged, and with the measure you use, it will be measured to you.

(Matthew 7:1–2)

57

What We Do When We Judge: Jesus on Judgment, Part 2

In the last chapter, looking at the phrase "do not judge," we saw that judgment is a fact. It will come, and it will be God who judges.

That historical truth—that ultimate judgment will happen at a set time in history—is the context for everything else the Bible says on this topic.

That's evident in the continuation of what Jesus says, because he moves on from "do not judge" to give some very self-interested reasons not to do so. This, by the way, sets talk of judgment apart from more relativistic notions of right and wrong. The biblical worldview assumes right and wrong are real and measurable and that everything will be called to account, but that we are not fully qualified to do the measuring.

What We Do When We Judge

Yesterday I sat on a friend's back deck overlooking Lake Erie, and we talked about what we do when we judge.

Since judgment is *not* the same as seeing something for what it is (i.e. "that is a sin" or "that behavior is going to hurt you"), and it's not the same thing as discernment, what is it?

My friend and I concluded that judgment happens when we cross the line from seeing to leveling consequences, whether we can actually enforce those consequences or not.

Jesus and the Pharisees could both clearly see that the local prostitutes were sinning and also hurting themselves.

The Pharisees leveled consequences: *Because you are doing these things, I will not speak to you, will not associate with you, will not bless you, will not pray for you. Because you are doing these things, I choose to cut you off.*

Jesus said judgment could wait till later and went about trying to save and dignify these women instead.

The Pharisees had labeled and socially exiled Zacchaeus. He was a traitor and a thief. Jesus invited himself over for dinner and transformed the tax collector.

(You have no hope of changing a man or woman you have declared your enemy. But you can have bottomless influence on a friend.)

The "sinners" might have deserved the first response. The second response was grace.

The Law of Freedom

Jesus warns us off the first response because none of us are without guilt. When we judge, to some degree we are setting the standard for our own lives, and God will take that into account at the judgment.

What exactly judgment will look like for us as Christians is not totally clear to me, but we *will* stand judgment,[1] and in that day, Jesus says the measures we used, the judgments we judged, will come into play.

In the short book bearing his name, James goes round and round on a few subjects, one of which is judgment.

> Don't criticize one another, brothers. He who criticizes a brother or judges his brother criticizes the law and judges the law. But if you judge the law, you are not a doer of the law but a judge ... Who are you to judge your neighbor? (James 4:11–12b)

---

[1] 2 Corinthians 5:10

James is saying that when we judge, we change our position relative to God's moral law. Instead of being people primarily concerned with *keeping* the law, we become people primary concerned with enforcing it.

There are people who have to do this. Judges and juries have to do it. Rulers have to do it. In some cases, elders in the church have to do it. But we are not all judges and juries and rulers.

There is a divine law, and we are to see ourselves as doers of it: people responsible to carry out the Word of God in our own lives.

We are not to see ourselves as judges of the law or of one another: as people capable of so fully understanding both the law and the hearts and actions of our neighbors that we can confidently pass sentence.

James says elsewhere:

> Speak and act as those who will be judged by the law of freedom. For judgment is without mercy to one who hasn't shown mercy. Mercy triumphs over judgment. (James 2:12–13)

The interesting inference of both James and Jesus is that we can expect God to be more merciful than we are. We can expect him to account for all factors, including the ones we can't see; we can expect him to act in love. Of ourselves, we unfortunately can't have the same expectation.

Why do you look at the speck in your brother's eye but don't notice the log in your own eye? Or how can you say to your brother, "Let me take the speck out of your eye," and look, there's a log in your eye? Hypocrite! First take the log out of your eye, and then you will see clearly to take the speck out of your brother's eye.

(Matthew 7:3–5)

58

The Comparison Trap: Jesus on Judgment, Part 3

One danger in human judgment is that we use the flaws, foibles, and sins of other human beings to make us feel better about ourselves.

We validate our lives and our choices by comparing them to the lives and choices of others, and so our judgment is not without bias and is actually extremely personal in nature.

We're *not* impartial; we're making our judgments of others based on what others' choices say about us.

That makes us dangerous.

As dangerous as a man with a log in his eye attempting to take a speck out of his brother's.

The likely outcome will be a lost eye. And when it comes time for us to face judgment ourselves, the eyes we gouged out will be held to our account.

Opting Out of Judgment

You'll be judged with the judgment you used, the standard of right and wrong you defined.

You'll be measured with the measure you adopted and wielded against others.

That's only fair.

You can, however, opt out. You can humble yourself and say, "I am not qualified. There's a log in my eye. I lack the necessary information and the necessary skill to judge. I am happy and content to be a doer of the law and to leave the judgment to a merciful God."

The beautiful thing is that when we do this, when we choose to vacate the judgment seat, we're set free from the entire sinkhole of judgment, of measuring, of comparing, of condemnation.

We can choose to relate to one another on a different plane, not because we can't see that someone else has problems, or because we can't see a better path that we ourselves may choose to take, but because we love mercy, and we wish to give it and to receive it.

The Rarity of Judgment

It's an interesting truth that God himself judges only rarely. A careful reading of the Old Testament shows that while God at all times saw and even announced the wrongdoing of Israel, he waited to bring judgment—sometimes for hundreds of years.

"I take no pleasure in the death of the wicked," he told Ezekiel.[1] In our era, Peter tells us why Jesus has not yet returned:

> The Lord does not delay His promise, as some understand delay, but is patient with you, not wanting any to perish but all to come to repentance. (2 Peter 3:9)

Our Father would rather release *everyone* from judgment, save every one of their lives, than condemn a single person.

And he is perfect. He sees it all. He isn't hanging his own sense of self-worth on comparing himself to his creation.

Be the same way, Jesus says. You can see, you can understand, you can discern. But you don't have to judge.

So don't.

Log Removal for Dummies

Of course, along with permission to quit judging, there's a disturbing truth in Jesus's words: we've got logs in our eyes.

---

[1] Ezekiel 33:11

Presumably these are affecting the way we see a lot of things, not just one another. Presumably our vision is universally skewed.

Is there any way to get the logs out?

(Not so that we can enthusiastically go into the speck-removal business. I submit that's the wrong motivation for trying to clean out our eyes.)

As it happens, I believe this is one reason Jesus came. To make blind eyes see, not only physically but also spiritually. To enlighten the eyes of our hearts, as Paul puts it in Ephesians 1:18.

Step 1: Stop comparing yourself to others. Comparison is the quickest way to cloud your vision.

Step 2: Get honest with God about how much you can't see.

Step 3: Ask him to reveal himself to your heart.

The more clearly we see him, the more clearly we see.

Do not judge, so that you won't be judged. For with the judgment you use, you will be judged, and with the measure you use, it will be measured to you. Why do you look at the speck in your brother's eye but don't notice the log in your own eye? Or how can you say to your brother, "Let me take the speck out of your eye," and look, there's a log in your eye? Hypocrite! First take the log out of your eye, and then you will see clearly to take the speck out of your brother's eye.

(Matthew 7:1–5)

59

How to Be a Judgment-Free Zone: Jesus on Judgment, Part 4

Earlier, I wrote that seeing, understanding, and discerning are intuitive, things we do automatically and instinctively, but judgment is a choice.

I believe that to be true, but it isn't obvious. For most of us, judging itself feels instinctive. We do it so fast we aren't aware we're doing it.

So Jesus's command, "Do not judge," calls us to slow down and notice what we're doing, and then to choose to do differently.

In practice it will mean a lot of backtracking: observe, judge, then consciously break the judgment and go backward in your thinking until you arrive somewhere else: to a place of receiving information but not of judging.

I find this challenging (see my earlier confession that this is, bar none, the most difficult of Jesus's commands for me to consistently walk out), so I have spent a lot of time trying to learn how to do it.

I'll confess: hard as it is, it's also rewarding. Being judge and jury is a lot of responsibility, and it's heavy. We aren't equipped or empowered to act like God in this respect, so when we quit doing it, we'll find life is lighter and more free. We are freed up to love better, give more generously, and focus on what really matters.

This is, in a nutshell, what humility will do for us. Pride is the heaviest weight there is. And ultimately, this thing of judging/not judging is a matter of walking in pride or walking in humility.

Humility = the glad acceptance that we are not God.

The Wisdom of Slowing Down

My best advice for becoming a judgment-free zone is this: slow down the process that comes before judgment, and learn to stay there.

It turns out that we're not as good at this intuitive process as we think we are anyway. We think we see. But do we? Really?

For many thousands of years humanity saw the sun rising and falling and concluded that it circled the earth. They could plainly see this to be true.

Except they couldn't. They didn't see as clearly

as they thought they did, because they lacked information that was not, at the time, available to them.

When they were finally able to gain that information, their sight deepened, and their understanding grew.

In the same way, we think we understand what we see. But do we, really?

I see a homeless man sitting on the corner, and I think I understand a host of things about him, about his life, about the conditions that put him there. But here again, it's likely that I don't understand as well as I think I do.

I can't see all the factors, much less truly comprehend them.

This is kind of the point of the log-and-speck analogy. We all have something in our eye.

Discernment, as a spiritual gift, is an interesting case. But here again, there are limits. I can sometimes discern the spirit a person is speaking from—whether it's their flesh, the Spirit of God, or something demonic. But on the back of that discernment, I'm tempted to make a host of assumptions about the person and what's really going on with them, many of which may be unfounded.

God doesn't give us limitless discernment of one another (or even of ourselves at times); that access is limited to himself. Here too, I don't see all that I think I see.

So I am learning not to judge.

I'm learning to walk in greater humility, to recognize that my information is always too limited, my understanding too subjective, my discernment too shallow.

When it comes to the hearts and lives of other people, God tells us what we need to know, but not usually much beyond that. And since we are *not* the judge, since that responsibility has not been given to us, what we need to know isn't really a whole lot.

Alternate Paths

Judgment is a bad habit that takes up a lot of room in our lives. If we jettison it, what then? What are supposed to do with the information we get if we're not supposed to judge on the basis of it?

I suggest three things:

1. Listen
2. Look
3. Inquire

This can be done with circumstances as well as with people, and it's a little safer to practice on the former.

For example, when you wake up and it's raining and you wanted to go for a walk, don't immediately snap to a judgment: "This is bad!"

Observe the rain. Look at it. Listen to the thoughts you're thinking about it, the knee-jerk responses rising up inside of you. And inquire about them.

Inquire about the rain: what it's there for, what it's doing. Inquire about yourself and your feelings: Why do you think this is bad? What exactly is your negative association—is it physical, emotional, linked to a memory, a matter of thwarted desire (you wanted to go for a walk and now you can't)?

Inquire of "bad." Question it. Is this bad? Or could this be good? Could the rain be an opportunity for you—to rest, to reflect, to spend some extra time doing something else, or even to go outside and get wet and remember when you were a kid and you loved to splash in the puddles?

Is it an opportunity for you to recover the joy of playing in the rain?

Peta Roberts, a musician and minister of my acquaintance, told me, "Every morning I pray, 'Father, I receive every gift you have for me today, and I ask you to help me to recognize them.'"

Sometimes gifts don't immediately look like gifts. Our quick, knee-jerk judgments may end up causing us to overlook a lot of them, and suffer a lot of bad moods besides.

We can do the same with people. Remember, we don't have to judge them. We're not even supposed to, so that pressure is off. We can instead listen, look, inquire.

Slow down that process. Learn to live in it. Don't get to the end. See it, not as a roadway that ends in inevitable judgment, but as a path that meanders through understanding and connection and grace.

And an unexpected consequence? When you quit judging others, you'll find it easier to quit judging yourself. Learning to listen, look, and inquire applies to you too. We don't know our own hearts. That's a universal truth. But it might help if we slowed down and paid attention.

One more thought: jumping to judgment is a convenient way to avoid getting really truthful about things. Inquiry leads to discovery, maybe of things we don't want to see and don't want to know. Judgment allows us to slap a label on things and thus cover them up; we never have to go the distance or look at what makes us uncomfortable.

Pharisees didn't spend time asking what was really going on with prostitutes.

Or with themselves.

A Word for Our Time

We live in a time of extreme polarization, where we all think we understand each other and don't like what we see.

Maybe more than ever, Jesus's words here offer us something vital.

If we'll actually do what he said, if we'll get up the gumption to face our own pride and jealousy and constant comparison and distaste for honest examination, if we'll do the hard and disciplined work of backtracking on our judgments and staying in the questions, it could change the conversation we're having spiritually, politically, morally, ethnically, and economically.

Jesus's words are an open door on the traps we've built for ourselves.

I hope we'll walk through it.

Don't give what is holy to dogs or toss your pearls before swine, or they will trample them with their feet, turn, and tear you to pieces.

(Matthew 7:6)

60

Pearls Before Swine: Jesus the Riddler and What He Might Have Meant

The Greeks and Romans didn't use paragraphs.

So when my Bible lumps Matthew 7:6 in with the discussion on judgment right before it, I take it on faith that they've got the flow right. In this case, though, I'm not sure they do. I think it may more rightly belong to the discussion just *after* it, on the need to continually seek.

Either way, it's curious that Jesus would follow up a long teaching on learning not to judge others with a harsh-sounding injunction against "casting your pearls before swine and giving what is holy to the dogs."

CLEAN AND UNCLEAN

Before we explore the deeper meaning of this statement, it's good to acknowledge a few foundational points that were obvious to Jesus's audience. The

Jewish people had a well-developed doctrine of holiness, expressed in the terms "clean" and "unclean." It was given to them in Leviticus 19 and other places, in a series of holiness laws that drew sharp distinctions between clean things and unclean things, holy things and unholy things. They were clearly differentiated, and clean and unclean things were never to be mixed.

Even in the law itself, it's fairly clear that these particular laws are largely symbolic in nature. For example, the Jewish people were forbidden from eating a number of "unclean" animals, even though all animals were given to the human race as a whole for food in Genesis 9:3.

These dietary distinctions, which we call the kosher laws, were given for the express purpose of setting the Jewish people apart from the nations around them. Mankind has always fellowshipped and found community around food: by declaring much of the pagan diet off-limits, God declared pagan-Jewish fellowship off-limits as well. This is the symbolic significance of Peter's vision in Acts 10, where God himself lowers a sheet full of "unclean animals" from heaven and instructs Peter to eat them. When Peter protests, God answers, "Do not call unclean what I have made clean."[1]

While most Christians have (rightly, I think) understood this as meaning that the kosher laws are

---

[1] Acts 10:15, paraphrased

not incumbent on believers, the bigger point is that the Gentiles, those who were once separated from the people of God, are no longer to be thus separated. The way has been made for the two to become one, as was the ultimate plan from the beginning.[2]

But to reiterate: Jesus's hearers had a strong sense of clean and unclean that stood at the core of their identity as a holy people, separated for God.

Dogs and pigs, which Jesus mentions here, were both unclean animals. In fact, it was common to refer to Gentile people as "dogs." Pigs are probably the most infamous of non-kosher meats. To turn over "that which is holy" to something unclean, something outside of the covenant that symbolizes separation from God, would be unthinkable. The image is that of feeding a dog consecrated meat from God's altar, or tossing pearls—a precious substance identified with holiness and the kingdom of God in various places throughout Scripture—into a pigpen. To do so wouldn't just be foolish, it would be a heinous insult to God—a desecration. For Jesus's hearers, it would make a mockery of their own set-apart identity as God's people.

An Awkward Juxtaposition

There are scholars who posit that the Sermon on the Mount is not a sermon, with a proper flow; that it is a collection of sayings given by Jesus at differ-

---
2 Ephesians 2:11–22

ent times and places and compiled by Matthew. But many scholars disagree. Jesus's teachings *do* follow on one another and create a master teaching on living by faith and walking by the Spirit.

So why the startling juxtaposition, here, of "do not judge" followed by what appears to be a harshly judgmental statement?

After all, many have taken Jesus's words to be about people. "View certain people as swine or dogs, and don't share holy things with them."

But if we've taken Jesus seriously for the previous five verses, we need to be very cautious before making that kind of value judgment against anyone. His own life also warns us against it, because he had a habit of associating with, eating with, healing, and helping people who were considered "unclean," including Gentiles, Samaritans, prostitutes, demoniacs, tax collectors, and lepers.

So maybe ...

This Isn't About People at All

Maybe the imagery of swine and dogs isn't about what we share with other people, but about how we ourselves use the holy things in our lives. The way we treat the gifts God gives us: our own chosenness, our own relationship to God, our right to approach him in prayer, the revelations and truths we've been entrusted with. Maybe it's about how we view and treat God's goodness to us. In this sense, choosing to judge someone else, when we ourselves are in desperate need of grace and understanding, is a "tossing your pearls before swine." It so misses the value of the pearl—God's mercy and forgiveness extended to us—that it uses it in a wrong way.

Who would ever choose to throw pearls to swine?

Only someone who doesn't understand the value of the pearl.

Or maybe ...

The People Are the Pearls

The people *are* the pearls. Maybe when Pharisees threw the prostitutes in their culture "to the dogs," Jesus said they were throwing away something holy.

Jesus came to redeem, literally to buy back, his people. He redeemed them from sin, renewed their covenant with him, and made them holy once more.

He drew pearls out of the mud, rescued them from swine, and polished them back to beauty again.

Maybe that is what he's saying here. Maybe his talk of swine and dogs is ironic, meant to call the attention of his audience to how judgmental and condemning they had been and how they were in fact reversing the truth: what they called clean was unclean, and what they called unclean could be made clean again.

When we miss the truth in such a soul-bending way, our mishandling of one another will certainly "turn again and rend us," as the KJV phrases it.

Or maybe ...

It's About Caring for the Pigs

The spiritual writer Dallas Willard wrote that this passage calls us to be careful in the way we "minister" to others: that even when we know we have all the right answers, if others are not ready for them, the right answers can do more harm than good. Pigs that try to eat pearls will be hurt by them. They can't be digested or made use of. The result is hurt, both to the minister and to the one ministered to.[3]

There is undoubtedly truth to this. Jesus exercised caution in what he said to whom, and when he said it. The deepest parts of his message he shared with no one but his closest disciples, and he told them to tell no one else until the time was right—after his death and resurrection. So maybe that is what he was saying. The reality is, not everyone is receptive. Not everyone will honor what should be honored. Some will take it, trample it, and do great harm to us and to our message. We are not to judge one another, but that doesn't mean we must be blind to plain facts.

When Mary was told she would bear the Son of

---
[3] Dallas Willard, The Divine Conspiracy (New York: HarperOne, 1997), 228–229

God by the Spirit of God, she "kept all these things and pondered them in her heart."[4] She was wise: she protected the pearl God gave her. She did not expose it to mockery or herself to unnecessary danger. In the church we can feel a certain amount of pressure to share everything, especially if it comes from God: we are after all people of the Great Commission. But Jesus here gives us permission to keep some things close, to keep them holy, personal, secret, treasured in our hearts where they transform us but do not invite the attacks of others.

So maybe that is what Jesus was saying.

Maybe.

The truth is, I don't know.

And this leads me to my favorite interpretation of them all ...

The Reason God Hides Things

God hides things. This is a fact, and it's stated all throughout Scripture. He doesn't hide things maliciously or for our harm—it's more like he has built riddles into the universe. "It is the glory of God to conceal a matter, and the glory of kings to investigate a matter."[5]

When Jesus is hardest to understand, I often ask myself if he's riddling. And sometimes, I believe

---

4 Luke 2:19, NKJV
5 Proverbs 25:2

he is. Like here. I think the gist of this passage may be something quite different than the first impression: that it's Jesus saying, "This is why God hides things."

Don't expect pearls to be lying around in the mud. Don't expect holy things to be scattered in the gravel, out in the open, where they will be trampled, scorned, misunderstood, misheard. If you want to go deeper with God, if you want to understand and walk in greater things, you have to put in more effort than just strolling around checking out the ditches. God's most precious treasures are not lying on the sidewalk like a misplaced ten-dollar bill.

So the correct paragraphing, maybe, isn't, "Don't judge ... don't cast your pearls before swine." It's "Don't cast your pearls before swine ... Seek."

The first part may be a proverb, a statement of the way things obviously are that's meant to make us ask what treasures might exist for us if we go seeking.

"Seek," Jesus says in the very next verse, "and keep on seeking. Ask, and keep on asking. Knock, and keep on knocking."

There is more here, more treasure, more beautiful and sacred and precious things, than you can dream of.

So lift yourself out of the pigpen and come looking.

Living with the Maybes

My friend Mercy Hope compares two different approaches to truth as a "checklist approach" and a "journaling approach." She and I are fans of the journaling approach, not because we don't think you can learn anything with certainty (you can, and absolute truth is a real thing), but because there's always *more*. Because we never really understand when we think we do.

So taking an approach to learning and receiving from God that is always digging another layer, always asking another question, and always being willing to question assumptions, revisit conclusions, and sometimes be wrong is a powerful way of life.

I don't know what Jesus means in Matthew 7:6.

I've found digging to be fruitful: in this chapter, I've outlined multiple possible explanations, and they all challenge me in helpful ways. They are all true on some level. And yet, maybe none of them are really what Jesus was getting at. Maybe that's something I've yet to learn.

I am committed to asking, seeking, knocking, and constantly looking for the holy and the true. I believe it is there to be found and that God rewards the seeker.

That means being often unsure, and living in a lot of maybes.

And that's okay. It turns out, it's a good way to live.

Keep asking, and it will be given to you.
Keep searching, and you will find. Keep
knocking, and the door will
be opened to you.

(Matthew 7:7)

61

To Seek and Keep on Seeking: Jesus's Call to Continual Exploration

Matthew 7:7 describes a fundamental way of life. It is an approach to every aspect of existence that changes who we become.

It summons us to cultivate hunger, to be curious, to look, to ask, to act like a child who wants to know. To know what, to know where, to know who, to know why.

Jesus doesn't tell us what to ask for, what to seek, what doors to knock on. He just says *do it:* make your life about seeking.

I'm an insatiable learner. I love this verse because I can apply it, and easily. I love it because it validates my inner drive to learn.

Of the many open invitations in Scripture, this is one of my favorites.

It's a call not to get bored. A blow against complacency. It strikes at laziness and apathy and jadedness like the call of an older brother urging a younger, "Come on, let's go! There's so much more to see."

I love Jesus for this: he stirs up my sense of wonder and makes me excited about life again.

When I was nine years old I lived on the edge of a Canadian wilderness: the rocky, marshy, blueberried woods and hills of the Canadian Shield around Lakes Huron and Superior in northern Ontario. There were bears out there, and wolves too. There were loons and herons and frogs that croaked and chirped all night. Sometimes from our back deck we could hear the long, haunting song of a whip-poor-will. We lived on the edge of a pond, and beyond that was a railroad track and then acres and acres of forest.

I loved it.

There was so much to see. In every season, something new to explore. That was childhood to me: the great outdoors calling, hinting at magic like I read about in books, thousands of secrets.

Ask, seek, knock.

With age, boredom threatens to set in. We've seen it all a million times, so we stop seeing it. We have things to do, usually the same things over and over again, so we lose our curiosity and our energy and our desire to explore.

Get it back, Jesus says.

This is how we live.

■■■■■

In the landscape of modern Christianity this is one trend I protest: that we tend to come at doctrine and spiritual things as something to learn, then shut the textbook and get on with life.

We may even look suspiciously at any suggestion that we should instead treat the Bible, theology, and relationship with God as something to explore. That we should try to find answers that aren't obvious, that we should suspect some of our conclusions, that we should keep asking, seeking, and knocking even if thousands of years of history assure us we've already got all the answers.

To be clear: I do believe we have all the answers.

But I don't think we've explored them.

You may possess a gold mine. That doesn't mean you've extracted all the gold.

You may have a door. But have you walked through it?

A life calling to ask, seek, and knock is humbling. You can't do it without embracing humility, because to live this way is to embrace being a learner, a novice, a disciple. You have to embrace what Seth Godin calls "the feeling of stupid" ("Stupid is the emotion we associate with learning—we are stupid and then we are not."[1])

Asking means you don't know. Seeking means you haven't found. Knocking means you need someone else to open the door.

To live this way means to be always open-handed, empty-handed, ready and eager to receive. It's the opposite of coming in as the teacher, the guru, the one who knows everything and may or may not dole it out.

You may end up teaching a lot along the way. Learners make the best teachers, passing along what they've found to those who are just behind them on the path, learning from those who are just ahead, and cross-pollinating with those who are coming alongside.

---

[1] Seth Godin, *What to Do When It's Your Turn (And It's Always Your Turn)* (New York: The Domino Project, 2014)

But you should never trust a teacher who doesn't want to learn.

Ask, seek, knock. Make that the posture of your heart.

Live to receive. Come humble and hungry.

When you do, the world is here for you.

Keep asking, and it will be given to you.
Keep searching, and you will find.
Keep knocking, and the door will
be opened to you.

(Matthew 7:7)

62

The Prayer that Listens: How to Practice a Lifestyle of Ask, Seek, Knock

There are two basic ways to pray.

One is to come with a list. It may be prewritten, or you may make it up on the fly. But it's a list of things to say, to check off. Petitions to make. Praises to give.

I'm not bashing it. The Lord's Prayer is a list, at least at first. And I pray it, line by line just like Jesus gave it, with my own personal additions added in (*where* I want to see his kingdom come, *how* I hallow his name, *which* daily needs need meeting, *which* debts I am releasing or seeking release from).

But it's not the only way to pray.

The other way is more tentative. It's conversational, and it goes like this: Bring something before God. And then ask. Wait. Seek. Wait. Knock. Wait.

In the waiting, listen.

Look.

Expect God to speak.

Jesus, The Speaking of God

Some Christians believe God does not speak to individuals today. At least not in any way except directly through the Scriptures, interpreted with as much exegetical and hermeneutical soundness as possible. I don't agree. Although God *does* speak through the Scriptures, and the Scriptures should be approached soundly, to say that he does not speak in any other way misses something profound about God's nature and also about his purpose in saving us.

Jesus, we are told in John 1, is the *Logos*, a Greek term usually translated "Word" that could also be translated "the Speaking."

He is the voice of God, the continual message, the ever-speaking of the Father, through whom the world was created (and is sustained) and by whom we know the invisible God.

The New Testament leads us to expect the continued speaking of God, in every possible way. We as his people should expect to dream dreams, to see visions, to prophesy.[1] These are the signs that our

---

[1] Acts 2:17–18

community is filled with the Spirit. It is this seeing and hearing and speaking that are the proof of Jesus's enthronement in heaven and the inauguration of the New Covenant.

"If any man speaks," says Peter, "let him speak as the oracles of God."[2] The Greek word translated "oracles" here is *logia*, meaning "divine utterances." When the Holy Spirit comes, Jesus told us, "he will teach you all things."[3]

This in fact is the fulfillment of one of the Old Testament's ancient promises:

> "Look, the days are coming"—this is the LORD's declaration—"when I will make a new covenant with the house of Israel and with the house of Judah ... I will put My teaching within them and write it on their hearts. I will be their God, and they will be My people. No longer will one teach his neighbor or his brother, saying, 'Know the LORD,' for they will all know Me, from the least to the greatest of them"—this is the LORD's declaration. (Jeremiah 31:31, 33–34)

The word "know" in Jeremiah is a Hebrew word stressing personal, experiential knowledge. We, God's people, will know God in the way we know our closest friends, our spouses, our children.

---

2 1 Peter 4:11, KJV
3 John 14:26

All this to say: It would be very odd for God to make these promises, to declare these intentions, and then *not* speak.

If God Is Speaking, We Should Listen

This being the case, we should practice a prayer that listens.

Ask, wait. Seek, wait. Knock, wait.

In very practical terms: Come to Jesus with a Scripture. Read it. Ask, "Lord, what do you want me to see?"

And then listen.

When something comes to you—as it will, not always, but at times—ask again. You might "hear" a word, "see" a picture, feel an impression. I place "hear" and "see" in quotation marks because for me at least, these are not strongly visual or auditory experiences. It's more like something rises up into my consciousness.

And then I ask God about it.

"What does that mean? What do you want me to see?"

Much of the time what comes up is a word or phrase from a Scripture, so I'll look it up and read it and ask questions about that too, or just bask in it for a while.

Be willing to risk looking silly. Maybe some of the things you ask about won't have come from the Lord at all, and you're chasing wild geese, going down rabbit trails. That's okay. It's a hazard of exploration: sometimes you get lost.

As long as you've got a compass and a guide, you'll get back on track.

Be willing to wait a long time for the answers. Sometimes they are immediate. Sometimes you ask a question, and the answer drops into your spirit three or five or ten years later. Sometimes you ask a question, and it takes a lifetime of experience to reach understanding.

Would you ever have heard the answer, if you hadn't asked?

Jesus indicates probably not.

The Prayer that Listens

This sort of listening prayer is my favorite way to pray, even though I'm frequently distracted, sometimes I doze off, and more often than not, I come away not having "heard" a single thing.

It's a beautifully relaxing, gentle thing—listening. You can't force the answers. You can't hold hot irons to God's feet and make him talk. You just come believing he wants to talk to you, and receiving it when he does.

I usually try to pray my way through a cup of coffee. I just slowly drink a cup of coffee, and I spend the length of time it takes me to do it asking and listening, and following up anything that comes to mind.

I have learned incredible, amazing things by studying the Bible in depth. Everyone should do it.

But everyone should do this too. Everyone should practice prayer that listens.

For me, the most personal revelations, the most life-changing moments of "seeing," they've all come through this kind of asking, seeking, knocking prayer.

Keep asking, and it will be given to you.
Keep searching, and you will find.
Keep knocking, and the door will
be opened to you.

(Matthew 7:7)

63

You Can Hear from God: Listening Prayer and the Choice to Believe

We should always come to God in prayer with an ask-seek-knock kind of approach—with an expectation that God will speak, so we should listen.

When you try to do this, you will be challenged.

By distractibility. By frailty. Mostly by doubt.

Don't Doubt

In James 1:5–8, we are told:

> Now if any of you lacks wisdom, he should ask God, who gives to all generously and without criticizing, and it will be given to him. But let him ask in faith without doubting. For the doubter is like the surging sea, driven and tossed by the wind. That person should not expect to receive anything from the Lord. An indecisive man is unstable in all his ways.

I think this applies to all forms of hearing from the Lord.

Recently someone told me she was uncomfortable with my talk of "hearing from God," because in thirty-some years of being a Christian, she couldn't honestly say she had ever heard him say a thing.

I am deeply sympathetic to this, by the way. My life has not been one unending, blissful string of chatting with the Infinite.

But then she said something fascinating: "Sometimes I think I've heard from God, but then I doubt."

I realized the difference between us is not that I hear from God and she doesn't, but that *when we both hear from God,* I choose to receive and she chooses to doubt.

We always have the option. I have chosen to doubt many, many, many times.

It was making the opposite choice, and then continuing to make it, that turned things around for me.

Can you know with 100% absolute certainty that God has spoken to you? Can you know with ironclad confidence that you hear, see, sense, and receive directly from God?

No.

You can't.

Even if you had a vision, or were directly lifted

into heaven, you couldn't know with 100% absolute certainty that you weren't hallucinating.

For that matter, you can't know with 100% absolute certainty that you exist.

Just ask a philosopher.

But.

You Can Choose to Believe

You can still choose belief over doubt. It is rational and reasonable to do so. I'm not saying you shouldn't test (see 1 Thessalonians 5:19–21). I'm not saying you shouldn't ask for confirmation. You should always hold your impressions, the things you "hear," with humility. I wouldn't run out the door and marry the guy down the street because one time, I got an impression that maybe I should do that. We are told to test spirits, we can recognize our own fallibility in hearing, and we are allowed to be wise.

Even so: If I ask God to speak to me, and (for example) he tells me he loves me—a statement that lines up 100 percent with the Scriptures, with God's nature and character—I am not going to talk myself into believing I just made that up.

Not only *can* we choose to believe, we *must* do so if we want to grow in faith and genuine relationship with our Father.

A caveat is warranted here: the things God

speaks to us may not be the things we want to hear at first. To be frank, most of us are pagans at heart in the way we initially approach God. When we come to God, we want him to tell us the future, give us perfect insight into our circumstances or the events in the world around us, or give us some kind of control over others. At times, we come dangerously close to practicing divination in our approach to God, both in the questions we ask and in the way we try to get answers (through the interpretation of omens, for example). I am not at all saying that we should never ask God for insight or even foresight, but our expectations need to align with the revealed purposes of God's Spirit and his role in our lives. We should not expect God to give us a horoscope. We *should* expect him to reveal himself, and to reveal our own hearts to us.

When we listen, God will give us insight into the Scriptures and help us connect what we read to our own lives—most of all in helping us discern how to be faithful to him in any given circumstance. We should expect him to reveal more of his nature and character to us. We should expect him to reveal his love. We should expect that he will help us grow in trust and holiness. He will give us insight into ourselves, he will convict us, and he will encourage us and build us up. When you listen for God, come with the expectation that he will speak these things. And then believe him when he does.

Again, our choice to believe is not based on wishful thinking. It is based on the revelation of God given in Scripture: as a God who indwells his people, who teaches, who enlightens, who seeks out open ears, who speaks.

The Spirit of Revelation in the Knowledge of Him

Paul wrote to the new believers in Ephesus:

> I pray that the God of our Lord Jesus Christ, the glorious Father, would give you a spirit of wisdom and revelation in the knowledge of Him. I pray that the perception of your mind may be enlightened so you may know what is the hope of His calling, what are the glorious riches of His inheritance among the saints, and what is the immeasurable greatness of His power to us who believe, according to the working of His vast strength. (Ephesians 1:17–19)

An ask-seek-knock prayer life is a life that expects the Spirit of wisdom and revelation in the knowledge of God. It's a life that expects true enlightenment in the perception of our minds as we seek God.

It's a kind of prayer that expects to come away with eyes that see, with ears that hear, and with a heart that understands—not because we have discovered some foolproof way to figure things out, but because God is a God who speaks and who invites us to engage with him.

This is the prayer life I endeavor to have: one in which I listen more than I speak, and as I hear the voice of the Eternal Father, I grow closer to him and see him more clearly.

Keep asking, and it will be given to you.
Keep searching, and you will find.
Keep knocking, and the door will
be opened to you.

(Matthew 7:7)

64

How to Read the Bible
(The Ask, Seek, Knock Approach)

Asking, seeking, and knocking are a posture of the heart. They are an approach to all of life, especially spiritual life. This posture is characterized not just by openness and seeking, but also by tenacity. The Greek stresses continual action: *Keep* asking, *keep* seeking, *keep* knocking.

This is a powerful way to approach prayer. It is also the best way to approach the Scriptures.

There are two ways to come to the Scriptures: passively and actively.

A passive approach just reads, receives what is understood on the surface, or maybe listens to a teaching. (Sometimes this is a good way to come, even the best way. It's not all one or the other.) An active approach is more aggressive. It doesn't just read the Word, it engages with it. It wrestles like Jacob wrestling the Angel at the River Jabbok, the night before facing all of his greatest fears and the most soul-baring truths about himself.[1]

It asks, seeks, and knocks.

Basic Skills: Noticing and Asking Questions

The Bible isn't a magic book. God does speak directly to our hearts through it, but mostly, you learn from the Bible the same way you learn from any other book: you work at it.

You ask, seek, knock.

The first basic skill when it comes to learning anything is noticing.

You can do this many different ways. One helpful way to notice what you're reading is to paraphrase it back to yourself, in writing or out loud or just in your thoughts.

Try unpacking single words into multiple words that better explain them. Like, when you read "The Lord is my shepherd," you can unpack "shepherd" into whatever components you know about shepherds: protector, caretaker, leader, owner, affectionate friend.

(If you're not so much a words person, you can also try noticing in other ways: draw what you're reading; put it to a tune and sing it.)

It doesn't matter that you don't know every-

---
[1] See Genesis 32.

thing, or that some of your assumptions might be wrong. The process of paraphrasing and unpacking will help you discover what you do know and what you don't, and it will suggest questions and things to dig into more deeply.

You can notice in other ways too, like by noticing allusions—where one Scripture or word or story reminds you of another Scripture or word or story, which you can then compare and contrast.

Or by noticing the way a Scripture impacts you, how it makes you feel, how it connects to the events of your life or the world around you.

We bring our own experience to the Bible.

This is not a bad thing, but it's good to recognize that we're doing it so we can get outside of our experience too. It's just another way that we come to greater understanding, of Scripture and of ourselves and also of the ways in which God's truths transcend time and culture.

Exegesis: Facts on the Table

All that said, if we really want to understand the Bible and avoid undue confusion, we need to be careful not to go transcending time and culture too quickly.

A lot of understanding comes from doing *exegesis,* which is a big word for "understanding what the text meant in its original context."

Now, let's be honest. There is a limit to how well we can do this, separated as we are by thousands of years from the cultures, languages, and events in which the original writers wrote. But even so, asking the question "What did this mean to the people who originally read it?" will get us a long way toward better understanding complex issues.

For example: in the famous story of John 4, where Jesus meets the woman at the well, we'll get more understanding of their conversation's impact if we understand that in times long past, a woman who had been married five times would be subject to a whole lot more social alienation than she would be now. We get even more understanding if we recognize that men didn't usually talk to women in a public social setting like a well, and that Jews and Samaritans of the time were ethnic and political and religious enemies.

The Bible tells us some of this and hints at other parts of it. Doing the work of exegesis just means that before we jump into asking "What do Jesus's words here mean to *me*?", we ask what they meant to the woman.

The understanding we get from asking that question will lead us to more water for our own souls.

Before we start interpreting for ourselves, we get the basic facts on the table. We notice what's said, how it's said, its context, its original meaning as far as we can tell.

This, by the way, is where word studies and original languages become important too. Translations are limited by nature: many words do not have a one-to-one correspondent in any other language, so even the best English or Spanish or German or Hindi or Chinese Bible will lose something from the original.

Using concordances and Bible dictionaries to dig into the nuances of Greek and Hebrew can really help us get our facts laid out.

Hermeneutics: Interpreting and Applying

That leads us to *hermeneutics,* another big word that basically just means "interpretation." We're in hermeneutical waters when we start asking how a Scripture given thousands of years ago applies to us—what a proper method of interpreting it might be.

For example, Paul writes extensively about how believers should deal with the matter of meat sacrificed to idols, which they could pick up fairly cheaply in the local markets. Should they eat it or not eat it?

It's a tricky moral question, but not one most of us will ever have to deal with ... until we start asking how to interpret and apply the underlying principles in our own lives.

In our own contexts, with our own idols, and our own tricky moral questions.

Bible Study Is Hard Work

If all this sounds like hard work, well, it is. Which is wonderful, because if it wasn't, we would quickly become bored with the written Word of God.

As it is, the Scriptures are rich and layered and powerful and inexhaustible, and they require us to work hard in the same way all rewarding things require us to work hard.

Climb a mountain, raise a child, get a PhD, read the Bible.

Worthwhile things are not easy, but they give the greatest rewards possible in life.

At the same time, the Bible isn't complicated.

Even a child can understand its truths.

Simple, but difficult. Hard, but rewarding. Infinitely complex and immediately accessible.

One tiny insight can change your life. You don't have to figure it all out.

Beyond Five-Minute Devotions

If you can only give five or ten or fifteen minutes to the Scriptures each day, give that time and know that God will meet you there.

But:

I encourage everyone to take Bible study seriously. Put in the work, the time.

Go to school, so to speak, and get an education in the words inspired by God. Get to know the Bible and its riches for yourself.

You will have to ask, seek, and knock, and it will take your whole life.

But it's worth it.

Keep asking, and it will be given to you.
Keep searching, and you will find.
Keep knocking, and the door will
be opened to you.

(Matthew 7:7)

65

What If We Are Not Entitled? Asking, Seeking, and Knocking in Community

What if we are not entitled?

What if we don't assume that anyone owes us anything, but in everything, we recognize that we have tremendous power through the simple act of asking?

Of seeking.

Of searching things, people, relationships, and understanding out.

Of knocking on doors and seeing who opens.

Relational Courage

It takes courage and humility to approach relationships this way.

Think immediate: The people closest to you. The ones who live in the next room, or on the other side of the bed. The people you always sit next to at church.

Think local. The barista at Starbucks. Your neighbors. The nice lady at the grocery store. The homeless man on the corner.

Think global. The Muslim from Pakistan. The church in Mexico you occasionally visit. The Japanese businessman you're flying out to see.

Not one of them owes you a thing.

Every one of them represents possibility: in relationship, in personal growth, in understanding.

In love.

But we will not realize any of that by accident.

We must be courageous and humble, and we must ask, seek, and knock.

Like People, Like God

Most of us understand, I think, that relationships will not give back to us if we don't invest in them. That we can't be purely selfish in any relationship and have it turn out well.

We understand innately that selfishness isn't the path to happiness, and neither is fear. The path to happiness, connection, community, and love are all the same: it's the path of seeking, risking, and investing ourselves.

In a weird way, though, we understand this when it comes to people but not when it comes to God.

We can be surprised, even affronted, to discover that relationship with God will take work, and that while we can count on his grace, his faithfulness, and his unconditional love, he doesn't owe us a thing.

If we want to know the richness of this relationship, we must come with courage and humility and give of ourselves.

Our time.

Our vulnerability.

Our efforts.

Sometimes our confused and hurt forgiveness.

(Yes, sometimes you have to forgive God. No, he isn't guilty, but your heart may not understand that. So forgive to move forward.)

What Does Not Work

What does not work in relationship is pride.

Refusal to ask. Refusal to seek. Refusal to knock.

Refusal to be dependent on anyone, to need somebody to respond to you. To put yourself out on a limb where you might be rejected.

(Or is that last one fear? Pride and fear may be more closely linked than we realize.)

We are afraid of people and afraid of God. We are afraid to give of ourselves. We are afraid of suffering.

Jesus invites you to overcome fear by embracing suffering. Die to yourself to find yourself. Take up your cross and follow him.

When we accept that some things will hurt us and that's okay, we can go through life without being controlled by fear, and we can overcome pride and walk in humility.

It takes humility to turn the other cheek.

The same humility it takes to be loved.

When Was the Last Time?

When was the last time you intentionally made yourself vulnerable to someone else? To God, or to another person?

When was the last time you turned the other cheek?

When was the last time you let curiosity, care, and connection lead?

Entitlement hurts us and others.

But *asking,* in a way that risks rejection and dares making us look foolish, will open doors.

When was the last time you made a friend?

When was the last time you were real with God?

A Way of Life

Asking, seeking, and knocking are a way of life. They will shape our approach to life, to learning, to prayer, to the Scriptures, to other people, to ourselves, and to God himself.

I love that Jesus doesn't tell us, in Matthew 7:7, *what* we are supposed to seek. It's open. Seek whatever you want to find. Ask whatever you want to know. Knock on any door you want to see opened.

Come at life actively, making choices, searching things out.

There are times to be passive, but if we do that all the time, we are probably dead.

God invites us into an adventure. He urges us to come exploring. To take initiative. To start things.

This is a way of humility and of risk, and it turns out, it's what freedom and joy really look like.

For everyone who asks receives, and the one who searches finds, and to the one who knocks, the door will be opened.

(Matthew 7:8)

66

Seeking and Finding: The Reason to Look, Ask, and Knock Is to Find

In Buddhist philosophy, desire is the cause of all pain. Since all is ultimately illusion, desire is futile. It is a meaningless yearning after nothing, and so it hurts us. To be enlightened, free, is to be freed from desire—to let go of the illusions entirely, become fully unattached, and therefore suffer no pain.

Christianity is different.

Christianity validates desire. It says we are right to desire, we are right to feel restless, we are right to be, in a sense, discontent.

These things are pointing us to truths about reality that are very different from an Eastern "all is illusion" kind of conclusion.

In Christianity, desire points us to the truth of our alienation from God, for whom we were originally created. It points us to the brokenness of the world, which was originally created to be perfect, to be paradise. It points us to the harmony and love we were intended to enjoy in human society.

And it points us to the hope of full restoration and redemption in Jesus Christ, a redemption we now know only partially until the day of resurrection comes and all is made new.

This role of desire is so central to Christianity that for many centuries, Christians have used it as an apologetics defense for the faith: our own souls bear witness to the truth. They signpost the way to heaven.[1]

Orientation and Promise

Jesus's command to ask, seek, and knock is a fundamental orientation toward life. It tells us how to approach the world and how to go through life: with our hands and hearts open, curious, eager to know more, to discover and enjoy.

But that orientation would ultimately only be a cruel trick if we could not find what we seek. In the end it would weary us, exhaust us body and soul, and leave us hungrier than we were when we began.

It's Jesus's next phrase, the promise attached to the command, that gives us the encouragement

---

[1] Thanks to Alister McGrath in A Brief History of Heaven for the wording here.

we need. He promises that if we seek, it won't be in vain.

Ask, for everyone who asks receives.

Seek, for those who seek find.

Knock, for to the one who knocks, the door will be opened.

The inverse is also true. He who never asks does not receive much. He who doesn't look won't find. He who doesn't bother to knock will never get inside.

Raising My Expectations

I find I am sometimes better at seeking than I am at believing there will be something, in the end, to find. Some of it's my personality, some is my life experience, but I tend to expect a long and sometimes arduous, sometimes exciting journey, but not necessarily a real reward at the end.

Jesus rebukes my lack of faith and tells me I'm wrong in this: that my low expectations do not do God justice. Our God has not set us on a hunt without reason and reward.

Nearly three thousand years ago, Solomon set himself to discover the secrets of the universe and concluded that all is vain, "vanity of vanities," empty and meaningless, because all ends in death.

Jesus, who comes to bring life everlasting, to restore to us what was lost, tells us the end of the search is no longer vanity. It is *finding what we're looking for.*

And as part of that: what we seek will, to some degree, determine what we find.

So the Questions Are ...

What are you seeking?

What are you asking for, that you don't already have?

What door are you knocking on, that has never been opened to you before?

You have Jesus's promise: it won't be in vain.

Your desires are pointing to something greater. The mysteries are there for you to find.

So seek.

What man among you, if his son asks him for bread, will give him a stone? Or if he asks for a fish, will give him a snake? If you then, who are evil, know how to give good gifts to your children, how much more will your Father in heaven give good things to those who ask Him!

(Matthew 7:9–11)

67

Is God Good?:
The Challenge of Faith in a World at War

With these words, Jesus forces us to reckon with our deepest false beliefs and the places we are wrong about God.

We've looked at Jesus's call to ask, seek, and knock in our relationship to God and to life generally.

But the thing about asking, seeking, and knocking is, it takes faith. Hebrews says it too: "He who comes to God must believe that He is, and that He is a rewarder of those who diligently seek Him." [1]

It takes a special kind of verve, a hope and courage, to keep coming when the answers aren't readily available, or when we meet resistance.

Which we will, always. The nature of this broken world is that it resists our attempts to break through to goodness and truth.

---
[1] Hebrews 11:6, NKJV

But most of us assume it's not the broken world, nor the enemy, resisting us, but God himself. Jesus is telling us we are wrong about that.

Checking Our Belief System

A few years ago I was undergoing one of the most difficult and painful seasons of my life. I was hurting so badly I couldn't see straight, but I kept trying to "submit" to God in this process, as though he was the cause of it.

For me the turnaround began when I heard him clearly say something into my spirit—this in a time when I had not been able to hear him say anything for months, though I begged him to speak.

Here is what I heard:

"Stop calling Me a thief."

Before that moment, I couldn't really draw close to God, because I believed he was the one inflicting this pain. I tried and tried to humble myself and surrender "to him," when all the time he was trying to draw near to me and fortify me against the attacks of the enemy.

It wasn't God hurting me. It was people, and it was spiritual powers in high places.

> The thief comes to steal, to kill, and to destroy, but I have come that they may have

life, and have it more abundantly. (John 10:10)

We live in a world of free agents. They can act, and they do. To blame everything they do on the master planning of God himself is to accuse God of heinous things.

Think about the implications of Jesus's words in this passage! Human beings are "evil," corrupt, and yet *even they* would not treat their children *the way we think God treats his*.

I didn't say this. Jesus did.

If we believe these things about God, it's no wonder if we don't seek him. It's no wonder we find it hard to run to him, to ask him for help, to dream big dreams with him. Instead of believing that God is good, we make him the author of evil, and then try to somehow justify that in our minds. I'm not going to name theological streams or leaders that have propagated this thinking. They're everywhere; it's not one group that's guilty. It's our humanity. It's our bitterness, disappointment, pain, and suffering trying to make sense out of itself and revise God's promises to fit our experience.

Because that's easier than saying God doesn't keep his promises.

Here's the thing, beloved: God does keep his promises. He is good. He gives out bread and fish and the Holy Spirit to those who ask him.

Yes, he does discipline his children, in the way that good fathers do, with patience and restraint and kindness and companionship. And yes, he does use the works of the enemy to glorify us and turn the enemy's own work back on him.

But that isn't the same as saying he causes all of the evil that comes into our lives, or that he resists and shames us for wanting and needing things from him. He is not an abusive father, nor does he withhold from his children.

The Central Challenge of Faith

The New Testament tells us that we are at war. We have a real enemy who hates us and is waging real warfare in an attempt to steal, kill, and destroy.

As people who live on the battlefield and in fact have a role to play in the outcome, we should not be surprised when we face hardship.[2] Moreover, in the battle we have the promise that God will be with us, suffer alongside us, cause us to shine with his glory, and work everything that happens to our ultimate good.

What the enemy brings into our lives to crush us, God will use to make us into gold.

Here's the central challenge of faith, then: to

---

[2] 1 Peter 4:12, Ephesians 6:11–13, Revelation 12:9–17

hang onto the conviction that God is good, that he is our loving Father, and that he has not lost control even when the battle is fiery. To hang onto his love, his goodness, and his everlasting mercy in times when we've got smoke in our eyes.

In the midst of the battle, the goodness of God is our hope and our salvation. After the battle, it's our victory cry.

If we forget that God is good, if we conflate him with the enemy and give up on expecting the best from him, we will lose something precious in this fight. We will lose intimacy with our Father and the childlike trust that sets us free and gives us full access to him.

But if we can believe, with Jesus, that God is a good Father with hands full of bread and fish and good gifts and the Holy Spirit, then we can keep coming, even when the fight is at its most intense.

Therefore, whatever you want others to do for you, do also the same for them—this is the law and the Prophets.

(Matthew 7:12)

68

The Golden Rule and the Glory of Being Good

This verse may be the best-known in the entire Bible. It's been incorporated so fully into our culture as the Golden Rule that I don't think most people even realize where it comes from—that Jesus said it. And that he based it on a surprising foundation.

Why should we keep the Golden Rule?

If you answered "because it sums up the law," you're right and wrong. It does, and Jesus makes that point. But *first,* he grounds his statement in the goodness of God:

> What man among you, if his son asks him for bread, will give him a stone? Or if he asks for a fish, will give him a snake? If you then, who are evil, know how to give good gifts to your children, how much more will your Father in heaven give good things to those who ask Him! (Matthew 7:9–11)

God is good, *so* we should treat each other the way we want to be treated. In other words, because God is good, we should be good too.

This is a glorious calling.

What Does It Mean to "Be Good"?

Few phrases have suffered as much violence in English as "be good." Even if you want to be good, it sounds like a rebuke. It also sounds like it won't be fun.

That couldn't be more wrong. A command to "be good" is a command to overflow, to be generous and gracious and giving, to be fruitful in all the best ways.

That is glorious, and it's a lot of fun. If we all did it, it would change the world.

God the Benefactor

At base, the word *good* doesn't mean quite the same thing as *moral* or *righteous*. Actually, *generous* is a closer match. The Greek word *agathos* ("good") means that which brings forth a benefit. The Bible applies it to fruitful trees and abundant ground (a good tree brings forth good fruit; good ground produces a full harvest). In both Greek and English, the plural noun form can refer to riches ("goods"). The word is a primary characteristic of God ("God is good").

Just as it does here in Matthew, when the Bible speaks of God's goodness it doesn't so much speak of God as moral in some abstract way, but of God as *giving,* as a source of life and benefit to all, even his enemies.

Psalm 103 famously exults:

> My soul, praise the LORD,
> and do not forget all His benefits.
> He forgives all your sin;
> He heals all your diseases.
> He redeems your life from the Pit;
> He crowns you with faithful love and compassion.
> He satisfies you with goodness;
> your youth is renewed like the eagle.
> (Psalm 103:2–5)

To say that God is good is to say that he is a benefactor. He is the kind of person who is constantly bringing benefit to those who know him. He's an opener of doors, a giver of resources, a networker of relationships, and a spreader of good cheer.

Many of us harbor "rich uncle" daydreams: one day we'll have a benefactor who changes everything for us in an instant through his riches and his unexpected generosity and favoritism toward us.

Turns out, that's God.

We Are Supposed to Be Good

God is good. We are supposed to be good too. That's what the Golden Rule, Matthew 7:12, tells us. But we tend to take the Golden Rule in its negative sense only. "Do unto others as you would have them do unto you" gets understand as *"Don't* do things you wouldn't want others to do to you."

But should we really limit how we want to be treated to this kind of "do no harm" mentality?

Or, when we're allowed to dream, would we like to be treated with grace and favor—in an outrageous, generous, joyful, and love-filled way?

What if we took the Golden Rule in its positive sense? What if we made an effort to do for others what we'd like—in our wildest dreams—others to do for us?

Jesus is pretty blunt that when it comes to goodness, our habits of giving our children bread and fish (instead of stones and snakes) don't even qualify us as "good." We are still "evil." *God's* goodness is so far beyond this as not to compare. "How much *more* will your Father in heaven give good things to those who ask Him!"[1]

What If We Were Good?

How would it affect our world if we chose to be

---

[1] Matthew 7:11

more like God in how we behave toward others?

What if we became benefactors, people who spread light, love, and life on a very different scale than the culture around us?

What if we became promoters, encouragers, givers, edifiers, mentors, friends, and lovers in the truest sense?

What if we flung grace wildly in every direction, not keeping track of who owes us what—just giving for the joy of giving?

I have argued that rather than believe God is good, we have tended throughout history to invent ways of redefining "good" so we can keep believing God is evil. When we do this, some of what we're doing is making God in our own image. Let's instead do the work of submitting ourselves to the Spirit so we can be remade in his.

If we do, we will give the world a far more accurate picture of who God is.

Enter through the narrow gate. For the gate is wide and the road is broad that leads to destruction, and there are many who go through it. How narrow is the gate and difficult the road that leads to life, and few find it.

(Matthew 7:13–14)

69

Enter through the Narrow Gate: The Hidden Way into the Kingdom

In 1678, an English Puritan named John Bunyan wrote *The Pilgrim's Progress from This World, to That Which Is to Come*, better known simply as *Pilgrim's Progress*. In 1985 Eerdmans released an illustrated version called *Dangerous Journey*, and this book with its wonderful and terrifying illustrations informed my view of the narrow road.

I think, for example, of the protagonist, Christian, making his way along the narrow road as it passes through the Valley of the Shadow of Death. In the illustration, the road is a winding, crumbling ledge, only wide enough to put one foot in front of the other, with a sharp drop-off on either side. To the left is a deep abyss, dark as pitch. To the right are the fires of hell, leaping and crackling in the air. Christian is edging his way forward with a drawn sword in his hand, every muscle taut as he tries to keep his footing and not fall into destruction.

In another illustration, Christian is approaching a place of refuge called the House Beautiful. In this case, the narrow road is marked out by a single, narrow beam of light shining from the front doors, where the doorkeeper awaits to welcome him. But before he can reach the doors, he must pass between two fierce, frothing, yellow-eyed lions, who are chained on either side of the path. They are so close that as they strain forward to tear Christian to pieces, their claws come within a mere breath of catching him. As long as he stays on the path of light, however, he will be safe.

As you can imagine, these illustrations depict one heck of a narrow road. One wrong step in either direction, and you are toast.

It wasn't until one afternoon at Disney World, of all places, that I realized I'd gotten it wrong. Alan Parry's paintings do a wonderful job of illustrating John Bunyan. But they don't really capture what Jesus's "narrow way" was meant to invoke.

Going through the Narrow Gate

Disney's Epcot theme park is divided into two sections, one of which, called the World Showcase, features pavilions from eleven different nations. Of these, the Morocco pavilion is unique in that the government of Morocco actually helped design it: King Hassan II sent artisans to create the pavilion's tile mosaics.

And, like any self-respecting ancient city, Morocco has a gate. Or rather, gates.

In the city wall, between two towers, a wide, welcoming gate stands front and center. It is easily thirty feet tall and fifteen wide, forming a broad passageway through the six-foot-thick wall.[1] This gate is designed for a wide flow of traffic. Everybody goes through that door, because it's prominent and inviting. If this were actually Morocco, or someplace else in the biblical world, the gate would be even bigger, and whole caravans would be able to go through it. Horses, donkeys, camels, wagons, carts, processions, armies.

In fact, if you were part of a caravan or a procession, or just one of the crowd on market day, you could go through that door without even really being intentional about it. You just have to let the flow of traffic sweep you along.

It's a wide gate.

But as I looked close, I noticed something else: on either side of that wide gate are two smaller, narrower ones—perhaps a third of the wide gate's height and only a quarter of its width. And off to the left, not at all fancy and really barely noticeable, there's a door ... just big enough for one person to get through.

That, my friends, is a narrow gate.

---

[1] My powers of estimation are notoriously poor. In no way should these be taken as real measurements. But they'll give you the right visual.

It's not designed for big caravans. It's not built for go-with-the-flow traffic. It's built for one person at a time. It's there for security and to let approved personnel in and out. Most people wouldn't even notice it.

In ancient castles and fortresses, this sort of narrow passage is a tight squeeze. Again, this isn't supposed to be a wide entry point.

And actually, that's what Jesus's words are referring to.

Tight Passages:
The Greek Behind the Narrow Way

If you'll indulge me a little Greek for a moment: Jesus said narrow (stenos, narrow or straight; tight) is the gate and difficult (*thlibo,* literally pressing, constricting, or confining) is the way, and few there be that *find* it.

In the pictures I grew up with, I always saw the narrow path as a road winding through wide open spaces, where a step off would lead to disaster. The trick was keeping your feet on this difficult path when you might lose your balance and go careening off at any moment.

And this is often how we talk about it. We picture the Christian life as a narrow path that is incredibly difficult to stay on, because at any time temptation or confusion might cause us to misstep.

We read "Narrow is the gate and difficult the way that leads to life, and few there are who can stay on it without losing their balance."

But the reality is quite different. The picture Jesus gave was that of a small, almost hidden door, and when you go through it, the passageway is tight—too tight to bring anything extra with you, too tight to admit more than one person at a time. You have to squeeze through it. For a moment it feels like the walls are closing in.

Lest you think I'm putting too much stress on a theme park, I'd encourage you to look up an image of the Bab Bou Jeloud, the actual gate in Morocco that inspired the Disney version. Once again you'll see it: a wide, central gate; two smaller gates on each side; and far off to one side, barely noticeable, a tiny door in the wall.

If you look at old fortresses, you'll always see these narrow gates. They make lots of sense: there had to be a way to let watchmen or guards or emissaries in and out without opening the broad gate for the whole world to come through.

The danger Jesus points out isn't that few people will have the balance and fortitude to stay on the path, it's that *few people will ever find it in the first place.* It's a narrow gate with a tight passage through. In crowded streets it may be almost impossible to see.

Not many ever find it.

The Hidden Way of Jesus

In Jesus's day, the people of Israel were waiting for the Messiah to come, overthrow the powers of Rome, and set up a throne in Jerusalem. They expected his coming to be obvious and political. No one could possibly miss it.

They expected a wide gate and a broad way.

Instead, Jesus came in a hidden way, a mysterious way. He *did* overthrow the powers of Rome. In fact, he overthrew all the dark powers of all evil empires, from that time forward. He did set up a throne. In fact, he sat down at the right hand of God.

The kingdom came.

But the door to life, the door to the kingdom, wasn't wide and broad after all. It was narrow, and tight, and not many people even noticed it was there.

That was in Jesus's time. In our time, it's not really much different. Anybody can (and most people do) go with the flow. We just get caught up in the crowd and sweep through whatever doors everybody else is going through.

To get into the kingdom, we have to unload our baggage, step out of the crowd, go in alone. It's tight and dark and hard to see, and we have to press our way inside, on faith, believing this is the right way to go and that we will be treated as authorized personnel, allowed to be here.

Surprise surprise, we find something unexpected on the other side of this tight, compressing fit: we find *life*.

GOING THROUGH THE DOOR

I'm convinced that as tight as the passage to life may feel, when you get through, the world on the other side is unimaginably expansive. It's a little (or a lot) like going through the wardrobe to Narnia. "He brought me out to a spacious place; He rescued me because He delighted in me."[2]

In spiritual terms, this makes good sense. On the one hand, faith in Jesus is narrow and constricting; on the other hand, it places us into the body of the Lord of the universe.

Obedience to Jesus's commands is much like this too. The need to forgive may make you feel like the walls are closing in, but on the other side of forgiveness is freedom. Loving one's enemies is incredibly hard, so difficult it may make you feel like you can't breathe—until you've broken through. Once you're through the passage, the other side is open and beautiful.

The door is open. The way is passable, though not easy. Each one of us is invited to go through—but we have to look closely, divest ourselves of anything that would prevent us from entering in, and push through.

---
2 Psalm 18:19

Beware of false prophets who come to you in sheep's clothing but inwardly are ravaging wolves. You'll recognize them by their fruit. Are grapes gathered from thorn bushes or figs from thistles? In the same way, every good tree produces good fruit, but a bad tree produces bad fruit. A good tree can't produce bad fruit; neither can a bad tree produce good fruit. Every tree that doesn't produce good fruit is cut down and thrown into the fire. So you'll recognize them by their fruit.

(Matthew 7:15–20)

70

Fruit, Sheep, and False Prophets: A Primer on Learning to Discern

For Jesus's early followers, this warning had an especially urgent character. Jesus was born at the close of a long window of time in which there had been a "famine of the word of the LORD."[1] After the era of the judges, kings, and prophets, no new major prophetic voice arose in Israel.

So it came like a thunderbolt out of the blue when Zacharias, the father of John the Baptist, encountered an angel in the temple who prophesied the birth of a son. It broke four hundred years of near silence when "the word of God came to John in the wilderness"[2] and he began to declare the kingdom of God. And it turned the world upside down when Jesus was born and declared to be not merely another prophet, but the long-awaited Messiah, the Son of God.

---

1 Amos 8:11
2 Luke 3:2

Thunderbolts invite irony. Jesus and John were both accused of being false prophets. And right on their heels came an outpouring of prophecy, a tidal wave of words from the Lord.

Some of it true.

Some of it false.

The need to tell the difference was suddenly urgent.

High-Stakes Heralds

Stakes were high in the first century. Under the oppression of Rome, Israel was aware that they were living in the era of Daniel's "fourth beast"—which meant the coming of the Messiah, the Son of Man who would receive the kingdom of God and give it to the saints forever, was imminent.[3] Messiah claimants were beginning to crop up from multiple quarters. Various religious groups and sects were claiming the status of "God's special people" for themselves, from the isolationist Essenes at Qumran to the legalistic Pharisees.

It was fairly clear to pretty much everyone that just being Jewish wasn't enough. You had to figure out who the real people of God were, the insiders with the correct claims and the true line to God's favour and support. On top of that, the Old Testament pattern gave a clear warning: wherever and

---
[3] Daniel 7:19–27

whenever God summoned his people, false prophets would try to draw them away.

What Is a False Prophet?

In the simplest terms, a false prophet is someone who claims to speak for God but does not. It's important to note that "prophecy" is not merely (or even primarily) future oriented. It is any claim to speak on God's behalf, to extemporaneously express what God is saying.

In the Old Testament, prophecy was limited to a few special individuals, but in the church, it's a different story. Prophecy is a prominent spiritual gift given to the church, open to everyone, and we are told to "eagerly desire" and pursue it.[4] The gift of prophecy is one of the clearest marks of God's New Covenant people.

But this makes things a little trickier than they may initially seem. In the context of prophetic words given to the church, by the church, 1 Thessalonians 5:20–22 tells us to test and discern all things and reject what is evil while holding on to what is good. At times a true prophet may be in error (this was true even in the Old Testament—see 1 Kings 13 or Numbers 20 for example). True prophets are still sinners and fallible human beings.

The confrontation between Paul and Peter is a

---

[4] 1 Corinthians 14:1, Acts 2:17–18

good example of this. Peter had a significant prophetic role in the church, but when he failed to live up to the gospel, Paul called him out as a hypocrite—but not as a false prophet (see Galatians 2:11–14). Apollos in Acts 18 preached an incomplete gospel in Ephesus, but rather than being treated as a false prophet, he was taken under wing and mentored by Paul and his companions Priscilla and Aquila.

So we can't simply denounce everyone who is ever wrong as a false prophet. Jesus's talk of "fruit" hints at something like this. Fruit isn't bad because it's immature, and a tree isn't bad because the occasional apple has a worm in it. In discernment, we need to look at a bigger picture.

Thistles and Thorns

Just as a true prophet may sometimes speak in error or do something sinful, so a false prophet may actually speak true things or even give true predictions. In fact, the ability of false prophets to "do signs and wonders" (including accurately predicting events) is one of the reasons they are so dangerous.

Again, this phenomenon was addressed in the Old Testament, along with the reason God allows it:

> If a prophet or someone who has dreams arises among you and proclaims a sign or wonder to you, and that sign or wonder he

has promised you comes about, but he says, "Let us follow other gods," which you have not known, "and let us worship them," do not listen to that prophet's words or to that dreamer. For the LORD your God is testing you to know whether you love the LORD your God with all your heart and all your soul. You must follow the LORD your God and fear Him. You must keep His commands and listen to His voice; you must worship Him and remain faithful to Him. That prophet or dreamer must be put to death, because he has urged rebellion against the LORD your God who brought you out of the land of Egypt and redeemed you from the place of slavery, to turn you from the way the LORD your God has commanded you to walk. You must purge the evil from you. (Deuteronomy 13:1–5)

So the real test of a true or false prophet is not whether the prophet is sometimes right in what he says. It is whether he (or she) leads people into loyalty to God or not. In the New Covenant era this will specifically mean loyalty to God *in Christ*. In an interesting twist, Paul treated the Christian "Judaizers," who taught loyalty to God by means of the Old Covenant in a way that minimized the role of Christ, as false prophets and ravaging wolves in the church.[5]

---
[5] Acts 20:29, Galatians 5:7–12

A false prophet leads the people away from loyalty to God in Christ and toward loyalty to idols or false gods. False prophets are not (usually, anyway) just misguided true believers with idiosyncratic understandings of a few doctrines. A false prophet claims to belong to the flock but does not. The false prophet is not just deluded; he is a deceiver and a wolf, and he has come to bring destruction and scatter God's sheep. Elsewhere Jesus connects "wolves" to the work of the devil.[6]

Interestingly, in Matthew the false prophet doesn't just bring forth sour or bitter fruit, he brings forth thorns and thistles. I think Jesus is deliberately referring to the original curse on creation, where Adam, who had listened to the deceiving voice of the serpent, is told that from now on his labor will bring forth thorns and thistles in the world outside the garden and away from the presence of God.[7] We who are part of the new creation are back in relationship with God, and our labor should bring forth good—not harmful or poisonous—fruit.

Pray that You May Discern

In a world where true and false matter so deeply, it's essential that we learn to discern. But how?

---

[6] John 10:12
[7] Genesis 3:18

First, we need to become mature in the Word of God and in the spiritual life.[8] Maturity is essential, and it plays into this discussion in two ways.

First, those who claim to speak prophetically can't always be judged immediately. Fruit may need to come to maturity before it can be judged as good or bad. At times it's necessary to watch and wait.

Second, we ourselves need maturity in order to discern properly! We are not necessarily good judges of "good" and "bad." The immature are particularly susceptible to being led astray by false prophets because they cannot necessarily discern between good and bad fruit. The writer of Hebrews puts this problem in strong terms:

> Although by this time you ought to be teachers, you need someone to teach you the basic principles of God's revelation again. You need milk, not solid food. Now everyone who lives on milk is inexperienced with the message about righteousness, because he is an infant. But solid food is for the mature—for those whose senses have been trained to distinguish between good and evil. (Hebrews 5:12–14)

A deep and intimate knowledge of Scripture is a major help in discernment. So is the input of ma-

---

[8] 1 Corinthians 2, 3:1–4; 2 Corinthians 5:16

ture believers. Discernment is also a spiritual gift, given by the Holy Spirit. We should ask for it and be intentional about sharpening it. The more we live and walk "by the Spirit" and not "by the flesh,"[9] the sharper our discernment will become, as we will be able to distinguish between the works of the flesh and the works of the Spirit more clearly.

It's also important to notice that we will *lose* discernment if we allow idols in our lives. Throughout the Old Testament, those who worship idols are said to have eyes but be unable to see; to have ears but be unable to hear; to have mouths but be unable to speak.[10] If our discernment is dull, we may need to surrender our idols and ask God to purify us from their effect and revitalize our senses.

In the end, the litmus test is this: Does this person lead others to loyal devotion to God in Christ? Or do they lead them into apostasy and idolatry? Are they growing food, or are they growing thistles?

By this, ultimately, we will know them.

---

9 Romans 8:4–9
10 Psalm 115:4–8

Not everyone who says to Me, "Lord, Lord!" will enter the kingdom of heaven, but only the one who does the will of My Father in heaven. On that day many will say to Me, "Lord, Lord, didn't we prophesy in Your name, drive out demons in Your name, and do many miracles in Your name?" Then I will announce to them, "I never knew you! Depart from Me, you who work lawlessness."[1]

(Matthew 7:21–23)

---

[1] The main text of the HCSB renders this last phrase "Depart from Me, you lawbreakers." I have used the literal text in the HCSB footnote, "You who work lawlessness," because I believe there is a difference between one who is guilty of breaking a law and one who is actually lawless.

71

Beyond "Lord, Lord": Where Reformations Go Wrong and How We Can Enter the Kingdom

I'm not sure there's a thoughtful Christian alive who hasn't found these words of Jesus a little frightening. Didn't Paul assure us that if we believe with our hearts and confess with our mouths "Jesus is Lord," we will be saved?[1]

Most of us hang our hope of heaven on exactly this declaration of "Lord, Lord."

So is Jesus telling us we can't rely on faith after all? That "getting in" will turn out to be all about our works?

This is an understandable question. But I think it reflects a false division in most of our minds between "faith" and "works," where these two things are different and often directly opposed to each other. Within a biblical framework, that's not the case at all.

---
1 Romans 10:9

Keep in mind that this passage comes directly after Jesus's warning against false prophets, with its very common-sense criteria for identifying them: what kind of fruit are they bearing?

Here, he continues with much the same thought. Jesus isn't trying to scare true believers. He's pointing out that true belief isn't about lip service, and it never has been. True belief has always manifested in obedient action—if we really believe something, we act on it. If we don't, we don't.

The fascinating twist of history, however, is how often we forget this.

God's Criteria for Entering the Kingdom

Jesus makes it very clear that God has no patience for pretending. He invented the word "hypocrite" as we use it today. We can't manipulate, flatter, or fake our way into the kingdom.

As much as this passage may (rightly) call up visions of a future judgment day, Jesus is not *just* talking about the future. After all, the invitation to enter the kingdom of heaven is a "now" invitation, not just a "later" expectation. In fact, he made the religious leaders of his day angry by informing them that prostitutes and tax collectors were already entering the kingdom—and the religious leaders were not.[2]

---

2 Matthew 21:31

This protects us from reading Jesus's warning as a return to Pharisaic legalism: a "doing God's will" in some list-checking way that none of us can ever hope to get right in order to gain entrance to eternity. Rather, God's will is that we believe in his Son, accept his forgiveness, and become the temple of his Holy Spirit on earth, all of which is a matter of receiving his undeserved grace. The works he wills for us to do, works of love and righteousness, are likewise the fruit of his grace.

At the beginning of this same Sermon, remember, Jesus declared that the kingdom of heaven belongs to the poor in spirit, to those with nothing to offer.[3] By its very nature (and ours), the kingdom has to be received and entered as a gift.

With that in mind, let's dig a little deeper into this passage.

It's About Knowing God, Not Giving Lip Service

Christianity as it has developed throughout history is strongly creedal and confessional. That's a good thing. Christianity is a faith with content: the "what" of our beliefs is essential. Any "Christianity" that doesn't hold to certain core historic beliefs is not Christian. Creeds and confessions allow us to center ourselves on the content of who God is and what he has done, and they give us a way to pass

[3] Matthew 5:3

on this essential foundation to future generations.

And yet, as many of us know from experience, there's a danger to creedalism. The danger is that we'll come to rely so much on confessing the "right things" that we forget to go beyond lip service to the heart of it all. And even worse, many will use confession as a cover-up for a lack of reality in our faith.

This isn't a New Covenant phenomenon. A major theme of nearly every Old Covenant prophet is the tendency of God's people to rely on lip service instead of actual faith and obedience. Isaiah 29:13 sums up God's complaint:

> These people say they are mine. They honor me with their lips, but their hearts are far from me. And their worship of me is nothing but man-made rules learned by rote. (NLT)

This is why Jesus parallels the idea of "not doing God's will" with the idea of "not being known by him"—in other words, not being in relationship with him, not being part of his family, not knowing God well enough to have a clue what he actually desires.

Before the birth of the prophet Samuel, God expressed what kind of service he wanted from his people:

> Then I will raise up a faithful priest for Myself. He will do whatever is in My heart and mind. (1 Samuel 2:35)

In other words, God seeks a people who actually *know* him, well enough to know and do what he wants.

The idea here isn't that God is seeking perfect, inhuman, flawless obedience at all times—as though God cares about us "getting it right" more than he cares about relationship. The idea is working toward the same goal as Jesus, caring about the same things, being on the same team.

If we don't know him, it shouldn't surprise us to hear that he doesn't know us.

Where Reformations Go Wrong

Church history is marked with peaks and valleys, revivals and depressions. In all of this, I've noticed a pattern—one that is probably inevitable, given human nature. Reforms and revivals seem to be driven largely by individuals who want to know God and walk with him in a way that is personal and immediate. But the movements these individuals spark soon feel the need to identify who is in and who is out, and the criteria typically becomes confessional—signing your name to the "right" set of beliefs.

Shortly after this, the movements go stale and give rise to power struggles and what Paul might call "biting and devouring one another."[4]

In other words, reforms and revivals begin when we want to know God and do his will, and they go sterile and sideways when we make them about merely saying "Lord, Lord" instead. That's an oversimplification, of course. But in broad terms, it helps me understand what's happening on the wide stage of Christian history.

Confessions and creeds are good things; truths written down and spelled out are helpful, even needful. But they also make it easy for people to fake it. Many who declare that Jesus is Lord do, in fact, know him. But many do not. And in the end, we'll know them by their fruit and not by the denomination they belong to or the creeds they repeat.

When I think about the evils that have been done by every branch of the church throughout history, this passage brings me comfort. Jesus surely foresaw this. Not everyone who attaches Christ's name to their activities should actually be understood as belonging to the kingdom or doing its work.

Many will say "Lord, Lord," but they do not know God, and they do not carry out his will.

---

[4] Galatians 5:15

An Invitation to Be Real

Every part of Jesus's message invites us into a more authentic, real, and grace-founded walk with God. We are invited to enter the kingdom. And while this will involve learning and believing true statements, true doctrine, ultimately that too is about relationship with the living God.

If we want in, we'll get in. If we aren't fakes, if we're real in our brokenness and our faith alike, Jesus's words don't need to scare us.

Instead, they declare that Jesus will always draw a line between those who love him and those who use his name for their own ends. The world may be fooled, but he isn't.

We can know God. We can know his heart and mind; we can do his will. We can enter his kingdom—now, today.

Given the choice between that and spending a lifetime building our own kingdoms and calling them God's, it's clear which is the better path.

Not everyone who says to Me, "Lord, Lord!" will enter the kingdom of heaven, but only the one who does the will of My Father in heaven. On that day many will say to Me, "Lord, Lord, didn't we prophesy in Your name, drive out demons in Your name, and do many miracles in Your name?" Then I will announce to them, "I never knew you! Depart from Me, you who work lawlessness."[1]

(Matthew 7:21–23)

---

[1] The main text of the HCSB renders this last phrase "Depart from Me, you lawbreakers." I have used the literal text in the HCSB footnote, "You who work lawlessness," because I believe there is a difference between one who is guilty of breaking a law and one who is actually lawless.

72

Beyond Success and Power: Walking by the Spirit and Doing God's Will

It's clear from Jesus's words that people in his day tended to measure spiritual fitness by two different criteria, both of which are insufficient. I think we tend to do the same today.

The first, as we just saw, is a kind of empty creedalism, where it's all about saying "Lord, Lord"—that is, thinking that as long as we give verbal assent to the right set of doctrines, we will be saved (as though belonging to the kingdom is about signing a legal form with all the right wording and not about entering into a living relationship with a living God).

The second is elevating acts of power and assuming they are the same thing as doing God's will.

The "lawless ones" who stand before Jesus protest that they have prophesied, worked miracles, and cast out demons in his name. They *must* belong to the kingdom. Their power proves it.

In our day, in the West, such supernatural acts of power are less commonly practiced and are viewed with suspicion by many Christians. Yet we are still guilty of using power as a marker of legitimacy.

Power, Success, and the Problem of Using What Doesn't Belong to You

A common theme of the New Testament is that the kingdom will benefit people who do not belong to it.

Sheep are not the only denizens of the New Creation world we live in. There are also thieves, robbers, and wolves. Wheat isn't the only crop growing in the field. It's full of weeds too.

Because this is true, many will use the blessings of the kingdom for their own ends. They may experience success and gain power by doing so, but this doesn't necessarily mean they are children of the kingdom themselves.

The seven sons of Sceva in Acts 19:13–16 are a vivid example. These seven were exorcists who discovered there was power in Jesus's name and began to invoke it as part of their practice. The text suggests this actually worked for a while—until they ran into a demonic power that was just too much for them.

> Then some of the itinerant Jewish exorcists attempted to pronounce the name of the Lord Jesus over those who had evil spirits, saying, "I command you by the Jesus that Paul preaches!" Seven sons of Sceva, a Jewish chief priest, were doing this. The evil spirit answered them, "I know Jesus, and I recognize Paul—but who are you?" Then the man who had the evil spirit leaped on them, overpowered them all, and prevailed against them, so that they ran out of that house naked and wounded.

In our own day, we all know of people who have pointed to their burgeoning bank accounts as proof of God's blessing on them and their ministries.

In recent North American history, European descendants have justified their abuse of power against Africans and indigenous peoples on the basis of God's supposed blessing.

If I may: we in North America still tend to claim that God is on "our side" against others in other parts of the world, and we often justify that claim by pointing to his blessings. We may not believe that might *makes* right, but we do tend to think it *proves* it.

The logic of success and power underlies all this. "Lord, Lord," we might ask, "didn't we take over the world in your name? Didn't we receive money, power, and blessing from you? Didn't you give us success in all our ways? We must belong to you!"

To many who would claim success as proof of belonging to God, I fear Jesus will say, "Depart from me. I never knew you."

When it comes to the kingdom, we can't claim success, power, or mere verbal assent as our proof of belonging, *even if much of the blessing we experience does actually come as a consequence of the kingdom's presence among us.*

For example, I strongly believe the degree of affluence we experience in the Western world is a direct result of kingdom principles at work in the world, blessing many with liberty, peace, and prosperity. That doesn't mean every wealthy person belongs to the kingdom or uses their wealth for good, or that every way of gaining and using wealth aligns with the principles of God's kingdom.

The way of Jesus, laid out from the start in the Sermon on the Mount, is deeply different.

The Way of Jesus: Walking by the Spirit

In the face of the dual "proofs" of creedal assent and acts of power, Jesus names two interrelated criteria for belonging to the kingdom.

The first is "doing the will of my Father in heaven." The second is "knowing him" (or "being known by him"—the word "know" suggests mutual relationship and experience).

Jesus strongly suggests these are two sides of the same coin. When we know God, we will do his will. When we do his will, we will know him.

As we saw earlier, based on his own teaching in the Sermon and elsewhere, when Jesus speaks of "doing the Father's will" he cannot be talking about living a law-based, box-checking life. That isn't the Father's revealed will for us.

Rather, Jesus is talking about a whole way of life that comes from placing our trust in him, entering his family, and walking with the Spirit of God. This is why, in John 3, he tells us that we cannot enter the kingdom of God unless we are "born from above," born of the Spirit.[1]

This is how Jesus himself lived. He spoke, acted, and related to the world around him by the Spirit of God.

Received, Not Earned

Walking by the Spirit will mean some very real and practical changes in how we live. Jesus is always very clear that those who truly love and know him also do his will:

---

1 John 3:5–8

> If anyone loves Me, he will keep my word. My Father will love him, and We will come and make Our home with him. The one who doesn't love Me will not keep My words. The word that you hear is not Mine but is from the Father who sent Me. I have spoken these things to you while I remain with you. But the Counselor, the Holy Spirit—the Father will send Him in My name—will teach you all things and remind you of everything I have told you. (John 14:23–26)

But lest we should view this as a "new law" that is even heavier than the old one, Jesus makes it clear that the kingdom is not earned, it is received. Moreover, it is given on the basis of Jesus's work, not ours. He does all the heavy lifting. Our part is to trust him, receive his Spirit, be adopted into his family, and continue to walk with him as part of a faithful community of believers.

In fact, the primary and most important element of the "will of God" that we are to do is to believe in Jesus.

> "What can we do to perform the works of God?" they asked. Jesus replied, "This is the work of God—that you believe in the One He has sent." (John 6:28–29)

Doing the Will of God

What is the will of God that we are to do?

If we read and believe the Sermon on the Mount, it is God's will that we come to him in faith, out of our mourning, our suffering, and our poverty, and receive his kingdom.

It is God's will that we believe in his Son and receive his Spirit, so as to be adopted into his family.[2]

It is God's will that we learn to forgive our debtors, trust our Father for provision, forgo worry, and release the normal human way of violence, power, and aggression. It is God's will that we give up anger and lust and learn to honor one another instead. It is God's will that we redefine "success" and ultimately learn to know him, even as we allow him to know us, in a relational way.

The will of God is our highest good, and through Jesus, we can know it, do it, and live by it.

---

[2] On that note: when I call believers to know God and be known to him, I want to be careful not to place an undue burden on those who don't feel that they've had a strongly experiential, subjective relationship with God to this point. While I do believe that an experiential relationship is God's ultimate will for all of us, long Christian experience can attest that we do not always *feel* this to the same degree, nor does everyone experience it in the same way. The "relationship" we need with God is an interpersonal relationship, yes, but first of all it's a family relationship—we need to become related to him as his children, through his Spirit, which relationship we enter by trusting in him and being baptized. Can you know God personally? Yes. Can you feel his presence with you? Yes. Can you hear his voice? Yes. Are you somehow subpar if, in truly trusting in Jesus and seeking to follow him, you don't seem to experience him to the same subjective degree as others do? No.

Believing in Jesus opens the door. It brings us into the kingdom.

From there we learn to live a kingdom lifestyle that lights, salts, and challenges the world. As Jesus later specified, this will largely be manifest through love—through our care for the needy and oppressed, our love and loyalty to one another, and our growing love for God. All of this flows first out of his love for us: "We love because He first loved us."[3]

When we walk with Jesus, we need not fear hearing the words "I never knew you." Ultimately, this is what it means to belong to the kingdom.

---

[3] 1 John 4:19

Therefore, everyone who hears these words of Mine and acts on them will be like a sensible man who built his house on the rock. The rain fell, the rivers rose, and the winds blew and pounded that house. Yet it didn't collapse, because its foundation was on the rock. But everyone who hears these words of Mine and doesn't act on them will be like a foolish man who built his house on the sand. The rain fell, the rivers rose, the winds blew and pounded that house, and it collapsed. And its collapse was great!

(Matthew 5:19–20)

73

Building on Rock: The Law of Christ and the Role of Works in the Christian Life

In Sunday school and VBS when I was a child, this passage was a favorite of teachers and pastors everywhere. Why not? It's one of Jesus's most powerful images. But as we do with many things, we misappropriated it in support of our favored soteriology. A good evangelical, I was taught that Jesus is the Rock, and to build one's life on the Rock means to invite him into our hearts.

That's not what Jesus said. Rather, this is his conclusion to the long-form teaching we know as the Sermon on the Mount, the most comprehensive collection of moral and spiritual teachings Jesus gave us.

The Sermon is not a tract on how to get saved. It's about *how to live*. It's about ordering our lives properly in relation to the kingdom, to God, to ourselves, and to others.

If we *do* this, Jesus says; if we actually *act* on his teachings, we will build our house on rock—stormproof.

On the other hand, if we allow his teachings to go in one ear and out the other, if we never turn hearing into action, they will do us no good. When the storms come, all our knowledge will not help us. It's only what we *did* with it that builds anything real in our lives.

If you recall, the opening salvo of Jesus's message was "Repent, because the kingdom of heaven has come near!"[1] Jesus then began the Sermon with the eight blessings of the kingdom. The kingdom is given to the spiritually impoverished. God himself is drawing near the hurting, depressed, and oppressed, and bringing peace. He has come to put everything right.

All of this comes with the kingdom, and the kingdom, Jesus is saying, is now. It's at hand. It has come, and it's about to come.

It's clear from everything Jesus says that we don't receive the kingdom by earning it. Or, to use more familiar "church" wording, we aren't saved by works. *But "saved," in this truncated sense, is not the point.* The point is new creation. The point is entering the kingdom and *living as kingdom people, kingdom citizens.*

---

[1] Matthew 4:17

The point is receiving a law written on our hearts and living and acting by it. The point is transforming and being transformed, from glory to glory, even as by the Spirit of the Lord.[2] And in a very real sense, this is salvation—it's the ultimate goal for which we are brought into God's family, filled with his Spirit, and granted eternal life.

"But as for me," Paul says in Galatians 6:14–15, "I will never boast about anything except the cross of our Lord Jesus Christ. The world has been crucified to me through the cross, and I to the world. For both circumcision and uncircumcision mean nothing; what matters instead is a new creation."

Choosing Our Foundation

As Christians, we can build our lives one of two ways.

We can build them on the teachings and commands of Jesus, on the law of freedom and love written in our hearts and described in the New Testament.

Or we can disregard what Jesus has to say and build our lives on something else. Anything else, really.

Jesus's point is that only one lifestyle, only one way of building, will withstand the storms that come to challenge and test us. A life lived Jesus's

---

[2] 2 Corinthians 3:18

way will stand strong. A life lived some other way will not.

This means if we want to live good lives, strong lives that matter and remain in some eternal sense, we need to take the way of Jesus seriously here in this world.

We need to get real about sin, and especially about anger, lust, disdain for others, and greed. We need to confront fear and worry and exchange them for trust and peace. We need to exchange judgment and vengeance for forgiveness and release. We need to engage with prayer and other spiritual disciplines. We need to learn to love our enemies, to turn the other cheek, and to embrace authenticity and receive God's blessings in our weakest areas.

We need to put the Lord's Prayer at the very center of our lives: living and working for the "kingdom come," forgiving those who sin against us and receiving the forgiveness of God. This is how we manifest the kingdom. This is how we change the world.

In other words, as kingdom people, we need to live like kingdom people. Jesus gives us a massive head start in doing this by laying out, in one place, so many of the key principles and lifeways of the kingdom of God.

Living these teachings out takes work. Real work. We have to change the way we think, and from there the way we feel. We have to swap out old identities for new ones. We have to act in ways that are hard and may feel unnatural at first. And we have to learn new actions, reactions, and habit patterns.

All of this takes concerted intention and action. But again, none of it is about "getting saved" in some eternity-only, ticket-to-heaven sense. It's about learning to be human, in a spiritual, Spirit-filled, righteous, and God-glorifying way.

Ultimately, it's about becoming what we were always created to be.

We may never get it down perfect while we're in this world. But I don't think that's the point either.

Whether we build on rock or we build on sand is our decision. Our "houses" may look quite different, depending on many factors (including our individual callings and situations in life). But the foundation is the same.

We don't get to opt out of the storms. Let's make a good choice, the good choice, and do the work of a kingdom life.

When Jesus had finished this sermon, the crowds were astonished at His teaching, because He was teaching them like one who had authority, and not like their scribes.

(Matthew 7:28–29)

74

The Unexpected Way: How We Lost the Gift of Discipleship —And Why We Need to Recover It

As we reach the end of the Sermon the Mount, we find the crowds responding to Jesus with astonishment. They recognized something in him that I believe we still grapple with today: the unusual merger of authority with teaching.

The Greek word translated "authority," *exousia,* denotes the right to exercise power. It is a word usually used of those in government: kings; their delegated agents such as governors, generals, and tax collectors; and the spiritual "rulers, authorities, and powers" we read of in Ephesians 6:12 and elsewhere.

The Jewish scribes—those who meticulously read, copied, and studied the Scriptures—taught the people regularly, but they did not have authority in this sense. In Jesus, the people recognized that they were not only hearing someone with the ability to accurately and intelligently transmit law, but someone with the power and authority to make and enforce it.

In other words, they recognized a king.

Kingly Expectations

As a teacher, a Jewish rabbi, I think that Jesus likely overturned the expectations of some. Recall that the Jews of Jesus's day were on the lookout for the prophesied Messiah identified in Isaiah and elsewhere as the king who would sit on the throne of David. He would overthrow the oppressive forces of the world (embodied at the time by the Roman Empire) and renew God's covenant with Israel.

Jesus is explicitly identified as this king from the very beginning of the gospel of Matthew. He is called "the Son of David" in Matthew 1:1. In Matthew 2 he is recognized as the shepherd of Israel, again a reference to kingly prophecy in the Old Testament. John the Baptist, of course, heralds Jesus's arrival with the words, "The kingdom of heaven has come near!"

And Jesus himself declares both his kingship and his kingdom in the opening words of the Sermon on the Mount: "The poor in spirit are blessed, for the kingdom of heaven is theirs."[1]

---

[1] Matthew 5:3

But here is where the story takes an unusual twist, for kings are not often also teachers. David certainly was not. David was a conqueror, a deliverer, and an ardent worshipper, but his "shepherding" of his people did not entail teaching them. David didn't make disciples.

Solomon, with his famed wisdom and collections of proverbs, is closer in this respect to being a picture of Jesus. In fact, David and Solomon together are a type of Christ, a picture in the Old Testament of the king who was to come.

The Spirit of God empowered David for military victory over Israel's enemies; the same Spirit of God empowered Solomon for wisdom and peace.

And so we have Jesus, the teacher with authority—the king and deliverer who is also a prince of peace, and who *teaches:* who brings wisdom and makes disciples.

Jesus is not one or the other. He is both.

THE ANSWER IS YES

I imagine that many of Jesus's early followers—not to mention the crowds and religious leaders who gathered around him—struggled with this both/and nature of Jesus's ministry.

If you were looking for a military commander to deliver your people from Rome, would you really expect to find that commander wandering around the countryside delivering sermons on the real meaning of God's law?

And if you were looking for a spiritual teacher to disciple you in the ways of God, would you really be looking for a rebellion-inciting king?

Of course, I may be overly westernizing (or overly modernizing) the issue. It's very possible that people in Jesus's time *didn't* see the dichotomy I do—that it was perfectly natural to them to expect their king to be a rabbi and vice versa.

But then again, they were astonished by *something*. And we're often told that what astonished and even dismayed them was Jesus's evident exousia. "Who gave you this authority?" the Pharisees often demanded.

In any case, whatever dichotomies confused the people of the first century, we have plenty of our own confusing us.

- Is Jesus Lord or is he Savior?
- Are we saved by faith or are we saved by works?
- Is Jesus a teacher or is he God?
- Does God speak through his Spirit or through his Word?
- Is the Christian life about love or is it about holiness?

- Are we children of God or are we servants of God?

To pretty much all of these, the answer is ...

Yes.

THE PENDULUM SWING: HOW WE BUILD FALSE DICHOTOMIES

In many areas of our lives and beliefs, we have set things in opposition to each other that do not need to be opposed and in many cases *should* not be opposed.

The reasons for this are usually historical.

For example, the Bible does not place faith and works in opposition to one another. It sees works as born out of and indicative of true faith. While works do not save us or justify us before God,[2] faith without works is just a sham ... it may pretend to be a living thing, but in reality, it's dead.[3]

Honestly, this should be self-evident. You may say you believe me if I tell you that the corner store is giving out million-dollar bills to anyone who walks in, but if you don't actually walk to the corner store to get your money, you don't really believe me at all.

Despite the Bible's teaching and the common-

---

2 Ephesians 2:8–9
3 James 2:6

sense relationship between faith and works, we still tend to think in terms of "faith vs works." Why? Well, mostly because of the historical circumstances in which a man named Martin Luther lived. Luther reacted to a religious system that was out of balance. His solutions were necessary correctives—but in some ways, they were also out of balance.

In his zeal, Luther even inserted a word into Scripture. Where Romans 3:28 reads "a man is justified by faith apart from the works of the law," Luther's translation says, "a man is justified by faith *alone* apart from the works of the law."

While in this context his addition may be justifiable, it did help to create a faith vs works paradigm that quickly departed from its biblical grounding.

This is how most of our dichotomies form. The pendulum swings one direction and then another. The truth is usually closer to the center—but it's natural for us, human beings who are moving with the momentum of history, to miss it.

And when we do, it may take some effort to get back to the center again.

Recovering the Grace of Discipleship

As history trembles and our thought-worlds divide along various fault lines, we may tend to lose important things down the cracks.

A modern example is the charismatic movement (of which I am a grateful part): as charismatics have emphasized the work of the Spirit, they have tended to create an opposition between the Spirit and the written Word, the Bible. This gap is (thankfully) beginning to close, yet it remains a significant problem for many charismatic groups.

In my opinion, one of the most important things we've lost down the cracks of history—or bypassed in the pendulum swing—is discipleship.

From the start of the Sermon on the Mount, it is crystal clear that Jesus does not just call people to "accept him," "invite him into their hearts," "be born again," "surrender all," "pray the Sinner's Prayer," or whatever wording you want to use.

Jesus was a rabbi, a teacher—and that meant he called (and calls) students. More specifically, he called disciples, and the purpose of discipleship is to learn a way of life.

If we accept the kingship of Jesus—his authority and power to save us and rule over our world—we also need to accept the teachings of Jesus. We need to do them, even if they take us a long time to learn and we never really walk them out perfectly.

We need to become people who build our lives on the rock and thus withstand the storms that batter us. We need to become people who take Jesus seriously as a teacher—not (again) because we think we can somehow perfectly "do" the Sermon and that will get us into heaven, but because the way of life laid out in the Sermon on the Mount is part and parcel of the gift of the kingdom.

It is part of what saves us, transforms us, and ushers us into new life, here and now, and into eternity.

Christianity is not just a set of beliefs to believe, principles to accept, or steps to take. It is not even "just" a relationship with God, whatever exactly that may mean. Christianity as Jesus gave it to us is a life to be lived.

As his disciples, we should be marked out not so much by our denominational affiliations or even our "works of power," but by our forgiveness, our love, our trust, and our self-giving lives.

We have the privilege of being not only children of God and subjects of the King of Kings, but his disciples as well—learning to think, feel, and live like he does. All of this is empowered by the Holy Spirit.

The call to discipleship is not a requirement for salvation. It is a *part* of salvation—a gift with the ability to transform our lives.

As much as we stand for the great doctrines of grace, faith, and salvation, let us not lose this unexpected and incredible gift. It too is a grace, given to us not by our own works but by the loving will and unmerited favor of God.

When He came down from the mountain, large crowds followed Him.

(Matthew 8:1)

Epilogue

Following vs Following: How to Step Out of the Crowd and Truly Follow Jesus

Jesus's ministry had an interesting problem: he was popular. The "large crowds" of the HCSB, translated "great multitudes" in the KJV, likely indicates thousands of people, as would later be present at the feeding of the five thousand.

It was in response to such "multitudes" that Jesus climbed the mountain to deliver the Sermon on the Mount in the first place. And in fact, this explains why the Sermon ends the way it does, on a note that feels suddenly negative—with a series of warnings about fake followers, false prophets, and broad gates that lead to destruction.

THE CROWD CONUNDRUM

Facing multitudes of people who had come to hear him and see what he would do, Jesus faced a conundrum. If he wanted to do the expected thing and establish a this-world kingdom in rebellion to

Rome, he could have leveraged his popularity to do it. Plenty of people would have followed. Plenty of people *were* following.

Instead, he was looking to bring the kingdom of heaven into the world, one heart and life at a time. He needed a different kind of follower.

Beginning in Matthew 7:6, Jesus began to draw lines between those who were truly following him and those who were just along for the ride, or worse, who were just trying to use Jesus to benefit their own agendas.

He contrasted "dogs and swine" with those who ask, seek, and knock, treating the holy and valuable as holy and valuable. He contrasted his hidden, narrow way with the broad and obvious path, where the crowds sweep one another along. And he contrasted false prophets, those who say "Lord, Lord" but have no real connection to the kingdom, with those who truly belong to the flock of Christ.

What's interesting is that just following didn't differentiate these groups. They were all following Jesus, literally—going where he went, listening to his teaching, and honoring him as a rabbi and as their possible king.

But Jesus wasn't just looking for this kind of follower: those who were in *proximity*. He was looking for followers who would go all-in, joining him in *purpose*.

Jesus always accepted that within the kingdom era he was ushering in, multitudes would "follow" without ever entering the kingdom.

Since they would all be in proximity to Jesus, it would sometimes be hard to tell the difference. But to him, there is a difference—a profound one.

The Difference between Following and Following

From our vantage point in history, we tend to associate following Jesus with placing our faith in his death and resurrection and thus becoming regenerate ("born again," or as Paul would put it, made a "new creation"[1]).

Yet Jesus draws a straight line between following him and "doing his will": that is, keeping and obeying his commands. This, he says, is how one builds a life that lasts:

> Therefore, everyone who hears these words of Mine and acts on them will be like a sensible man who built his house on the rock. The rain fell, the rivers rose, and the winds blew and pounded that house. Yet it didn't collapse, because its foundation was on the rock.
> But everyone who hears these words of Mine and doesn't act on them will be like a fool-

---

[1] John 3:7, 2 Corinthians 5:17

ish man who built his house on the sand. The rain fell, the rivers rose, the winds blew and pounded that house, and it collapsed. And its collapse was great! (Matthew 7:24–27)

Don't miss this: as Jesus's life progressed and his mission became clearer, it did become evident that the first order of doing God's will *is* placing our trust in Jesus's work as carried out in his death and resurrection and thus becoming regenerate through the grace and power of God.

But this doesn't mean that as regenerate followers of Jesus, we have nothing more to do.

There is a grander plan, a grander purpose for our lives.

Jesus said those who enter the kingdom will be those who do the will of the Father,[2] and the will of the Father is the redemption and transformation of the world, starting with the human race. The teachings of Jesus, taken seriously and implemented in our lives, are an integral part of that transformation.

The Sermon on the Mount and the Redemption of Our Souls

The Old Testament prophet Micah gives a powerful vision of the kingdom era ushered in by Jesus.

---

[2] Matthew 7:21

Note the role of teaching in the transformation of the nations:

> In the last days
> the mountain of the LORD's house
> will be established
> at the top of the mountains
> and will be raised above the hills.
> Peoples will stream to it,
> and many nations will come and say,
> "Come, let us go up to the mountain of the LORD,
> to the house of the God of Jacob.
> *He will teach us about His ways*
> *so we may walk in His paths."*
> *For instruction will go out of Zion*
> *and the word of the LORD from Jerusalem.*
> He will settle disputes among many peoples
> and provide arbitration for strong nations
> that are far away.
> They will beat their swords into plows,
> and their spears into pruning knives.
> Nation will not take up the sword against nation,
> and they will never again train for war.
> But each man will sit under his grapevine
> and under his fig tree
> with no one to frighten him.
> For the mouth of the LORD of Hosts
> has promised this.
> (Micah 4:1–4, emphasis mine)

Micah envisions an era in which the nations of the world voluntarily stream to the "mountain of the Lord" to learn from him, to receive his instruction. This teaching of God will bring peace and prosperity to the entire world.

When he "climbed the mountain" to deliver the Sermon on the Mount, Jesus began to fulfill this prophecy. And in fact, the teachings of Jesus have already brought almost unimaginable change to the world.

As much as our world still has many problems, and as much as it sometimes seems like they are getting worse, a long view tells a different story. We live in an era of unprecedented freedom, wealth, health, peace, and human rights; and in all of these areas, the teachings and the people of Jesus Christ have long been at the forefront of the change.

We are likewise called to be part of the change—part of the kingdom expansion. We are called to do the will of God; in other words, *to join him in his purposes*. We don't do this in order to earn redemption, but because it is *part* of redemption—ours and that of the people and societies around us.

Part of redeeming, transforming, and restoring creation is teaching us how to live in the way we were originally intended to live. That's what the teachings of Jesus are all about.

Following Jesus All Over Again

As someone who came to Jesus in the classic way of praying a prayer (at the age of four) and who learned to "follow" him through the tripart method of going to church, reading my Bible, and praying, I find the teachings of Jesus in the Sermon challenging—and revitalizing.

More and more, it's becoming evident that we don't just need a belief system, we need a way of life. Thankfully, that's exactly what Jesus gave us. Yes, it's a way of life that has relationship, covenant, and "redemption by the blood" at its core. But it's still a way: a path, a lifestyle.

Isaiah 58:12 in the King James Version says of God's faithful people, "And thou shalt be called, The repairer of the breach, The restorer of paths to dwell in." I love that last phrase: *paths to dwell in*. Jesus has given us this: a path in which to live, a way of life that can become a home for us and for those who come after us.

I'm challenged by this to renew my faith and my commitment to following Jesus: to stepping out of the crowd, differentiating myself from those who are merely "near" Jesus, and becoming someone who is truly "with" him—participating in his plans for the world through my own commitment to living out a Sermon on the Mount lifestyle of trust, forgiveness, purity, honor, and continual seeking.

Where I have fallen away from the path and been content to camp out near the road, watching Jesus go by but not really going with him, I look forward every day to getting back on the path again. The journey is exciting. The company is unbeatable. And the destination is the restoration of all things.

I can't think of a better way to build my life.

Or a better path to dwell in.

Rachel would love to hear from you!

You can visit her and interact online:

Web: www.rachelstarrthomson.com
Facebook.com/RachelStarrThomsonWriter
IG: Instagram @rachelstarrthomson

FEARLESS

You can live free from fear.

Fear steals our lives from us. It steals our impact and cripples our joy.

In our modern world, there are a million reasons to be afraid.

But what if your default mode was courage and faith, not fear and timidity?

True freedom is possible— through the presence of Jesus and the practice of his Word.

In this book, we expose the insidious roots of fear and explore the answers found in the Bible. Learn how:

- THE FEAR OF THE LORD WILL BREAK THE POWER OF LESSER FEARS

- HOLINESS WILL CHANGE YOUR IDENTITY— AND GIVE YOU COURAGE TO STAND AGAINST THE TIDE

- THE PRESENCE OF GOD IS THE ANSWER TO THE WORLD'S TROUBLES

- YOU CAN PRACTICE THE GIFTS OF POWER, LOVE, AND A SOUND MIND

Available from Amazon and everywhere books are sold.

THE SEVENTH WORLD TRILOGY

For five hundred years the Seventh World has been ruled by a tyrannical empire—and the mysterious Order of the Spider that hides in its shadow. History and truth are deliberately buried, the beauty and treachery of the past remembered only by wandering Gypsies, persecuted scholars, and a few unusual seekers. But the past matters, as Maggie Sheffield soon finds out. It matters because its forces will soon return and claim lordship over her world, for good or evil.

The Seventh World Trilogy is an epic fantasy, beautiful, terrifying, pointing to the realities just beyond the world we see.

"An excellent read, solidly recommended for fantasy readers."
– MIDWEST BOOK REVIEW

"A wonderfully realistic fantasy world. Recommended."
– JILL WILLIAMSON, CHRISTY-AWARD-WINNING AUTHOR OF *BY DARKNESS HID*

"Epic, beautiful, well-written fantasy that sings of Christian truth."
– RAEL, READER

Available everywhere online or special order from your local bookstore.

THE ONENESS CYCLE

The supernatural entity called the Oneness holds the world together. *What happens if it falls apart?*

In a world where the Oneness exists, nothing looks the same. Dead men walk. Demons prowl the air. Old friends peel back their mundane masks and prove as supernatural as angels. But after centuries of battling demons and the corrupting powers of the world, the Oneness is under a new threat—its greatest threat. Because this time, the threat comes from within.

Fast-paced contemporary fantasy.

"Plot twists and lots of edge-of-your-seat action,
I had a hard time putting it down!"
—Alexis

"Finally! The kind of fiction I've been waiting for my whole life!"
—Mercy Hope, FaithTalks.com

"I sped through this short, fast-paced novel, pleased by the well-drawn characters and the surprising plot. Thomson has done a great job of portraying difficult emotional journeys . . . Read it!"
—Phyllis Wheeler, The Christian Fantasy Review

Available everywhere online or special order from your local bookstore.

TIME TO ALIGN:
FREE EMAIL COURSE

Join Rachel Starr Thomson and the 1:11 team for a personal journey through 8 key areas of life in our free email-based course, "Time to Align."

This free, 11-week course is a spiritual recalibration: a chance to bring your heart, soul, mind, and strength into alignment with the nature and will of God.

To get your first lesson straight to your inbox, sign up here:
One11Ministries.com/Align

www.ingramcontent.com/pod-product-compliance
Lightning Source LLC
Chambersburg PA
CBHW030314100526
44592CB00010B/423